Cromosys Publication

Teach Yourself CorelDRAW

NIRANJAN JHA SHOWMAN

Founder - Niranjan Jha Showman

Education and Technology Research Center

Patankar Park, Nallasopara (W), Mumbai. +91-9561450045

Education, Technology, Publication, Healthcare, Newsmedia, Realtor, Filmmaking

www.facebook.com/cromosys

+91-9561450045
Learn Advanced Skills
And Get Job Instantly
GERMAN
Python
FRENCH
C++
SPANISH
Java
ENGLISH
HTML5
RUSSIAN
CSS
JavaScript
Cromosys
Education and Technology Research Center
Nallasopara (W), Mumbai

Learn Web Programming
Demo-Class Free
HTML
CSS
React
JavaScript
Typescript
Bootstrap
Cromosys
20 Years of Experience
Nallasopara (W), Mumbai
+91-9561450045

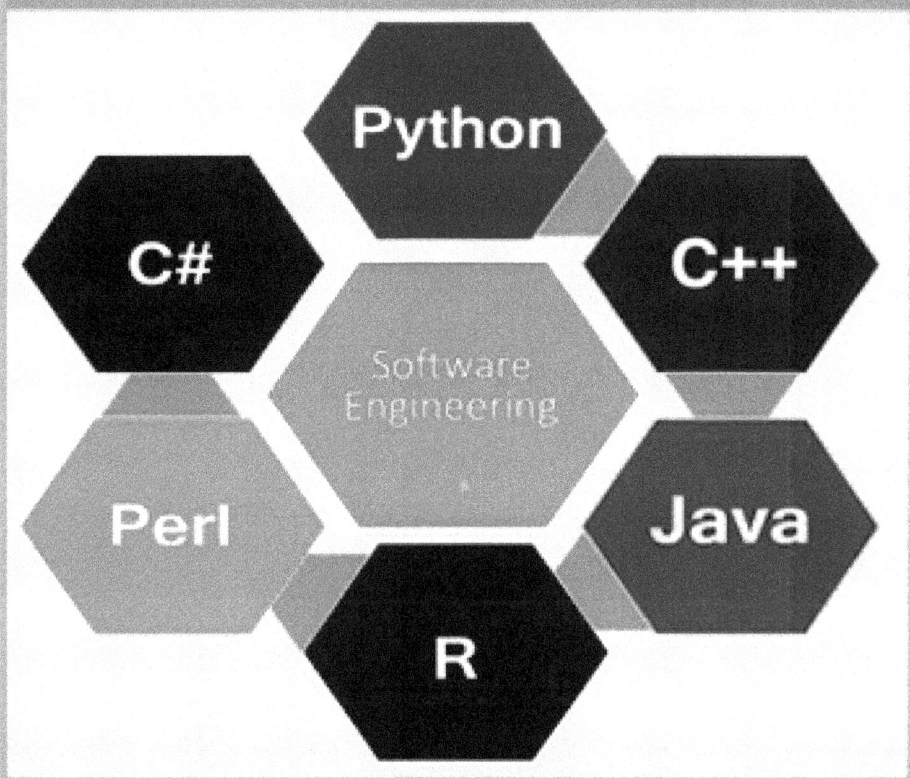
+91-9561450045
Learn Software Engineering
Demo-Class Free
Python
C#
C++
Software
Engineering
Perl
Java
R
Cromosys
20 Years of Experience
Nallasopara (W), Mumbai
+91-9561450045

25 Years of Experience
Learn Visual Multimedia
Animation VFX
Movie Editing
Game Development
Cromosys
+91-9561450045
Education and Technology Research Center
Nallasopara (W), Mumbai
www.facebook.com/cromosys

Jobs Available
For Candidates Who Know

German
French
Spanish

Vacancy in Germany, France, Spain

For Hospitality, Engineering, IT Sector
With Free Visa, Airfare and Accommodation

Cromosys

Education and Technology Research Centre
Nallasopara (W), Mumbai
+91-9561450045
20 Years of Experience

+91-9561450045
Foreign Languages Institute
German, French, Spanish
Basic and Advanced - All Levels
3 x 6 = 18 Courses
FRANCHISE
Business Offer
Teaching Materials Provided
We have 1 Million Students Globally
Great Income Assured
Global Exposure
Cromosys
20 Years of Experience
Nallasopara (W), Mumbai
+91-9561450045

Book:	Teach Yourself CorelDRAW
Author:	Niranjan Jha Showman
Publisher:	Cromosys Publication
ISBN:	Acquired
Category:	Computer Education
Subcategory:	Drawing and Designing

Preface

Cromosys Publication's **Teach Yourself CorelDRAW** book is an optimal quality guide to the beginners and advanced learners. We are the leading book publisher of languages and technology. Our research and education center working for last fifteen years has made tremendous efforts to simplify the learning of CorelDRAW, and so we assure you that this book will walk you through in the simplest way in your entire course of learning, and will make you a master of this application in just one month of time. This all-inclusive book provides a thorough, step-by-step introduction to CorelDRAW X6 and advanced versions. It also explains the core concepts of objective illustrations used in vector graphics. This easy, effective, and reliable book provides an ideal introduction to the world of graphic design and is intended to enhance the skills required for designing. The lessons of this book also cover the new and enhanced features in CorelDRAW X6 and its basic geometrical tools to create objects on the Drawing page. An easy-to-understand language and step-by-step approach to the concepts are some of the features that make this book unique. The latest CorelDRAW X6 version helps you to transform your creative imagination into new and innovative concepts. This book explains the key as well as new features, such as Smear, Twirl, Attract, Repel, and complex script types of CorelDRAW X6. As you practice, you learn to work with curves, lines, and outlines; and to modify objects by using the fillet, scallop, chamfer, and envelope tools. The lessons conceived and prepared by us will help you start learning from real basic making your move amazing, astonishing, and exhilarating for you. It's cool, simple, and sublime!

Niranjan Showman, the author of this and fifty other books published online, is the coiner, founder, and owner of Cromosys Corporation. His dedication in technological and linguistic research is significantly known to millions of people around the world. This book is the creation of his avowed determination to make the learning of CorelDRAW easy to the people. After you install the application on your system, you just have to follow the instructions of this book doing the same on your computer, and you will see that you are quickly learning everything. Just an hour of practice per day, and in a month of time you'll get a lot of knowledge, tips and tricks to work with this software. This is an unmatchable unique book of its kind that guarantees your success. The lessons are magnificently powerful to bring you into the arena of graphic design. With the industrial growth from the year 2014, the accurate and profound knowledge of this software has influenced millions of minds; therefore we conceived the idea of making this book a guideline to those who want to be perfect in this application starting from real basic. What CorelDRAW does, no other software can do. The quick and precise lessons with screenshots will help you enhance your creativity of crafting sophisticated high-quality designs. This book will get you acquainted to the object handling processes, such as duplicate, scale, mirror, combine, break, group, envelop, blend, contour, transparency, drop shadow, and extrude. In this book, you also learn the procedure by which you can work with new complex script types, and the process to create, format, merge, split, and set margins for tables. This book also includes the procedure to create, show, hide, edit, move, and delete layers from the Drawing page of CorelDRAW X6. Towards the end, you learn about image conversions and work with image adjustment lab command, as well as exporting a CorelDRAW drawing in the PDF format, for Web and MS Office applications. It is the need of time and that is why many people have been sharpening their knowledge to be good in it.

The CorelDRAW application is widely known as a graphics designing application, which is highly used to create illustrations, page layouts, and Web graphics, as well as to edit photos. This application was formerly developed by one of the world's leading software development company, Corel Corporation of Ottawa, Canada. Corel Corporation, founded by Michael Cowpland in 1985, was intended to be a research laboratory aimed at introducing the latest graphics manipulating technologies.

Cromosys, our education and technology research center, saving human efforts from being wasted, is committed to help you gain profound and contemporary knowledge. The world growing with density has brought enormous opportunity to graphic design talents irrespective of their geographical boundaries. We strongly believe that this book is useful for people working for picture editing, graphics and animation, media houses, and entertainment world. After you start the lesson, you don't need to worry about anything but just follow each and every step carefully. This book is designed to fulfill the instant need of learners in a very economical way, as it is easy to find on Internet and affordable to buy and share. Cromosys, our path-breaking pioneer training institute for Computer Courses, English Speaking, Foreign Languages, and Competition Coaching, is dedicated to enlightening human mind with educational endeavors, and we are doing the same for last successful fifteen years. And recently we have come up with 'Worldwide Online Teaching System' for languages and technology. We not only hope but believe that your success is in your hand, as this book will take you miles ahead in your expectation. We always respect the views and comments of readers, so for any communication with regards to assistance, enquiry or collaboration, we are always there at your reach as it helps us improve our quality.

Niranjan Jha Showman
Founder: Cromosys Corporation
Web: facebook.com/cromosys
Contact no.   +91-9561450045
Email address: cromosys@yahoo.com
Facebook link: www.facebook.com/niranjanshowman

Books by the same author: Teach Yourself Photoshop CS6, Teach Yourself Premiere Pro CS6, Teach Yourself After Effects CS6, Teach Yourself Adobe Flash, Teach Yourself Adobe Dreamweaver, Teach Yourself Autodesk Maya, Teach Yourself Autodesk Combustion, Teach Yourself Autodesk 3ds Max, Teach Yourself Tally ERP 9, English Voice Accent and Pronunciation, English Word Power, English Dictionary of Modern Slang, Teach Yourself Spanish, Teach Yourself French, Teach Yourself German

Cromosys
Education and Technology Research Center
Education, Technology, Publication, Healthcare, Realtor, Filmmaking
Nallasopara (W), Mumbai, India

Caution: All the writing works that include all the educational, non-educational books, novels, and articles of the author Niranjan Jha, are the registered contents of Online Digital Services and also published contents of his registered magazine FACE OFF - Inventing Truth, which carries registration no. MAHENG12112/13/1/2009-TC and the endorsement no. 3244 28/5/2009 with the Ministry of Information and Broadcasting, Govt. of India. Any plagiarism in this regard will attract strict legal action. Any further publication of any of his books requires his written permission. Copyright certificate of this book is attached at the end of this book.

Lesson 1
Introduction
Corel is an abbreviation of Cowpland Research Laboratory. CorelDRAW X6 is the latest version of CorelDRAW. This application offers a host of new and enhanced designing, managing, and modifying tools that allow you to create the most intricate of illustrations and perform other graphics manipulation tasks more quickly and easily than ever before. CorelDRAW X6 is designed for professionals and aspiring designers alike. It provides an intuitive workflow, high-value digital content, and market-leading file compatibility which make it easy to create impressive results without professional training.

The chapter begins by introducing CorelDRAW Graphics Suite X6, wherein you learn about the various applications of the suite. You also learn about the image types supported by the CorelDRAW application. Next, you explore its new and advanced features. Further, you learn about the system requirements that are mandatory to install the CorelDRAW X6 application. Then, you learn to launch this application and discuss the procedure to create a new document. This chapter also describes the components of the CorelDRAW user interface. After this, you learn the process to undo and redo a series of actions, which are previously performed in a drawing. This chapter also discusses the procedure to save a drawing and open an existing drawing. Towards the middle of this chapter, you learn to preview a drawing, in which you discuss to preview a drawing in the full screen and selected objects mode.

Understanding CorelDRAW Graphics Suite X6
CorelDRAW is developed by Corel Corporation, which revolutionized the graphic design industry when it introduced the first version of CorelDRAW in 1989. Today, the company continues to lead the market with its excellence in the designing approach. Corel Corporation introduced the latest upgraded sixteenth version, known as CorelDRAW Graphics Suite X6. This version is supported by all the Windows-based operating systems, such as Windows Vista, Windows XP, Windows 7, and Windows 8. CorelDRAW is also at the forefront of the digital media, which delivers the broadest and most innovative portfolio of photo and video conceptions to the design industry.

CorelDRAW Graphics Suite X6 is a collection of various applications, such as CorelDRAW X6, Corel PHOTO-PAINT X6, Corel PowerTRACE X6, Corel Website Creator X6, Corel CAPTURE X6, Corel CONNECT X6, PhotoZoom Pro 2, and Corel ConceptShare. The suite includes major enhancements, particularly related to design tools, color management, and Web graphics. These enhancements help you to express your ideas creatively and translate them into professional results easily and quickly. In addition, you can easily switch between applications while working in CorelDRAW X6. The main applications in CorelDRAW Graphics Suite X6 (version 16) are as follows:

CorelDRAW X6: Refers to the vector-design application used for designing page layouts.
Corel PHOTO-PAINT X6: Refers to the image-editing application, which can be used to adjust the color and tone of an image, retouch images, or mask images.
Corel PowerTRACE X6: Lets you accurately convert raster images to vector graphics.
Corel Website Creator X6: Refers to prevailing website design software that works automatically.
Corel CAPTURE X6: Provides the facility to capture a shot of the screen with one click.
Corel CONNECT: Refers to a full-screen, built-in content finder, which enables you to find files, templates, and images from your computer and selected websites.
Corel PhotoZoom Pro 2: Refers to the convenient PHOTO-PAINT plug-in, which helps in enlarging digital images.

Corel ConceptShare: Helps you to share feedback, concepts, and ideas on CorelDRAW projects with other online users.

After briefly describing the various applications present in CorelDRAW Graphics Suite X6, let's discuss the image types supported by CorelDRAW X6 in the following section.

Understanding the Image Types in CorelDRAW

Before working with images in CorelDRAW, you must have knowledge of two important types of images, namely bitmap image and vector image. While working in graphic software, as a professional or a beginner, one should be knowledgeable enough about the different image types. Let's have a look at these image types in detail in the following sections, starting with bitmap images.

Defining Bitmap Images

Bitmap images are mode up of dots (or pixels). The number of dots or pixels determines the resolution of the image: the greater the number of pixels in the image, the higher is its resolution. Bitmaps are useful if you want to achieve photographic quality images with complex color gradients or bitmap effects. You can import a variety of bitmap formats into your CorelDRAW document, such as .jpeg, .tiff, and .png. After importing the bitmap image, you can modify the image in different ways. For example, you can trace a bitmap image, apply an effect on it, and modify it color mode, brightness, and contrast. Picture 1.1 shows a bitmap image:

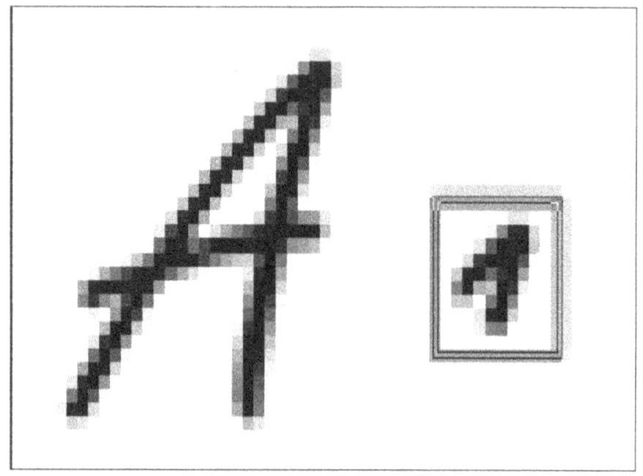

Picture 1.1

Defining Vector Images

Vector images are created or defined by using algebraic equations. Unlike bitmap images, vector images are resolution independent. These images consist of curves and lines instead of pixels, and are easier to manipulate than bitmaps as individual objects. Vectors can be rescaled without any loss to their clarity or quality. Examples of common vector formats are CorelDRAW (.cdr) and Adobe Illustrator (.ai). Both the bitmap and vector images look identical. You can distinguish their type by zooming (or magnifying) them to a specific level of the image. Picture 1.2 shows an example of a vector image:

Picture 1.2

Now that you have a brief understanding of the bitmap and vector images, let's next explore the new and enhanced features in the CorelDRAW X6 version.

Exploring the New and Enhanced Features in CorelDRAW X6

CorelDRAW X6 includes various new features that aim at enhancing both the performance and the productivity of a user. Some of the features include the advanced OpenType support, vector shaping tools, object styles, page layout, website design, alignment guides, and page numbering. Let's discuss some of the new and enhanced features in CorelDRAW X6 in the following points:

Freehand Pick Tool: In CorelDRAW X6, you can save time by controlling the object selection and transforming by using the Freehand tool. You can use this for selecting curved and non-linear shapes in a complex drawing. In addition, this tool also enables you to drag a freehand marquee around the desired object or shape that you want to modify.

Advanced OpenType Support: In CorelDRAW X6, you can create creative and attractive text by using the OpenType typography features. You can create contextual and stylistic texts, such as alternates, ligatures, ornaments, small caps, and swash variants. In the OpenType platform you can work with various inclusive languages that allow you to customize characters to suit the desired language that you want to use. You can manage the OpenType options from a centralized menu and can create contextual changes with the interactive OpenType features.

Shape Tools: In CorelDRAW X6, four supplementary shaping tools, such as Smear, Twirl, Attract, and Repel, are launched. These tools help you to refine the objects on the Drawing page. By using the Smear tool, you can shape an object by pulling extensions or making marks besides its outline. You can specify the size of the brush nib and the Pressure setting for controlling the intensity of the effect. In the Smear tool, you can also select from the smooth curves or curves with sharp corners. By suing the Twirl tool, you can apply circle motion effects to objects. You can specify the size of the brush nib to control the size of the twirls. The Rate setting allows you to control the speed of the effect. While twirling the object, you can specify the counterclockwise or clockwise option, according to your requirements. The new Attract and Repel tools enable you to shape curves by attracting nodes or by pushing nodes away from other nodes within proximity. While using these tools, you can manage the shaping effect by altering the size of the brush nib and the speed specified for the nodes to be attracted to or repelled from each other.

Custom-Built Color Harmonies: In CorelDRAW X6, you can create desired complementary color palette for your designs. The Color Harmonies tool introduced in X6 enables you to access the Color Styles docker, which combines Color Styles into Harmony. By using this option, you can modify colors collectively in a single docker. In addition, it also helps you to analyze colors and hues for complementary color schemes.

Alignment Guides: In CorelDRAW X6, the introduced Alignment Guides help you to position objects more precisely and accurately in a Drawing page. In this way, you can quickly adjust the alignment of objects having the suggested alignments fly within the existing artwork on your page. The alignment guides are temporary and remain for a small instance of time when you create, resize, and move objects with respect to the center or edges of other adjacent objects. The Alignment Guides are used to connect the centers and edges of objects. These can also be selected for displaying them from the edges of one object to the center of another object. In addition, you can also indentify the required margins for Alignment Guides to help you align objects placed at a distant location.

Page Layout Tools: In CorelDRAW X6, you are enabled with a reserves location for placing the text or graphics by using the new empty PowerClip frames. The new Placeholder Text command helps you to make a page layout presentable and designed in a professional manner.

Complex Script Support: In CorelDRAW X6, the Asian and Middle Eastern languages are added. By using these languages, you can support complex scripts that can be applied in the same way the other OpenType fonts are applied.

Native 64-Bit and Multi-core Support: The CorelDRAW X6 application now comes with a high speed and multi-core processing power. You can also use the applications of X6 versions in 64-bit support. By using this enhanced speed, you can quickly process larger files and images. In addition, the system will produce more output and will be more responsive while running multiple applications at the same time.

Bitmap and Vector Pattern Fills: In CorelDRAW X6, the new transparent background support is created by using the vector pattern fills. The new bitmap fills and vector pattern fills allow a transparent background with the use of collections of fills.

Page numbering: You can inset page numbers in multiple documents instantly. The Insert Page Number command helps you to insert instant page numbers on all pages of a document. You can initiate the page numbering from a specified page and can also start with the desired number. By using this feature, you can work ideally with various documents in a single file by arranging and giving them numbers. In CorelDRAW X6, you can also select the desired alphabetic, numeric, or roman format from the options. In addition, the page numbering can also be set according to the lower or upper case lettering.

The System Requirements to Install CorelDRAW X6

The CorelDRAW X6 application provides you a flexible development stage to create specialized designs. For installing CorelDRAW X6, you are required to fulfill the following system requirements in your computer system. For a complete installation of CorelDRAW X6, you also need to consider minimum hardware requirements on your computer. The table below shows the hardware requirements to install CorelDRAW X6-32 bit in your computer:

Hardware Requirements to install CorelDRAW X6

Components	Requirements
Central Processing Unit (CPU)	Intel Pentium 4, AMD Athlon 64 or AMD Opteron
Random Access Memory (RAM)	1GB RAM
Hardware Support	Mouse or tablet
Screen Support	1024 x 768 screen resolution
Drives	DVD drive
Hard Drive	1.5 GB hard disk space (for typical installation without content - additional disk space is required during installation)
Operating Systems	Microsoft Windows 8 (32-bit or 64-bit Editions) with latest service packs installed
	Microsoft Windows 7 (32-bit or 64-bit Editions) with latest service packs installed
	Windows Vista (32-bit or 64-bit Editions) with latest service packs installed
	Windows XP (32-bit) with latest service packs installed
Internet Explorer	Microsoft Internet Explorer 7 or higher

Launching the CorelDRAW X6 Application

After installing CorelDRAW on your computer, you can open this application and start working with a new blank page, create a document by using a template, or open an existing document. You can start CorelDRAW by selecting Start> All Programs> CorelDRAW Graphics Suite X6> CorelDRAW X6.

When you click, the CorelDRAW X6 launching splash screen appears on your computer screen. After that, the CorelDRAW X6 Welcome screen appears, as shown in picture 1.3. You can perform the following activities from the Welcome screen of CorelDRAW X6:

1. Start working with a new drawing in CorelDRAW X6 by clicking the **Quick Start** link.
2. Learn about the new features of CorelDRAW X6 by clicking the **What's New** link.
3. Learn about the various designing tools in CorelDRAW by clicking the **Learning Tools** link.
4. View a sample of predefined design patterns in CorelDRAW by clicking the **Gallery** link.
5. Explore the updates available for the CorelDRAW X6 application by clicking the **Updates** link.

Picture 1.3

Let's proceed by clicking the **Quick Start** link to open a new document in CorelDRAW X6. The Quick Start page appears, as shown in picture 1.4.

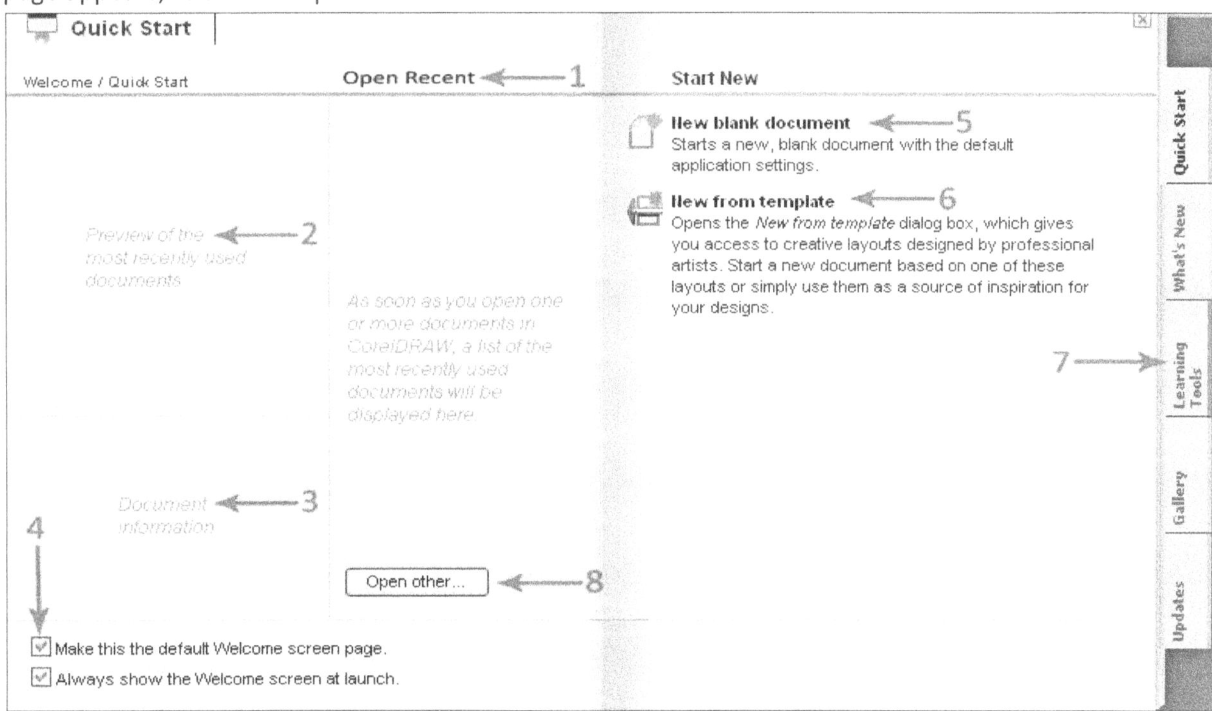

Picture 1.4

The Quick Start page of CorelDRAW (as shown above) includes various options which are numbered in the picture:

1. Open recent documents
2. The document preview area

3. The document information area
4. Select to personalize the screen
5. Create new blank document
6. Open template dialog box
7. Tabs for Quick Start page
8. Click to locate and open document

After a brief understanding of the various options in the Welcome screen of CorelDRAW, let's quickly proceed ahead and learn to create a new document in CorelDRAW X6 in the following section of this lesson.

Creating a New Document in CorelDRAW X6

You can create a new document to start with CorelDRAW tools. In CorelDRAW, you can create a new blank document either from Menu bar or from Welcome screen. The new document appears white in color having no objects on the Drawing page. In CorelDRAW, you can create multiple documents at a single time. The new scene refreshes the application while keeping the previous session settings. In this section, you learn to create a new document from the Menu bar. Let's perform the following steps to create a new document in CorelDRAW X6 by using the Create a New Document dialog box:

1. **Launch** the CorelDRAW X6 application.

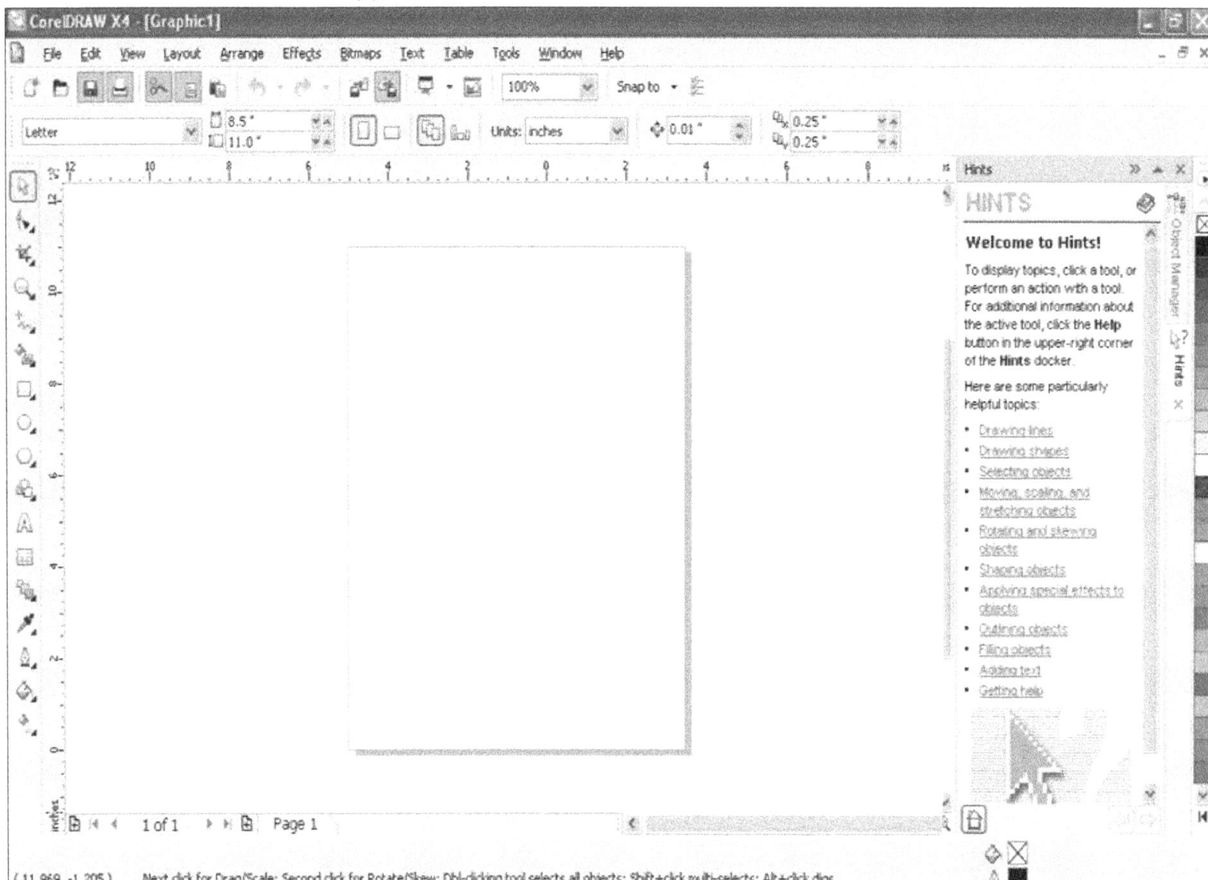

Picture 1.5

2. Select the **File**> **New** option from the <u>Menu</u> bar. It opens the **Create a New Document** dialog box on the screen.

3. **Type** a name for your document in the **Name** text box in the Create a New Document dialog box. In our case, we type **Untitled-1**.

4. Click the **OK** button at the bottom in the dialog box. It opens the workspace of CorelDRAW X6, as shown in picture 1.5.

After learning the procedure to open a blank CorelDRAW document, let's next explore the user interface features of CorelDRAW X6 in the following section.

Exploring the User Interface of CorelDRAW X6

In CorelDRAW X6 application, wide range of features and tools help you to work with the different designing approaches. Before working in CorelDRAW, you are required to get a little familiar with its user interface and its various components.

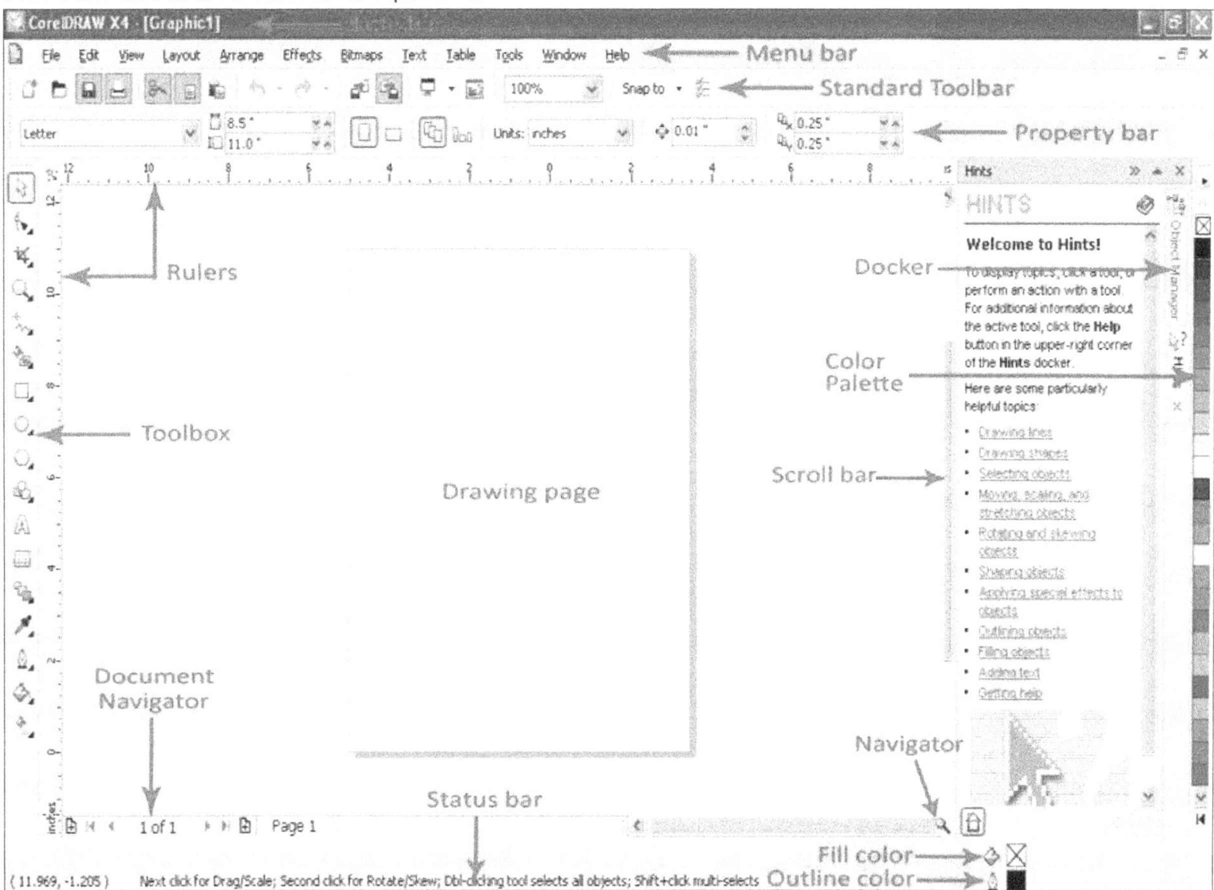

Picture 1.6

In other words, you should know about the various components in the user interface, including the Color palette, the Document Palette docker, and the various other dockers that are available by default. The user interface also includes the toolbox, drawing page, status bar, and the property bar that allows you to configure the page settings, units, and layout of your document. Moreover, the CorelDRAW X6 user interface includes a library that you can use to customize the workspace (the area comprising the Document window, which includes the Drawing page). The library contains various tools and applications that you can select to include in the workspace according to your requirements and convenience. The user interface of CorelDRAW X6 is shown in picture 1.6. You can see in picture 1.6, the various user interface features available in the CorelDRAW X6 application. Let's next discuss some of these components in the following sections.

The Title Bar

You can view the Title bar (shown in picture 1.6) at the top of the interface of the application, which displays the title of the currently-opened document. For example, when you open the CorelDRAW application for the first time, a blank document appears on the interface with the name, CorelDRAW X6 (Evaluation Version) – [Untitled- 1], by default proceeding with the application name, and then the document number, which is [Untitled- 1] in our case. On the left side of the Title bar, there is an icon called the Control Menu. When you click this icon, a dropdown list appears, containing options such as Restore, Move, Size, Minimize, Maximize, and Close. The right side of the Title bar contains a button panel that has three buttons from left to right: Minimize, Restore Down / Maximize, and Close. These buttons are used to minimize a CorelDRAW window, restore the size of the window to its default size or maximize the window, and close the window, respectively.

The Menu Bar

You can view the Menu bar below the Title bar of the CorelDRAW window. It comprises dropdown list having commands, such as File, Edit, View, Layout, Bitmaps, and Text. Each menu opens a dropdown list from where you can select other options according to your requirement. The right side of the Menu bar also contains a button panel that has three buttons, namely Minimize, Restore Down / Maximize, and Close. However, these buttons are specific to the current document.

The Standard Toolbar

In CorelDRAW X6, the Standard Toolbar comprises various shortcuts to basic menus and commands, such as opening, saving, and printing documents. Additional toolbars contain shortcuts for more specific tasks. These shortcuts appear as buttons on the Standard Toolbar. The table below displays a brief description of the various buttons on the Standard Toolbar:

Table: Standard Toolbar Buttons

Button Name	Description
New	Allows you to open a new CorelDRAW document
Open	Allows you to open an existing document in CorelDRAW
Save	Allows you to save the changes made in a new or existing file
Print	Allows you to print the currently opened document
Cut	Using this option, you can move items from one location to another location on the Drawing page
Copy	Using this option, you can create a duplicate copy of selected items or objects in CorelDRAW

Paste	Allows you to paste the items that you cut or copy from one location to another location either within the same CorelDRAW document or to an external application, such as MS Paint or Adobe Photoshop
Undo	Allows you to reverse the last action performed in the document
Redo	It lets you restore the action of the Undo button
Search Content	Allows you to display the Connect docker. You can also search for content in times of clipart, photos, and fonts
Import	Allows you to import a graphics file in a CorelDRAW document
Export	It lets you export a CorelDRAW document in a different file format
Application launcher	Allows you to open the applications of CorelDRAW X6 Graphics Suite, such as Corel PHOTO-PAINT X6, directly from the CorelDRAW X6 workspace
Welcome screen	Allows you to open the Welcome screen of the CorelDRAW X6 application
Zoom levels	Using this option, you can set the zoom level for the CorelDRAW document
Snap to	Allows you to disable or enable the alignment for the grid, guidelines, objects, and dynamic guides automatically
Options	Allows you to open the Options dialog box, from where you can edit properties for the workspace, document, and options related to printing

The Property Bar

You can view the options according to the tool activated at that time under the Property bar. In CorelDRAW X6, you can use the Property bar to edit or change the properties of that tool according to your requirement. For example, if you select the Text tool from Toolbox, the controls on the Property bar change to display tools related to creating and editing text, such as font size, font style, and font color. Therefore, you can say that the options on the Property bar keep changing according to the actions performed by the user.

The Toolbox

You can view the Toolbox on the left side of the Document window. Toolbox comprises of a collection of tools that can be used to perform specific drawing and editing tasks, such as creating, filling, and modifying objects in the drawing. Each tool in the Toolbox, except the Pick tool, the Text tool, and the Table tool, contains a small arrow at the lower right corner of the tool icon. When you click this arrow, a flyout appears containing a set of tools related to the respective tool. The table below displays the various tools available in Toolbox of CorelDRAW X6:

Table: Tools in Toolbox

Name of tool group	Tool Name	Description
Selection Tool	Pick tool	Allows you to select, resize, skew, and rotate objects or Images in a CorelDRAW document
	Freehand Pick Tool	Allows you to select the objects by creating a marquee selection around the specified object
Shape Edit tools	Shape tool	Allows you to edit the shape of objects by manipulating their nodes and segments
	Smudge Brush tool	Allows you to change the shape of an object by dragging its outline

	Roughen Brush tool	Allows you to distort the outline of a vector object by dragging its outline
	Free Transform tool	Allows you to transform an object, by rotating, mirroring, scaling, and skewing the object
	Smear tool	Allows you to shape the object by creating extensions or marks along the outline of the object
	Twirl tool	Allows you to create swirl effects by moving beside the edge of the object
	Attract tool	Allows you to shape objects by attracting the specified nodes with the cursor
	Repel tool	Allows you to shape objects by driving the nodes away from the cursor
Crop tools	Crop tool	Allows you to resize a drawing by selecting the required portion from it
	Knife tool	Allows you to cut an object to create two or more separate objects
	Eraser tool	Allows you to remove or erase unwanted portions of your drawing
	Virtual Segment Delete	Allows you to delete the portions of objects that lie between intersections
Zoom tools	Zoom tool	Allows you to change the magnification level of the Drawing page
	Pan tool	Allows you to drag the hidden areas of a drawing into view without changing the zoom level
Curve tools	Freehand tool	Allows you to create single line segments and curves
	2-Point Line tool	Allows you to create a straight line that begins from the starting point and terminates at the endpoint
	Bezier tool	Allows you to draw curved line segments
	Artistic Media tool	Allows you to access the Brush, Sprayer, Calligraphic, and Pressure tools
	Pen tool	Allows you to draw straight as well as curved line segments
	B-Spline tool	Allows you to draw curved lines by setting control points that shape the curve without breaking it into segments
	Polyline tool	Allows you to draw and connect lines and curves in one continuous line
	3-Point Curve tool	Allows you to draw a curve by dragging from the starting point to the endpoint, and then position the center point
Smart tools	Smart Fill tool	Allows you to indentify the enclosed area when one object overlaps the other one, and fill the enclosed areas
	Smart Drawing tool	Allows you to convert freehand strokes to basic shapes and smoothed curves
Rectangle tools	Rectangle tool	Allows you to draw a rectangle
	3-Point Rectangle	Allows you to draw rectangles with a rotation angle

Ellipse tools	Ellipse tool	Allows you to draw an ellipse
	3-Point Ellipse tool	Allows you to draw an ellipse with a rotation angle
Object tools	Polygon tool	Allows you to draw symmetrical polygons
	Star tool	Allows you to draw a perfect star
	Complex Star tool	Allows you to draw complex stars with intersecting sides
	Graph Paper tool	Allows you to draw a grid of lines
	Spiral tool	Allows you to draw the symmetrical and logarithmic spirals
Basic Shapes tools	Basic shapes tool	Allows you to select from a set of shapes, including a hexagon, a smiley face, and a right angle triangle objects
	Arrow Shapes tool	Allows you to draw arrows of different shapes and directions, and add arrow heads at the starting and ending points
	Flowchart Shapes tool	Allows you to draw the symbols of a flowchart
	Banner Shapes tool	Allows you to draw banners
	Callout Shapes tool	Allows you to draw callouts and labels
Text tool	Text tool	Allows you to type words in the form of Artistic or Paragraph text on the Drawing page
Table tool	Table tool	Allows you to draw and edit a table
Dimension tools	Parallel Dimension tool	Allows you to draw parallel dimension lines. Dimension lines are those lines whose dimensions can be specified on the Drawing page
	Horizontal or Vertical Dimension tool	Allows you to draw horizontal or vertical lines
	Angular Dimension	Allows you to draw angular dimension lines
	Segment Dimension	Allows you to display the distance between end nodes on single or multiple segments
	3-Point Callout tool	Allows you to draw callouts with a two-segment leading line
Connector tools	Straight-Line Connector tool	Allows to draw a straight line to connect two objects
	Right-Angle Connector tool	Allows you to draw a right angle to connect two objects
	Right-Angle Round Connector tool	Allows you to draw a right angle with a rounded corner to connect two objects
	Edit Anchor tool	Allows you to modify the anchor points of objects. This tool is helpful when you want to modify the anchor points of two lines connected to each other
Interactive tools	Blend tool	Allows you to blend objects by creating a progression of intermediate objects and colors
	Contour tool	Allows you to apply a series of concentric shapes that radiate inward or outward to the base object
	Distort tool	Allows you to transform objects by applying the Push and Pull, Zipper, or Twister effects
	Drop Shadow tool	Allows you to apply shadows behind or below objects

	Envelope tool	Allows you to change the shape of an object by dragging the nodes of an envelope around the boundary of the object. Applying an envelope on an object provides the object with additional nodes that you can use to edit the object
	Extrude tool	Applies 3D effects to objects to create the illusion of depth
	Transparency tool	Allows you to apply transparency to objects
Eyedropper tools	Color Eyedropper	Allows you to sample colors, and apply them to objects on the Document window
	Attributes Eyedropper	Allows you to copy object attributes, such as fill, outline, size, and effects, and apply them to other objects
Outline tools	Outline Pen tool	Allows you to change the appearance of outlines by using the options available in the dialog box that appear on clicking this tool. For example, you can specify the color, width, and style of the outlines
	Outline Color tool	Allows you to set the options to define the outline color of an object from the dialogue box that appears on clicking this tool
	No Outline	Allows you to remove the outline of a shape
	Hairline Outline	Allows you to create a thin line similar to a human hair
	1 pt	Allows you to create a 1 point thick outline
	Color	Allows you to set the color model and color values while filling an object or applying color to its outline from the Color docker that appears on clicking this tool
Fill tools	Fill Tool	Allows you to fill objects or closed paths in different styles
	Uniform Fill tool	Allows you to apply a solid color to an object
	Fountain Fill tool	Allows you to blend two or more colors to add depth to objects
	Pattern Fill tool	Allows you to fill an object with 2-color, Full color, or Bitmap color
	Texture Fill tool	Allows you to apply a texture on objects to give them a more natural or realistic appearance. CorelDRAW provides a variety of preset textures and each texture has a set of options that you can change as per your requirements
	PostScript Fill tool	Allows you to apply PostScript texture fills to objects. The PostScript texture fill is created by using the PostScript language
	No Fill tool	Allows you to import no color to an object
	Color tool	Allows you to set the color model and color values while filling an object or applying color to its outline from the Color docker that appears on clicking this tool
Interactive Fill tools	Interactive Fill tool	Allows you to fill an object with uniform fills, pattern fills, texture fills, and fountain fills
	Mesh Fill tool	Allows you to apply a mesh grid to an object

The Document Window

In CorelDRAW X6, the Document window can be defined as a workspace area that is bordered by scroll bars and various controls. The Drawing window comprises of the Drawing page and the surrounding area. The Drawing page is a rectangular region inside a Document window. It is the printable area of your work area. When you open CorelDRAW, the Drawing page appears with the default size. However, you can set the size and orientation of the Drawing page from the Property bar as per your requirements.

By the way, the region outside the Drawing page is known as the Document window, and it can be used to place objects that you frequently use in your drawing. For example, you can create a rectangle and place it outside the Drawing page and use the rectangle any number of times by making copies of it from the Document window. Objects placed outside the Drawing page are not printed but they increase the size of the file. Therefore, after finalizing the document, it is recommended to remove all the objects present outside the Drawing page to keep the file size low.

Document Navigator

You can view Document Navigator at the bottom of the CorelDRAW X6 window. It is located just above the Status bar. Document Navigator comprises the controls that allow you to add pages in your document and move between the pages. There are two such controls with the + sign. The first control (located to the left of Document Navigator) is used to insert a page to the left of the selected page, while the second control is used to insert a page to the right of the selected page.

The Dockers

You can define the dockers as a component in the user interface, which contains controls, such as command buttons, options, and list boxes. The dockers are somewhat similar to the dialog boxes but with the difference that you can keep a docker opened while working on a document, whereas a dialog box needs to be closed before resuming work on a document. Object Manager is an example of a docker, which displays elements, such as the Fill Type list box and the Color palette, and buttons, such as Advanced and Apply. Picture 1.7 shows the Object Manger docker.

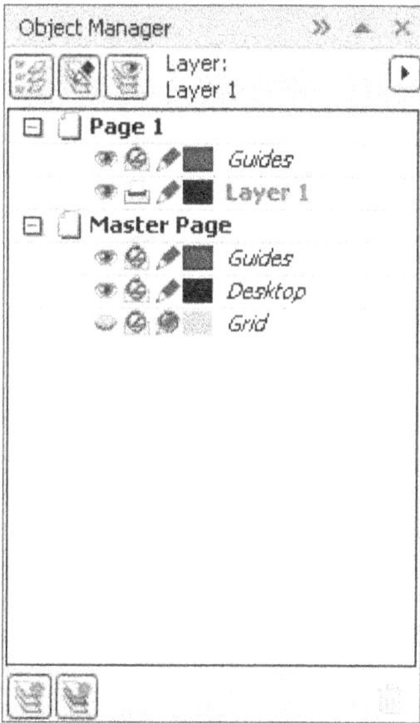

Picture 1.7

The Color Palette

You can view the Color palette at the right side of the CorelDRAW window. The Color palette is a dockable bar consisting of a collection of solid colors used for filling, outlining, and highlighting objects. You can only view some colors at a time on the bar. The rest of the colors can be viewed by scrolling the bar by using the up and down buttons present at the top and bottom of the bar respectively.

The Status Bar

You can view the Status bar at the bottom of the CorelDRAW window. The Status bar displays information about the properties of an object, such as type, size, and color. This bar also displays information, such as color proofing status, color profiles, and the current position of the mouse.

The Navigator

The Navigator button in CorelDRAW provides a smaller display of the Document window, which helps to move around a drawing page.

The Ruler

The rulers are specified by the horizontal and vertical borders and used to determine the size and position of objects in a document. They are used to accurately place objects on the document page. After understanding the various components of the CorelDRAW X6 user interface, let's learn to work with some of the navigation tools, such as zooming and panning of CorelDRAW X6 in the next lesson.

Lesson 2
Navigation by Using the Zoom and Pan Tools

You can use the Zoom tool to get a magnified or distant look of a drawing in CorelDRAW. Sometimes, when you view an object by using a high magnification level, you may not be able to view the entire object. In such a case, you can pan the object by using the Pan tool to view the areas that were not visible earlier. Panning allows you to view those areas of the object that are hidden from the view, by moving the Drawing page around in the Document window. When the Zoom tool from Toolbox is selected, the Property bar displays the buttons related to the tool. These buttons can be briefly discussed as follows:

Zoom level: Allows you to select the various zoom levels, such as To Page, To Width, To Height, 10%, 25%, and 50%
Zoom in: Allows you to view the Drawing page with a high level of magnification
Zoom out: Allows you to view the Drawing page with a reduced level of magnification
Zoom to selected: Allows you to view only the selected objects in a magnified form
Zoom to all objects: Helps you to zoom on all the objects in the Drawing page
Zoom to page: Fits the Drawing page in the Document window
Zoom to page width: Allows you to view the Drawing page width-wise
Zoom to page height: Allows you to view the Drawing page height-wise

Zooming the View of a Drawing

The Zoom tool allows you to magnify or reduce the view of your drawing according to your requirements. In CorelDRAW X6, you can use the zoom tool to either zoom in or zoom out of the Drawing page. The Zoom tool helps you to view the required objects clearly and precisely on the Drawing page. In CorelDRAW, you can access the Zoom tool from Toolbox. In this section, you learn to zoom a drawing with the help of Zoom tool. Let's perform the following steps to zoom a drawing:

1. **Open** any drawing (any .cdr file) in CorelDRAW X6.

2. Select the **Zoom tool** from the <u>Toolbox</u>.

3. Click the **Zoom in** button on the <u>Property bar</u>. As a result, the enlarged view of the drawing appears on the screen. You can also change the magnification level to view your drawing by using the Zoom tool in CorelDRAW.

Panning the View of Drawing

While working with large images having complex and various designed objects, you need to move the drawing in the required position. For this, the Pan tool helps you to move and drag the huge images in the desired directions. In other words, if you are viewing an image at a high level of magnification, it may be that some part of the image is not visible. In such a case, you can use the Pan tool to view the part that is not visible. Let's perform the following steps to pan the view of an object:

1. **Open** a drawing in CorelDRAW X6.

2. **Select** (click and hold) the arrow on the right side of the Zoom tool from Toolbox. It opens a flyout on the screen.

3. Select the **Pan tool** from the flyout.

4. **Click** and **drag** the drawing towards the left side to view the right section of it.

In the same way, you can also view the left section of the drawing by panning the page towards the right with the help of the hand pointer that appears on the CorelDRAW interface. You can also scroll left and right by using the horizontal slider to view the spiral. After learning to pan a drawing in CorelDRAW, let's proceed to the next section and discuss how to undo and redo a series of actions performed on a drawing.

Undoing and Redoing Series of Actions

In CorelDRAW X6, you can undo or redo a series of actions performed on the Drawing page. All actions you perform on the objects of your drawing are recorded and displayed in the Undo docker. Sometimes, you may make a mistake while creating or modifying a drawing and realize it only after you have performed a series of actions on the drawing. Now, after realizing the mistake, you want to bring your drawing to the state it was before you made the mistake. In such cases, CorelDRAW provides the facility to undo the actions to the specified point of your choice. If you want to undo a series of actions, you need to select the action from where you want the undo operation to be performed, from the Undo docker. All the actions, which are listed below the selected action, are undone. Similarly, you can also redo a series of actions from the Undo docker by selecting the action from where onwards you want to perform the redo operation.

You can also perform a single undo action by selecting Edit> Undo and a single redo action by selecting Edit> Redo from the Menu bar. Let's perform the following steps to undo and redo a series of actions in a drawing:

1. **Open** a new CorelDRAW document. In our case, we open a document having multiple objects drawn on the Drawing page.

2. Select **Tools**> **Undo** from the Menu bar.

The Undo docker appears on the right side of the Document window having various actions that have been performed previously or from the start of the drawing. The actions enrolled under the Undo docker are stacked in the order of use of specific tool or action implemented in the drawing page.

3. Select the **Create** action (in our case), which is second from the top. The second create action appears in the Drawing page.

4. Select the **Create** action (in our case), which is third from the top. The second create action appears in the Drawing page.

The actions that are listed below the selected Create action are undone. The operation results in the deletion of the rectangle on the Drawing page. By the way, when you select an action to undo it from the Undo docker, all the actions listed below the selected action are undone. Similarly, to redo an action, you need to select the action from the docker, which you want to be redone.

Saving a Drawing in CorelDRAW X6

In CorelDRAW X6, you have learned to draw basic geometric figures, such as a line, rectangle, ellipse, and spiral. After working on the drawing, you can save your document at a location of your choice so that you open and work on it later according to your requirements and convenience. Saving a document in CorelDRAW is not different from any other application. Documents are saved as files with the name and format specified by you. Let's perform the following steps to save a CorelDRAW document:

1. **Open** a drawing in CorelDRAW X6. In our case, we open the drawing created in the previous section.

2. Select **File> Save As** from the Menu bar. It opens the Save Drawing dialog box on the screen.

3. **Navigate** to the location where you want to save your document.

4. **Type** a name for the document in the File name combo box. In our case, we type the name: **My First Drawing**.

5. Click the **Save** button to save the document as a file with the specified settings. As you click the Save button, the name of the document and its location appears on the Title bar.

Opening an Existing Document

In addition to creating and saving new documents in CorelDRAW, you can also open and use existing documents. Documents in this application are saved in the .cdr format by default. You can open the existing document and several built-in files (.cdr files) as well as the files of different formats created by other users. You can open and directly work on those files. In this section, we are opening the document, which we saved in the preceding section. Let's perform the following steps to open an existing CorelDRAW file:

1. **Lanuch** the CorelDRAW application, and select **File> Open** from the Menu bar. It opens the Open Drawing dialog box on the screen.

2. **Navigate** to the location where the document you want to open is stored.

3. **Select** the document that you want to open from the location. Then click the **Open** button in the Open Drawing dialog box. As the result, the selected document opens.

Previewing a Drawing

Before printing or exporting a drawing in CorelDRAW, you can preview the drawing to see how it will look. When you preview a drawing, all the objects in the drawing on the Drawing page and the objects in the intermediate area of the Document window area are displayed. You can preview either all the objects or a particular object in the drawing. While previewing a particular object, the remaining objects of the drawing are hidden. When you want a preview of all the objects in your drawing, you need to use the Full Screen Preview mode, as discussed in the following section.

Previewing a Drawing in the Full Screen Preview Mode

In Full Screen Preview mode, a preview of the Drawing page appears in full screen. In this mode, you can view all the objects present on the Drawing page. You can return to the CorelDRAW window by pressing any key from the keyboard. Here are the steps to preview a drawing in the Full Screen Preview mode:

1. **Open** a drawing in CorelDRAW, and select **View> Full Screen Preview** from the Menu bar. The drawing appears in the Full Screen Preview mode.

2. **Click** anywhere on the screen or press any key from the keyboard to return to the Document window.

Previewing Selected Objects

In CorelDRAW, you can preview the selected objects in a drawing. Selecting objects for preview allows you to view these objects on the Drawing page, while keeping the other unselected objects hidden. In this section, we show you how to preview the selected objects of the drawing used in the preceding section. Let's perform the following steps to preview the selected objects in a drawing:

1. **Open** a drawing in CorelDRAW, and select the **Pick tool** from Toolbox.

2. **Select** the object or objects by using Pick tool, which you want to preview.

3. Select **View> Preview Selected Only** from the Menu bar. As a result, a preview of the selected object appears in the Drawing page.

Viewing a Drawing in Different Views

In CorelDRAW, you can view your drawings in various diverse modes. These view modes apply certain predefined values to various elements in your drawing, such as color, toning, linings, contrast, and shades effects. You can select a view mode that best suits your requirement, to enhance your drawing or to modify the drawing in a desired manner. These view modes can be described as follows:

Simple Wireframe: Displays the bitmap in a drawing in monochrome, that is, in black and white. This view mode shows the outline of the drawing while hiding complex properties, such as fills, contours, drop shadows, and intermediate blend shapes. This view mode allows you to quickly preview the outlines of a drawing, as shown in picture 1.8.

Picture 1.8

Wireframe: Refers to a view mode that is similar to the Simple Wireframe view mode, except that Wireframe also shows the intermediate blend shapes in the drawing. Picture 1.9 shows the same picture in Wireframe mode.

Picture 1.9   Picture 2.0   Picture 2.1

Drafts: Displays the fills and bitmap of a drawing, but this mode displays low resolution, as shown in picture 2.0.

Normal: Displays a drawing without the PostScript fills or high resolution bitmap, as shown in picture 2.1 above.

Picture 2.2   Picture 2.3

Enhanced: Displays a drawing with the PostScript fills, high-resolution bitmaps, and anti-aliased vector graphics, as shown in picture 2.2.

Pixels: Refers to a type of view mode, which helps you to create drawings in pixel units. In this way, it provides you a better idea and way to represent your design on the Internet. The Pixels view mode is shown in picture 2.3. You can quickly switch between the selected viewing mode and the previous viewing mode by pressing the Shift+F9 keys in combination.

Working with Page Layout

When you open CorelDRAW X6, the drawing page appears with the default size, orientation, background, and layout style. However, you can change all these attributes according to your requirement. You can also add guidelines on the Drawing page, which help to place the objects in the drawing with precision. In addition, you can add any number of Drawing pages in your document, rename the pages, as well as delete them according to your requirement. Let's begin this section by learning to modify a Drawing page by adjusting its size and orientation.

Modifying the Size and Orientation of a Drawing Page

CorelDRAW provides two ways to define the size of the Drawing page: by selecting a preset page size, and by creating a custom page size by specifying the dimensions of the page. You can customize the size of the Drawing page by defining its dimensions (width and height) when the available preset page sizes do not fulfill your requirements.

Similar to a page size, there are two ways in which you can set the orientation of the Drawing page: Landscape and Portrait. When the width of the Drawing page is greater than its height, the orientation of the page is Landscape, and when the height of the Drawing page is greater than its width, the orientation of the Drawing page is Portrait. Let's perform the following steps to modify the size and orientation of a Drawing page:

1. **Open** a drawing in CorelDRAW, and **click** the down arrow button of the Page size list box on the Property bar. It opens a dropdown list, as shown in picture 2.4.

2. **Select** a size for your Drawing page from the dropdown list. In our case, we select the **Tabloid** size.

3. Type a value in the **Page dimensions** spin boxes to specify the height and width for the Drawing page, as shown in picture 2.5 with the red arrow numbered 3.

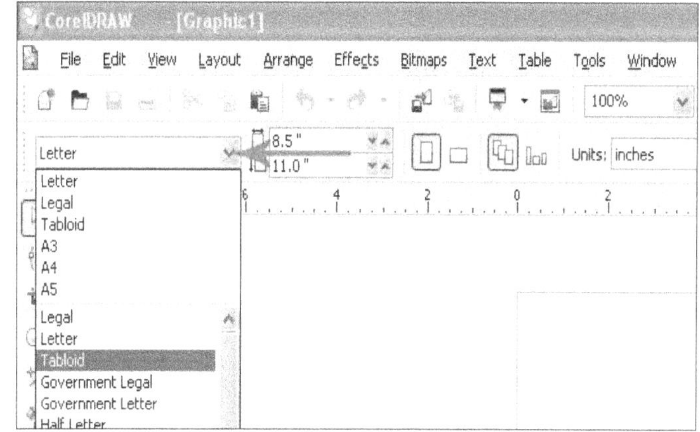

Picture 2.4

In our case, we **type**: 14.0" as the width and 10.0" as the height of the Drawing page.

By the way, when you set the width of the Drawing page to be more than its height, the orientation of the page sets to Landscape. On the other hand, if you set the height of the Drawing page to be more than its width, the orientation of the Drawing page sets to Portrait.

4. Type a value in the **Zoom level** combo box (picture 2.5 with arrow numbered 4) to specify the level of zoom you want. In our case, we type: **40%**.

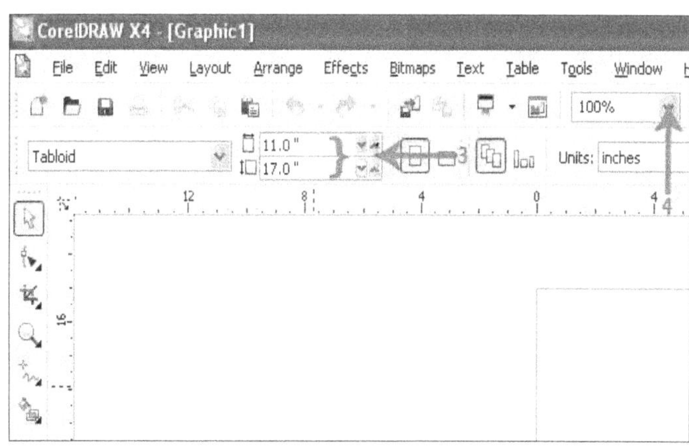

Picture 2.5

5. **Click** anywhere on the Drawing page to apply changes.

You can also click the **Apply Page Layout to All Pages** button on the Property bar of the CorelDRAW window, to apply page size and orientation settings to all the Drawing pages of your document. On the other hand, if you want to apply the settings only in the current Drawing page, click the **Apply Page Layout to Current Page Only** button on the Property bar.

Setting the Background of the Drawing Page

In CorelDRAW, the background of a new, blank Drawing page appears white by default. However, you can change this default setting and apply any color of your choice and set it as the background of the Drawing page. An appropriate background color helps to enhance the look of the page. In CorelDRAW, you can also use solid colors or even images as a background for the Drawing page. Let's perform the following steps to set the background for the Drawing page:

1. **Open** a drawing in CorelDRAW, and select **Layout> Page Background** from the Menu bar. It opens the **Options** dialog box, as shown in picture 2.6.

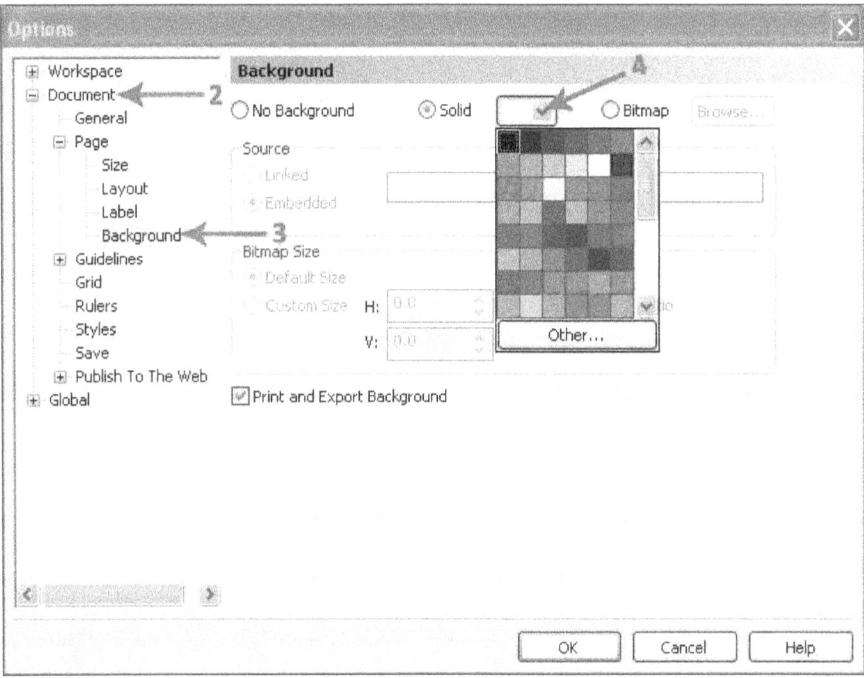

Picture 2.6

This dialog box is divided in two panes, namely the left pane and the right pane. The left pane shows different categories and the right pane displays the options related to the category selected in the left pane.

2. **Click** the (+) key beside the <u>Document</u> category from the left pane of the Options dialog box. The selected category expands to display various subcategories.

3. Select the **Background** subcategory. The options to set the background of the Drawing page are displayed on the right pane.

4. **Select** a radio button under the Background section to specify the type of color you want to apply to the background. In our case, we select the **Solid** radio button.

5. **Click** the down arrow button of the list box to open the Color palette. Then **select** a background color form the palette.

6. Click the **OK** button in the Options dialog box. As a result, the selected color is applied as a background to the Drawing page.

If you want to remove a background color, you can select the No Background radio button under the Background section of the Options dialog box. Let's next learn to add, rename, and delete a Drawing page in CorelDRAW X6.

Adding, Renaming, and Selecting a Drawing Page from a Document

CorelDRAW provides the facility to add new Drawing pages in your document. The Drawing page you add is named Untitled- 1 by default. You can change the default name and provide a name of your own to better reflect the contents of the Drawing page. In addition, you can delete Drawing pages that you feel are no longer required in your document. Performing these basic activities is easy and provides a way to keep the content of the document updated and organized at all times. Let's begin this section by learning how to add the Drawing page in a document.

Adding a Drawing Page

You can add any number of Drawing pages in your document. The inserted pages can be added before or after the current page as per your requirement. Let's perform the following steps to add a Drawing page in a CorelDRAW document:

1. **Open** a drawing in CorelDRAW X6. You can open the same drawing which was created in the previous section.

2. **Select** location where you want the new page to be inserted in the document, from **Document Navigator**, as shown in picture 2.7 with red arrow numbered 2. In our case, we select **Page 1**.

3. Select **Layout> Insert Page** from the Menu bar to open the Insert Page dialog box.

In this dialog box, you can set the number of Drawing pages that you want to insert in the document. You can insert the pages before or after any existing Drawing page in the document.

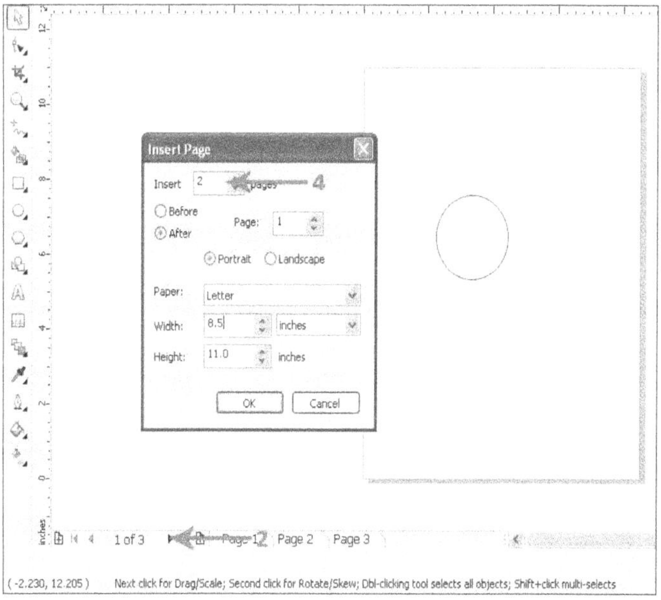

Picture 2.7

4. **Type** a value to specify the number of Drawing pages you want to insert, in the <u>Number of pages</u> spin box, as shown in picture 2.7 with red arrow numbered 4. In our case, we type **2**.

5. **Select** a radio button beside the <u>Place</u> option, to specify the location of the Drawing page in relation to the other existing pages in the document. In our case, we select the **After** radio button.

6. Click the **OK** button in the Insert Page dialog box. As a result, the two Drawing pages are inserted at the specified location (after Page 1) and displayed on the Document Navigator which is at the bottom of the Drawing page.

Renaming a Drawing Page

When you need to add a Drawing page, it appears with the default name on Document Navigator. However, you can rename the Drawing page according to your requirements. Let's perform the following steps to rename a Drawing page:

1. **Open** a drawing in CorelDRAW X6. You can open the same drawing which was created in the previous section.

2. **Select** the page that you want to rename from the Document Navigator. In our case, we select **Page 2**.

3. Select **Layout> Rename Page** from the Menu bar. It opens the <u>Rename Page</u> dialog box.

4. **Type** a new name for the Drawing page in the text box under the <u>Page name</u> option. In our case, we type the name **Cromosys-2**.

5. Click the **OK** button in the Rename Page dialog box. The Drawing page is renamed, and can be viewed in Document Navigator.

Deleting a Drawing Page

You can delete an individual Drawing page or a range of Drawing pages from your document by using the Delete Page option under the Layout menu. Let's perform the following steps to delete a Drawing page:

1. **Open** a drawing in CorelDRAW, and select **Layout> Delete Page** from the Menu bar. It opens the <u>Delete Page</u> dialog box.

2. **Type** the Drawing page number that you want to delete, in the <u>Delete Page</u> spin box. In our case, we type page **3**.

3. Click the **OK** button in the Delete Page dialog box.

Inserting Page Numbering in Multiple Drawing Pages

You can insert page numbering to specify the sequence of numbers, such as precedence of the Drawing page that you want before or after another. In CorelDRAW X6, now, you can insert page numbering in multiple Drawing pages document. In other word, you can display the page numbers on each Drawing page of the document. For inserting page numbering in CorelDRAW, you just need to select the Layout menu from the Menu bar, and then go for the Insert Page Number option. This option allows you to insert page numbers, such as On Active Layer, On All Pages, On All Odd Pages, and On All Even Pages. CorelDRAW X6 has many preformatted page number designs so that you can quickly insert page numbering in the Drawing area. You can also set the size of the digits that appears on the Drawing page. Let's perform the following steps to insert page numbers in CorelDRAW X6:

1. **Open** a drawing in CorelDRAW, and select **Layout> Insert Page Number> On All Pages** from the Menu bar. The page number appears in all the pages of the drawing.

2. **Click** the down arrow of the <u>Font size</u> combo box in the Property bar.

3. Select the **100 pt** option from the list. The figure number automatically appears in all the pages with the specified font size.

Exploring the Online Help in CorelDRAW X6

The Help feature of CorelDRAW X6 provides comprehensive information about the application from the online, Corel.com Corporation. When you use the Help feature, CorelDRAW X6 displays the CorelDRAW Help window consisting of three tabs that appear to the left of the Internet Explorer window. Each tab consists of various categories that can be expanded on clicking, to display further topics related to the category. When you select a particular topic from a category, the information of the topic appears on the right side of the window. The three tabs of the CorelDRAW Help window are as follows:

Contents: Displays a list of categories that you can expand to view the corresponding information
Index: Allows you to use the index to find a topic
Search: Allows you to use words or phrases to find information

In this section, you learn to use the Help feature to get information about a particular topic related to CorelDRAW. In our case, we are using the Search tab to get the required information. Let's perform the following steps to use the Search tab present in the CorelDRAW Help window:

1. **Open** a drawing in CorelDRAW, and select the **Help> Help Topics** option from the Menu bar. The CorelDRAW Help in the Internet Explorer window appears.

2. **Select** a tab depending on the information you want. In our case, we select the **Search** tab which is at the top in the middle of the Internet Explorer window.

3. **Type** a word or phrase in the **Type in the word(s) to search for** text box option. In our case, we type **Smear Tool**.

4. Click the **Go** button. The list of options searched from the online Corel help appears under the CorelDRAW Help window.

5. Click the **Smudging and smearing objects** link appearing in the window. The details and help about the specified options appear.

The information related to the selected topic is displayed on the right side of the CorelDRAW Help window, with the searched text highlighted. Let's next learn to close the drawing, and then quit the CorelDRAW application in the next section.

Closing a Document and Quitting the CorelDRAW Application

After you have finished working in CorelDRAW, you can close the application. However, before you do that, you need to make sure that the documents you have been working on are saved. This is important because saving helps to retain the changes made in a document so that the next time you open the document, you can continue working with all the changes intact. In case you try to close CorelDRAW without first saving your opened documents, a message box appears, asking you whether you want to save changes made in the documents. You need to ensure that all opened documents are saved and closed before quitting the CorelDRAW application. You can close the documents by selecting **File> Close** from the Menu bar. Now, you quit the application by selecting **File> Exit** from the Menu bar. By the way, you can also quit the CorelDRAW application by clicking the Close button on the Title bar.

Lesson 3
Drawing Shapes in CorelDRAW

Shapes are the basic elements of any drawing, which are created by the combination of the lines. The shapes can be drawn in different ways and by using various tools available in the CorelDRAW application. A straight line between two given points links the points together by traversing the shortest distance between them. Lines are used to create different shapes, which can be regular, enclosed geometric shapes, such as rectangles and squares, or irregular, and open shapes such as curves. The boundary of a shape is also known as its outline. When you create an object in CorelDRAW, you can edit the outline of the object to change its shape. You can also add colors to objects or shapes to make them attractive and make the drawing more realistic. CorelDRAW provides a number of drawing tools, such as Freehand, Bezier, Artistic, Pen and Polyline, which you can use to create lines, outlines, shapes, and curves. Objects are the basic elements of a design in CorelDRAW. These objects can be modified in different ways to create the design of your choice. Toolbox provides various tools to not only create objects, but also make modifications in the properties of objects. For example, you can draw a rectangle with the help of the Rectangle tool from Toolbox, and also modify the properties, such as increasing or decreasing the thickness of the stroke used to draw the rectangle or changing the height and width or the fill color of the rectangle.

In this lesson, you first learn to work with basic geometric tools in CorelDRAW by using the Freehand, Rectangle, Ellipse, and Spiral tools. You also learn to use curves by drawing a curve specifying the width and height and setting the options for the Freehand and Bezier tools. Next, you learn to work with lines and procedures to draw the Calligraphic, Pressure-Sensitive, and Preset lines. The chapter also discusses the procedure to work with outlines, wherein you learn to define outline settings, create a calligraphic outline, add an arrowhead, and edit an arrowhead. Further, in this chapter, you learn to work with newly-created vector shape tools, such as the Smear, Twirl, Attract, and Repel tools. In addition, you learn to modify shapes and lines and the procedure to apply the Convert command to convert an ellipse into a pie, crop a line, and split a line. Towards the middle of the chapter, you learn the procedure to perform the advanced operation with line objects, by using the Fillet, Scallop, Chamfer, and Envelope tools, copying an envelope, editing the nodes and segments of an envelope, altering the mapping mode, and creating an outline around an object. Towards the end of this chapter, you learn to work with brush stroke, wherein you learn to use a preset brush stroke and create a custom brush stroke. At the end, you learn to work with grids and guidelines in CorelDRAW, in which you learn to se the distance between grid lines, snap objects to the grid, and snap objects with the guidelines. Let's start the chapter and learn to work with basic geometric tools of CorelDRAW X6 in the following section.

Working with Basic Geometric Tools

The geometrical figures commonly comprise of line structure. Any design, simple or complex, which you create in CorelDRAW, consists of geometric figures that are made by using lines on the Drawing page. Therefore, if you want to create designs in CorelDRAW, you need to begin by creating simple geometrical figures and knowing the tools used to create them. Basic figures include line, rectangle, ellipse, polygon, and star. To draw these shapes on the Drawing page, you need to be adept in handling the mouse. In CorelDRAW, there are number of tools that you can use to draw the basic shapes. The tools are easy to use, and in most cases, their names suggest their functions, such as the Rectangle tool, which is used to draw rectangles, and the Ellipse tool, which is used to draw ellipses. Apart from this, there is the Freehand tool, which is used to draw simple lines and curves. In this section, you learn to use these tools in your CorelDRAW document.

Using the Freehand Tool to Draw a Line

The Freehand tool enables you to draw the straight and curved lines. You can also use this tool to adjust the smoothness of the lines. Let's perform the following steps to draw a line by using the Freehand tool:

1. **Open** a new drawing in CorelDRAW X6, and select the **Freehand tool** from Toolbox, as shown in picture 2.8 with the red arrow.

2. **Click** to specify the starting point of the line on the Drawing page.

3. **Click** the desired location on the Drawing page to specify the endpoint of the line. Now, a straight line appears on the Drawing page, as shown in picture 2.8.

This line is formed by specifying two points on the Drawing page. You can also use the Freehand tool to draw a series of connected lines. In this case, each line begins from where the previous line ends.

4. Select the **Freehand tool** again from Toolbox.

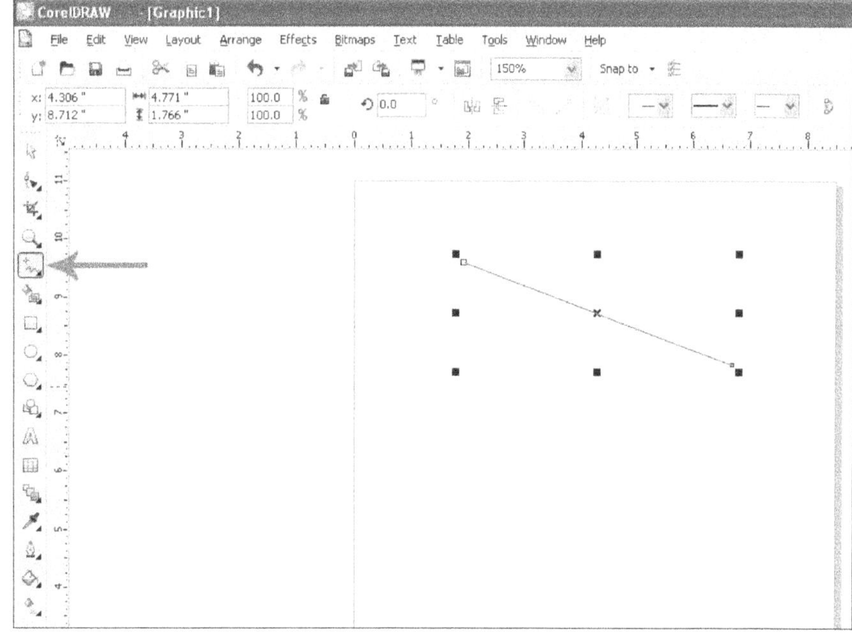

Picture 2.8

By the way, rotating a line at an angle requires you to move the mouse pointer, at the time of specifying the points of the line, and then draw the line. Likewise, erasing requires holding the Shift key, and then dragging backwards. You can also draw a curved line by using the Freehand tool. For this, click the point where you want to start the curve on the Drawing page, and drag the mouse pointer.

5. **Click** anywhere in the Drawing page to specify the starting point of the second line. The mouse pointer changes into the cross head pointer shape having a line initiated from the selected starting point, (picture 2.9).

6. **Double-click** the point where you want to end the second line. This point will act as the starting point of the third line, (picture 2.9).

7. **Click** the final point where you want to end the third line, as shown in picture 2.9 with red arrow numbered 7.

This picture shows a line pattern of connected lines with the help of the Freehand tool.

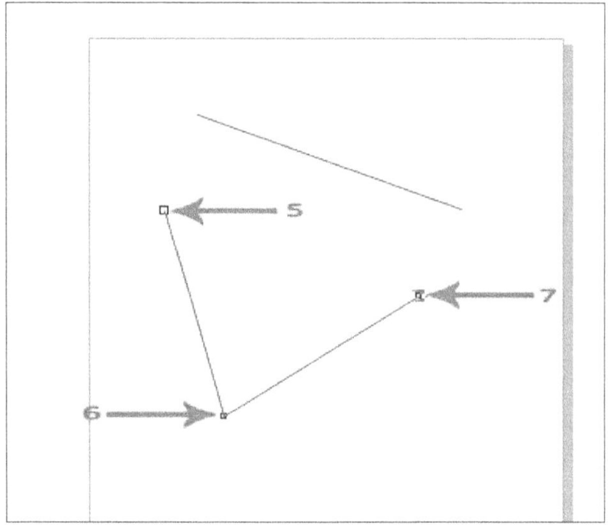

Picture 2.9

Till now, you have learnt that a single line can be drawn by selecting the initial and final positions of the line on the Drawing page. On the other hand, in case if you want a line in continuation, you can draw it by selecting the initial position and continuing by double-clicking to end the first line on the way to give continuation to the proceeding line.

Using the Rectangle Tool

The Rectangle tool is used to draw rectangles. After drawing the rectangle, you can resize it by using the handles on its boundary or specifying its height and width on the Property bar. Let's perform the following steps to draw a rectangle:

1. **Open** a drawing in CorelDRAW, and select the **Rectangle tool** from Toolbox.

2. **Click** and **drag** the mouse pointer to draw a rectangle on the Drawing page.

3. **Type** some values in the <u>Object Size</u> text boxes on the Property bar to specify the width and height of the rectangle. In our case, we type **7.0"** as the width and **4.0"** as the height, as shown in picture 3.0 with red arrow numbered 3. The rectangle is drawn according to the specifications you set.

Creating shapes involves changing or editing one shape to another until you have the shape of your choice. For example, you can edit the shape of a rectangle or square by rounding its corners to create a capsule. In CorelDRAW, changing the shape of objects is an easy and a simple process.

By the way, you can draw a square or rectangle by selecting the Rectangle tool from Toolbox, and then holding down the Ctrl key from keyboard and dragging the mouse pointer on the Drawing page until you have a square of the desired size.

4. **Set** appropriate values in the <u>Corner radius</u> spin boxes on the Property bar to specify the roundness of the corners of the rectangle. In our case, we set the value: **8"** in all the Corner radius spin boxes, as shown picture 3.0 with red arrow numbered 4.

As a result, the rectangle appears with rounded corners according to the specifications we have set.

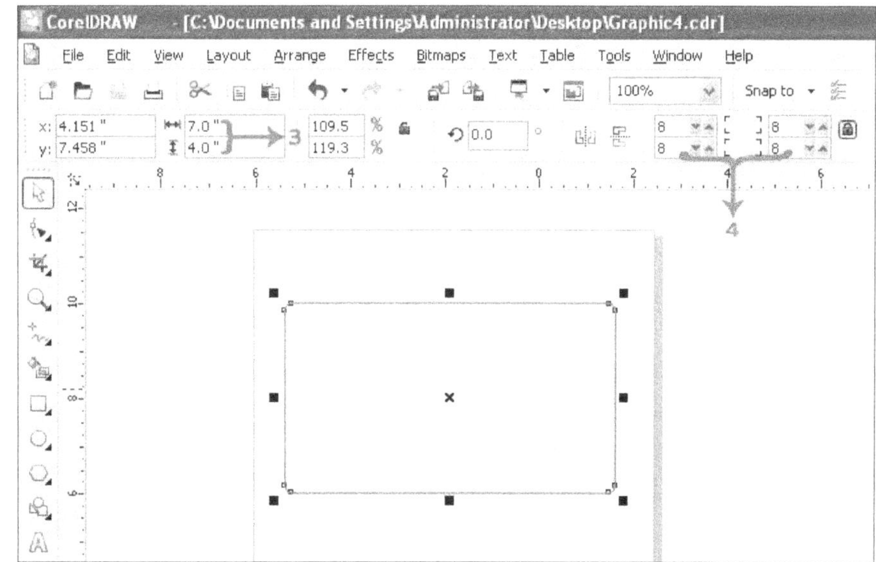

Picture 3.0

If you want to draw a rectangle by specifying its height and width, use the 3-Point Rectangle tool present in the flyout menu of the Rectangle tool. You can click the Round Corners Together button on the Property bar, to apply the same roundness for all corners of the rectangle. Let's next learn to use the Ellipse tool in the following section.

Using the Ellipse Tool

You can draw an ellipse by using the Ellipse tool. After drawing the ellipse, you can change its height and width by either dragging its handles diagonally or by setting its height and width from the Property bar. Let's perform the following steps to draw an ellipse:

1. **Open** a new drawing in CorelDRAW, and select the **Ellipse tool** from Toolbox.

2. **Click** and **drag** the mouse pointer to draw an ellipse on the Drawing page.

3. **Type** some values in the <u>Object Size</u> text boxes on the Property bar to specify the width and height of the ellipse. In our case, we type **7.0"** as the width and **3.0"** as the height. The ellipse is drawn according to the specification you set.

Using the Spiral Tool

You can draw a spiral by using the Spiral tool. There are two types of spiral shapes in CorelDRAW, symmetrical and logarithmic. You can set the number of revolutions of the spiral from the Property bar. A high value results in an increased number of spirals, whereas a low value results in a reduced number of spirals. Let's perform the following steps to draw a spiral:

1. **Open** a new drawing, and **select** the arrow on the right side of the **Object tool** in Toolbox. It opens a flyout, as shown in picture 3.1.

2. Select the **Spiral tool** from the flyout.

3. **Type** a value to specify the number of revolutions for the spiral in the **Spiral Revolutions** spin box on the Property bar, as shown in picture 3.1. In our case, we type: **6**.

4. Click either the **Symmetrical spiral** or **Logarithmic spiral** button on the Property bar, according to the type of spiral you want to draw. In our case, we select the **Symmetrical spiral** button, as shown in picture 3.1.

5. **Click** and **drag** to draw the spiral on the Drawing page.

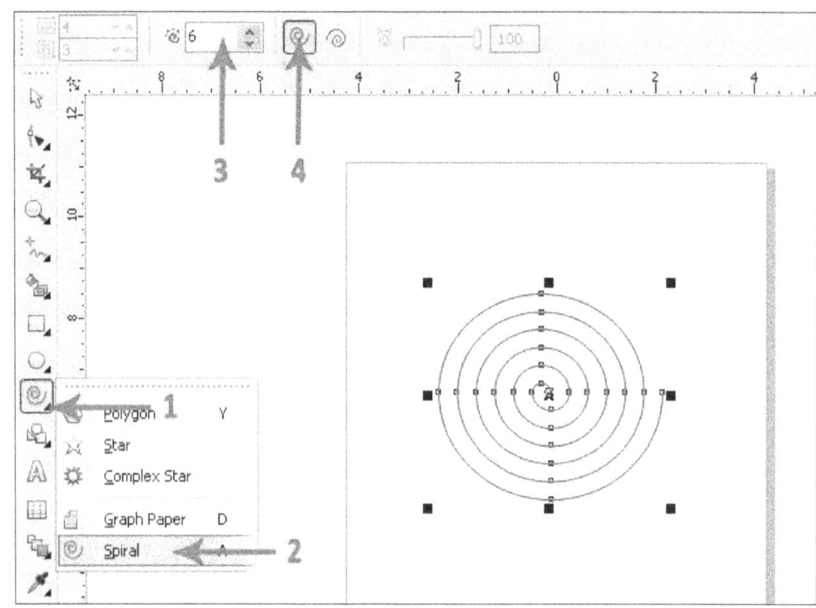

Picture 3.1

Using Curves in CorelDRAW

CorelDRAW provides various tools to create and design graphics that are not only pleasing to the eye, but are also professional in appearance. A drawing is an art that reflects the creativity of the user. CorelDRAW X6 provides a platform, where you can combine lines and shapes to communicate effectively in different ways, by designing logos, graphics, brochures, newsletters, posters, signs, and other types of visual communications. CorelDRAW provides you with different tools to draw lines, such as the Freehand, Polyline, Bezier, and Pen tools. These tools also provide various styles and options to edit the lines. Let's begin this section by learning to draw a curve by setting its width and height.

Drawing a Curve by Setting Width and Height

A line that deviates from a straight path in a smooth and constant manner is known as a curve. CorelDRAW provides various tools to draw curves, such as the Freehand, Bezier, Artistic Media, Pen, Polyline, and 3-Point Curve tools. All these tools are available in the Curve tools flyout on Toolbar. The Freehand tool is selected by default in the Curve tools flyout. Let's perform the following steps to draw a curve by using the 3-Point Curve tool, as well as set the width and height of the curve:

1. **Open** a new drawing, and **click** the arrow on the right side of the **Curve tools** from Toolbox. It opens a flyout, as shown in picture 3.2.

2. Select the **3-Point Curve tool** from the flyout (picture 3.2).

3. **Click** the Drawing page and **drag** to specify the starting and ending points of the curve. A straight line is created, as shown in picture 3.2.

4. **Click** the desired location on the Drawing page to specify the third point to form a curve, as shown in picture 3.3. A curve is formed at the specified point.

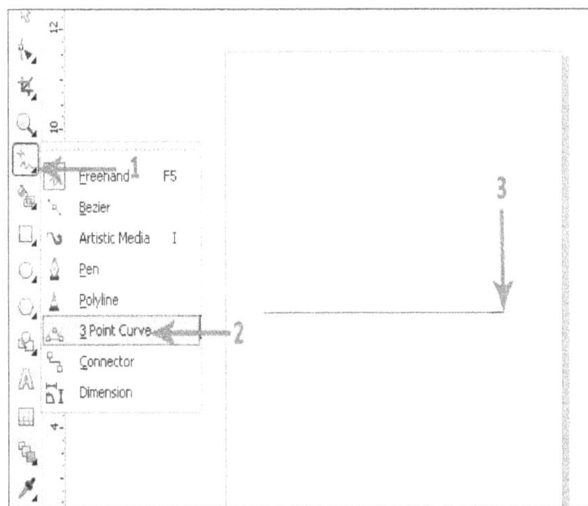

Picture 3.2

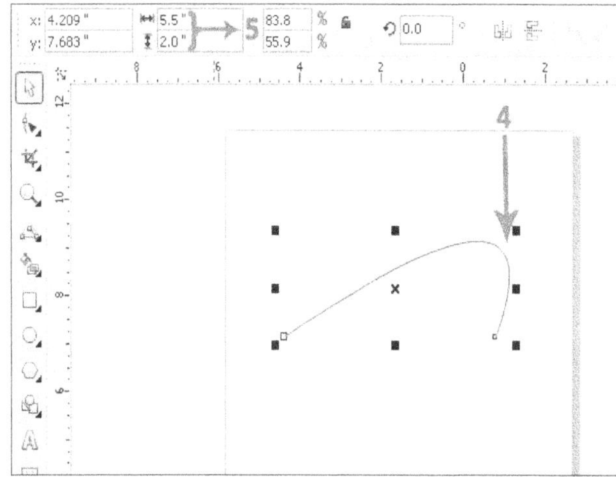

Picture 3.3

5. Type values in the **Object Size** text boxes on the Property bar to specify the width and height of the curve. In our case, we type **5.5"** as the width and **2.0"** as the height of the curve, as shown in picture 3.3 with red arrow numbered 5.

The shape of the curve is set according to the specified values. Let's next learn to set the options for the Freehand and Bezier tools in the following section.

Setting the Options for the Freehand and Bezier Tools

In CorelDRAW, the Freehand and Bezier tools include various options that you can set for the curves you create by using these tools.

These options allow you great flexibility and precision while manipulating the curve to enhance its usability. For example, you can control the smoothing of the curve by changing the values of the Corner threshold, Straight line threshold, and Auto-join options. These options are available in the Options dialog box. Let's perform the following steps to set options for the Freehand and Bezier tools:

1. **Open** a new drawing, and select **Tools**> **Options** from the Menu bar. The Options dialog box appears on the screen, as shown in picture 3.4.

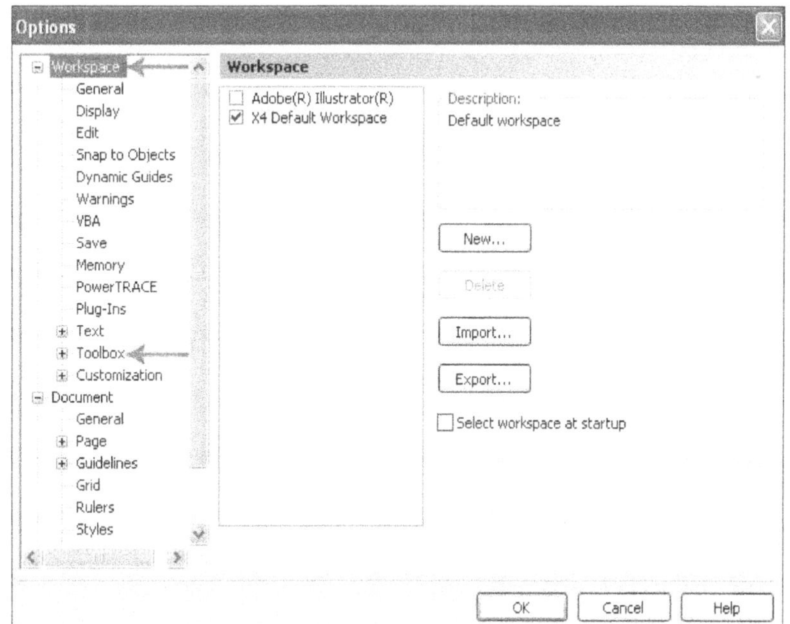

Picture 3.4

The Options dialog box is divided in two panes, namely the left pane and the right pane. The left pane displays various categories. When you select any of these categories, the options related to that category are displayed on the left pane.

2. **Click** the (+) sign beside the **Workspace** category on the left pane of the Options dialog box. The category expands to display various subcategories.

3. **Click** the (+) sign beside **Toolbox** subcategory under the Workspace category.

4. Select the **Freehand/Bezier Tool** option to display the related options on the right pane of the Options dialog box, as shown in picture 3.5.

5. Type a value in the **Freehand smoothing** text box to specify the level of smoothness you want for the curve. In our case, we type **80**.

6. Type a value beside the **Corner threshold** spin box, for the corner nodes of the curve. In our case, we type **7**.

7. Type a value beside the **Straight line threshold** spin box. This spin box determines the way the shape of the curve is created.

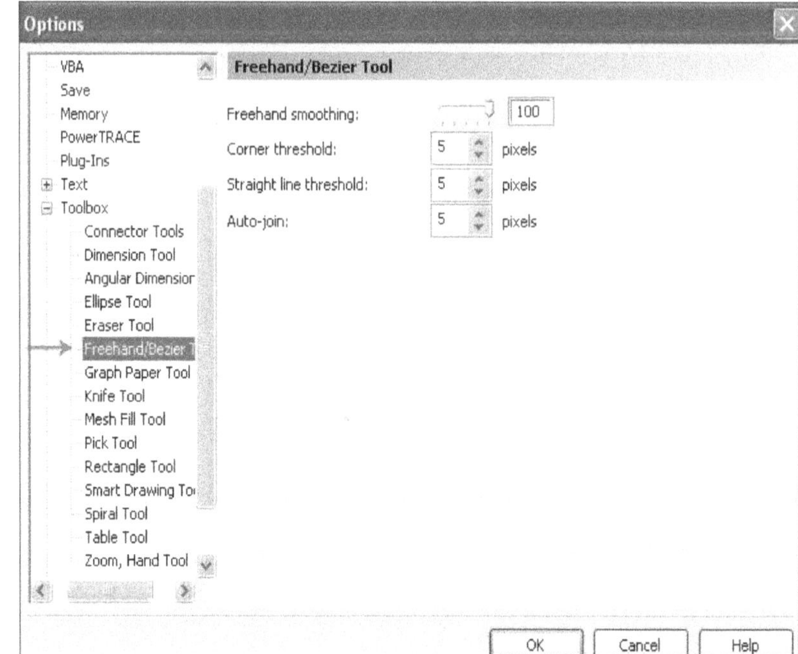

Picture 3.5

A lower value causes the nodes to be set on straight lines, whereas a higher value causes the nodes to be set on a curved line. In our case, we type 6.

8. Type a value beside the **Auto-join** spin box. This value represents the distance in pixels that the mouse pointer must be when clicking the first node of a newly-created path to close the path automatically. The default value is 5. In our case, we type **4**.

9. Click the **OK** button at the bottom to save the changes.

You can also drag the slider up and down beside the Freehand smoothing option to increase or decrease the value. In addition, the values of Corner threshold, Straight line threshold and Auto-join can be increased or decreased by the up and down arrow button provided along the respective spin boxes.

Working with Lines

CorelDRAW offers a wide range of line patterns. You can draw calligraphic, pressure-sensitive as well as preset lines. These lines are used for artistic effect and can be created by using the Brush tool with the color and pattern of your choice. These lines vary in thickness, depending on the direction of the line and the angle of the pen nib. You can apply thick strokes to a line with the help of preset lines and apply them on various objects. In this section, you learn to draw a calligraphic, pressure sensitive, and preset line. Let's first learn to create a calligraphic line in the following section.

Drawing a Calligraphic Line

You can create the calligraphic line in a similar way you create line by hand using a paintbrush. The calligraphic lines are referred as stylized lines whose thickness changes with a change in the angle of the line. In CorelDRAW, the Artistic Media tool provides the Calligraphic mode, which is used to create calligraphic lines. Let's perform the following steps to draw calligraphic lines:

1. **Open** a new drawing, and **click** the arrow on the right side of the **Curve tools** from Toolbox. It opens a flyout on the screen (picture 3.6).

2. Select the **Artistic Media tool** from the flyout.

3. Click the **Calligraphic** button from the Property bar, as shown in picture 3.6.

4. Type the value: **0.7"** in the **Stroke width** spin box on the Property bar, to specify the width of the stroke.

5. Type the value: **80** in the **Calligraphic angle** spin box on the Property bar, to specify the angle for the strokes.

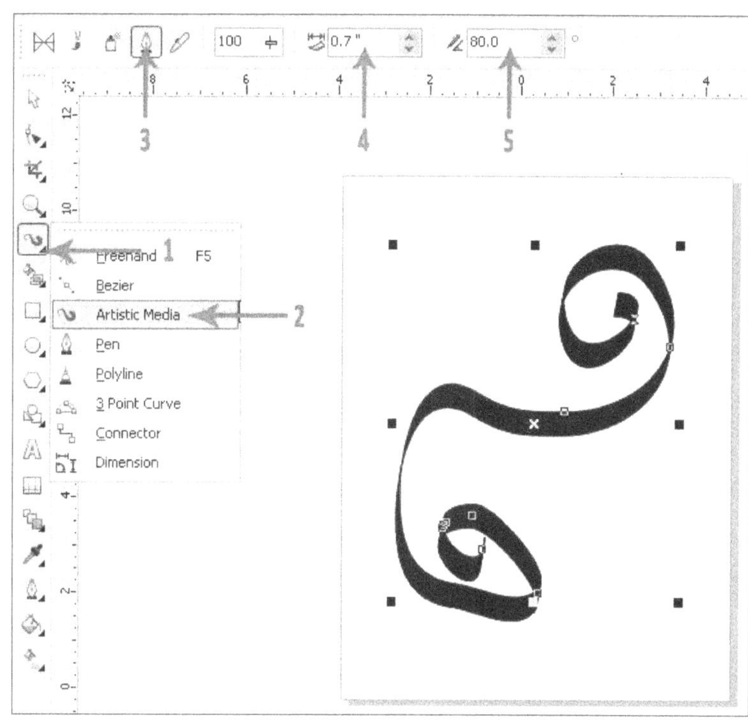

Picture 3.6

You can also increase or decrease the values of Stroke width and Calligraphic angle by clicking the up or down keys provided beside the respective spin boxes.

6. Click the **Drawing page** and drag to create calligraphic curves and shapes, as shown in picture 3.6. If required, you can access the options related to calligraphic lines by selecting the Artistic Media option in the Effects menu.

Drawing a Pressure-Sensitive Line

As the name suggests, pressure-sensitive lines are susceptible to pressure. The width of these lines is determined by the amount of pressure you apply when creating them. In CorelDRAW, you can draw pressure-sensitive lines with the help of the Artistic Media tool. The lines created using this method have curved edges and varying width. Let's perform the following steps to draw a pressure-sensitive line in CorelDRAW:

1. **Open** a new drawing, and **click** the arrow on the right side of the **Curve tools** from Toolbox. It opens a flyout on the screen.

2. Select the **Artistic Media tool** from the flyout.

3. Click the **Pressure** button from the Property bar.

4. Type the value: **0.35"** in the **Stroke width** spin box on the Property bar, to specify the width of the stroke.

5. Click the **Drawing page** and **drag** to specify the starting and ending points to create pressure-sensitive curves and shapes according to your requirement.

Drawing a Preset Line

In CorelDRAW, the Preset lines are defined as a set of predefined lines, which can be used under the CorelDRAW workspace. There is wide variety of Preset patterns available in the CorelDRAW application. The appearance of these lines resembles with a readymade curve patterns having definite attributes, such as stroke, width, and angle. Therefore, the advantage of these lines is that they do not need to be created from scratch. You can simply select the one you want and directly apply it to your document without needing to modify its properties. You can select a curve pattern from the dropdown list that appears on clicking the Preset stroke located on the Property bar. Let's perform the following steps to draw a preset line:

1. **Open** a new drawing, and **click** the arrow on the right side of the **Curve tools** from Toolbox.

2. Select the **Artistic Media tool** from the flyout.

3. Click the **Preset** button from the Property bar, as shown in picture 3.7 with the red arrow numbered 3.

4. Click the **Preset stroke** down arrow button on the Property bar. A dropdown list of stroke options appears (Picture 3.7).

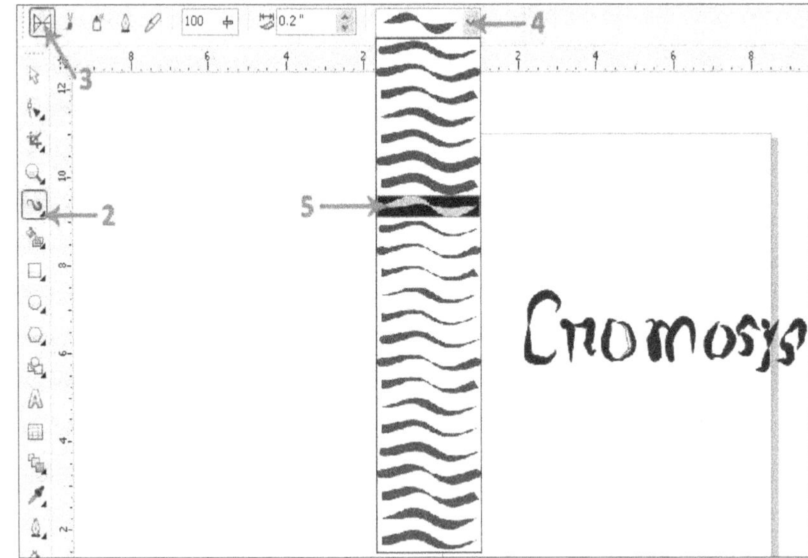

Picture 3.7

5. **Select** a stroke option from the dropdown list. Then click the **Drawing page** and **drag** to create curves and shapes of your choice by using the selected stroke option.

You can smoothen the edges of a preset line by typing a value in the **Freehand smoothing** text box with a range slider on the Property bar. You can also increase the width of the preset line by typing an appropriate value in the **Stroke width** text box on the Property bar.

Working with Outlines

You can use the Outline Pen tool to change the thickness and color of the boundary or outline of an object. In CorelDRAW, the Outline Pen tool appears in the flyout of the Outline tools, located on Toolbar. The flyout of the Outline tools also includes various thickness options for your outline. In addition, when you select the Outline Pen tool, from the flyout, the Pen Outline dialog box appears which includes advanced settings for the outline. In addition to the Outline Pen, the flyout of the Outline tools includes the Outline Color tool, which allows you to create your own custom colors, add the colors to the Color palette, and apply them to the outlines. In this section, you learn to define outline settings, create a calligraphic outline, add an arrowhead, and edit an arrowhead. Let's first learn to define the settings for outlines of objects created in CorelDRAW in the following section.

Defining Outline Settings

An outline marks the outer boundaries of an object. In CorelDRAW, you can define various properties with regard to outlines. For example, by using the Outline Pen dialog box, you can change the appearance of an outline by changing its color, width, and style. You can also set miter limits for the outlines. The miter limit is a value that defines how pointed (mitered) joints of two lines will be smoothened (beveled) when the lines make a sharp curve. Let's perform the following steps to define the settings for the outlines of an object in CorelDRAW:

1. **Open** a CorelDRAW document containing shapes. In our case, we open the document (picture 3.0) having a rectangle drawn on the Drawing page.

2. Select the **Pick tool** from Toolbox, and then **select** the rectangle on the Drawing page, as shown in picture 3.8.

3. **Click** the arrow on the right side of the **Outline tools** from the Toolbox.

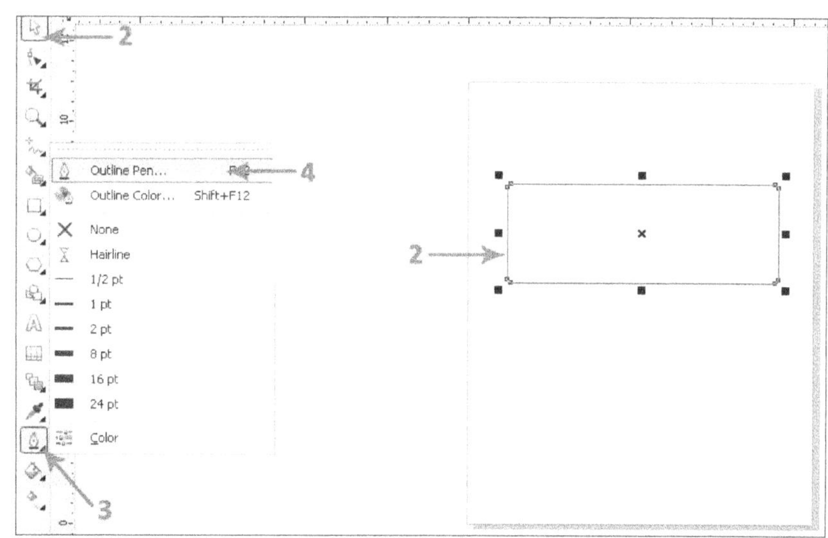

Picture 3.8

4. Select the **Outline Pen** tool from the flyout, as shown in picture 3.8. The Outline Pen dialog box appears on the screen (picture 3.9).

5. **Click** the down arrow beside the **Color** option (picture 3.9), and **select** a color of your choice from the Color palette for the outline. In our case, we select the **Red** color.

6. Type a value in the **Width** combo box to specify the width for the outline. In our case, we type the value: **13.0 pt** (picture 3.9).

7. Click the down arrow below the **Style** option, and **select** a style option for the outline from the dropdown list that appears. In our case, we select the first style option from the dropdown list.

8. Type a value in the **Miter Limit** spin box. In our case, we are continuing with the default value, **45.0**.

9. Select the **Behind fill** check box, if you want the outline color behind the object.

10. Select the **Scale with object** check box, if you want the width of the outline to increase at the same rate as the shape itself.

11. Click the **OK** button to apply the values set in the Outline Pen dialog box, as shown in picture 3.9.

As the result, the outline of the rectangle changes according to the specifications you have set in the dialog box.

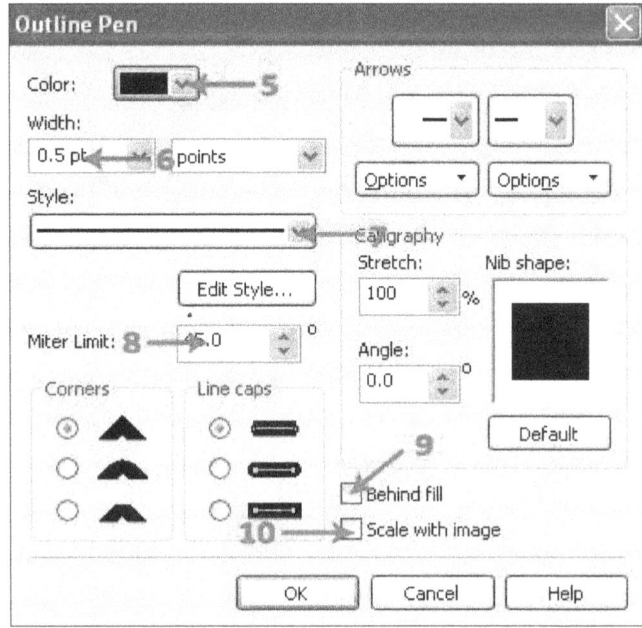

Picture 3.9

By the way, you can also change the outline width of a selected object by typing the appropriate value in the **Outline width** combo box on the Property bar.

Creating a Calligraphic Outline

In CorelDRAW, the calligraphic outlines can be defined as the outlines to objects similar to those created by hand using a calligraphic pen. These outlines have varied thickness, similar to a handmade sketch created by using the calligraphic pen. Let's perform the following simple steps to create a calligraphic outline:

1. **Open** a CorelDRAW document, and **draw** an ellipse with the help of the Ellipse tool.

2. Select the **Pick tool** from the Toolbox, and then **select** the ellipse on the Drawing page.

3. **Click** the arrow on the right side of the **Outline tools** from the Toolbox.

4. Select the **Outline Pen** tool from the flyout. The Outline Pen dialog box appears.

5. **Click** the down arrow beside the **Color** option, and **select** a color of your choice for the outline from the dropdown list. In our case, we select the **Orange** color.

6. Type a value in the **Width** combo box to specify the width for the outline. In our case, we type the value: **20.0 pt**.

7. Click the down arrow below the **Style** option, and **select** a style option for the outline from the dropdown list that appears. In our case, we select the third style option from the dropdown list.

8. Type a value in the **Miter Limit** spin box. In our case, we are continuing with the default value, **45.0**.

9. Select the **Behind fill** check box, if you want the outline color behind the object.

10. Select the **Scale with object** check box, if you want the width of the outline to increase at the same rate as the shape itself.

11. Type a value in the **Stretch** spin box under the Calligraphy section to apply a stretched effect on the outline. In our case, we type the value, **60**.

12. Type a value in the **Angle** spin box under the Calligraphy section to specify the angle of rotation for your calligraphic outline on the Drawing page. In our case, we type the value, **30.0**.

13. Click the **OK** button to apply the changes. As the result, the outline of the ellipse changes to show the calligraphic effect according to the specifications we set in the Outline Pen dialog box.

By the way, if you want to reset the **Stretch** and **Angle** values to their default settings, click the **Default** button under the Calligraphy group in the Outline Pen dialog box.

Adding and Editing an Arrowhead

In the CorelDRAW application, the arrowhead signifies a mark used on a line or curve to show it direction. Arrows are used to indicate the flow or continuity of a process. CorelDRAW X6 provides several options to insert and edit arrowheads. Using arrowheads in diagrams or figures help you to explain difficult processes or concepts easily. In this section, you learn to add an arrowhead to a line. Let's perform the following steps to add an arrowhead to a line:

1. **Open** a new drawing in CorelDRAW, and **create** a line on the Drawing page using the **Freehand tool** from the Toolbox, as shown in picture 4.0.

2. Select the **Pick tool** from the Toolbox, and **select** the line on the Drawing page.

3. **Click** the arrow on the right side of the **Outline tools** from Toolbox.

Picture 4.0

4. Select the **Outline Pen** tool from the flyout. The Outline Pen dialog box appears, as shown in picture 4.1 below.

5. Type a value in the **Width** combo box to specify the width of the arrow and the line (picture 4.1). In our case, we type the value, **16.0** pt.

6. **Click** the first down arrow button present on the left side of the **Arrows** section (picture 4.1). A dropdown list with options appears.

7. **Select** an arrowhead type from the dropdown list of the options. In our case, we select the **Arrowhead 5** option.

8. **Click** the second dropdown arrow button present on the right side of the **Arrows** section (picture 4.1). A dropdown list with options appears.

9. **Select** a tail for your arrowhead from the dropdown list. In our case, we select the **Arrowhead 10** option.

10. Click the **OK** button to set all the changes made in the Outline Pen dialog box. Now you can see on your screen that the line appears with a selected arrowhead and tail.

You have learnt to create an arrowhead. After creating an arrowhead in CorelDRAW, let's next learn to edit the arrowhead in the following section.

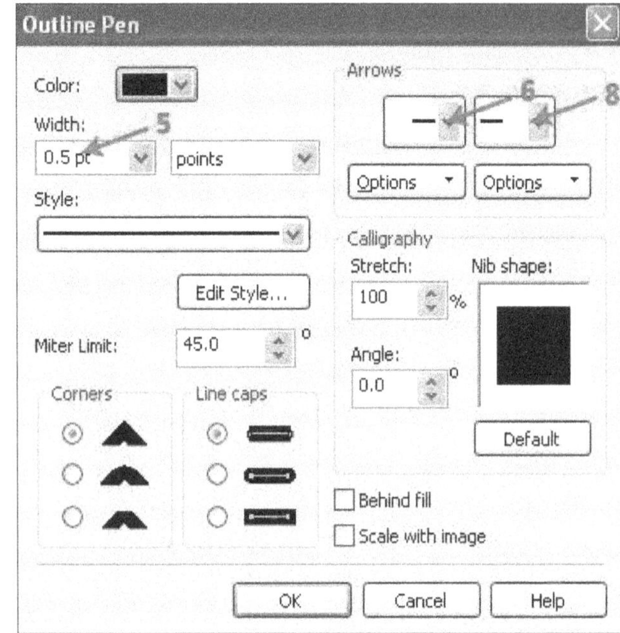

Picture 4.1

Editing an Arrowhead

In CorelDRAW, you can easily edit an arrowhead according to your requirements. The arrowhead can be edited in various ways by switching the arrowhead with the tail and vice versa, creating a new arrowhead and tail, changing the appearance of an existing arrowhead, and deleting an arrowhead. CorelDRAW provides the following options to edit arrowheads:

None: Allows you to remove the selected arrowhead or arrow tail from a line
Swap: Allows you to switch the arrowhead with the arrow tail and vice versa
New: Allows you to create a new arrowhead or arrow tail in a line
Edit: Allows you to change the appearance of the arrowhead or arrow tail applied to a line
Attributes: Allows you to specify the arrowhead or arrow tail properties, such as size, mirror, offset, and rotation, in the Arrowhead Attributes dialog box
Delete: Allows you to delete the selected arrowhead or arrow tail from the line as well as from the arrowhead or arrow tail options from the list in the Outline Pen dialog box. Let's perform the following steps to edit an arrowhead:

1. **Open** a drawing in CorelDRAW. In our case, we are continuing with the drawing of the line with arrowhead created in the previous section.

2. Select the **Pick tool** from the Toolbox, and **select** the line with the arrowhead from the Drawing page.

3. **Click** the arrow on the right side of the of the **Outline tools** from Toolbox.

4. Select the **Outline Pen** tool from the flyout. The Outline Pen dialog box appears.

5. **Click** the first option button to the left of the **Arrows** section in the Outline Pen dialog box. A dropdown list of options appears.

6. Select the **None** option from the dropdown list, and then click the **OK** button in the Outline Pen dialog box to apply the settings. Now you can see on your Drawing page that the line appears without the arrowhead.

Lesson 4
Working with Creative Vector Shape Tools
In the CorelDRAW X6 application, new tools, such as Smear, Twirl, Attract, and Repel, are introduced. These tools enable you to modify and transform the shape of vector objects drawn on the Drawing page. The object shapes, which are composed of line structures, can be edited by using these tools. The tools work and produce results in different manners, which you will learn in this lesson. The patterns, such as simple or complex, can be edited to create designed and desired appearances. If you want to create designs in CorelDRAW X6, you need to work with these four new vector editing tools. In this lesson, you learn to use the Smear, Twirl, Attract, and Repel tools.

Using the Smear Tool
In CorelDRAW X6, the newly introduced Smear tool allows you to edit the shape of object. You can make the outline of an object either inwards or outwards by using this tool. The shape can be edited to produce depth strokes, pointed strokes, and various other creative patterns. In this section, you learn to edit the star object created on the Drawing page with the help of the Smear tool. Let's perform the following steps to use the Smear tool:

1. **Open** a new drawing in CorelDRAW X6.

2. **Create** an object on the Drawing page. In our case, we create the **star** object by using the Star tool, as shown in picture 4.2.

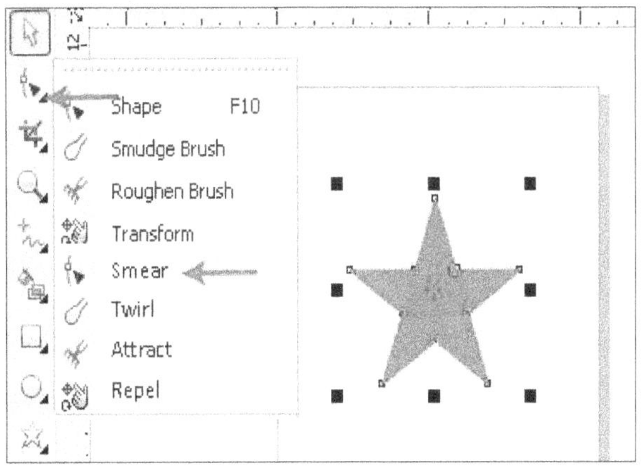

Picture 4.2

Picture 4.3

3. **Click** the arrow on the right side of **Shape Edit tools** from Toolbox (picture 4.2).

4. Select the **Smear tool** from the flyout, as shown in picture 4.2.

5. **Click** the point of the **star** object on the Drawing page, where you want to apply the Smear tool. In our case, we click the **top** point of the star on the Drawing page (picture 4.3).

6. **Drag** the selected point of the star either outward or inward to modify the shape (or outline), as shown in picture 4.3. In our case, we drag the selected point in the outward direction.

Similarly, you can drag the object inward, outward, up, below, and in any desired direction to reshape it by using the Smear tool. The shape of the start object will be changed and it will look as shown in picture 4.4.

Let's next learn to use the Twirl tool in the following section.

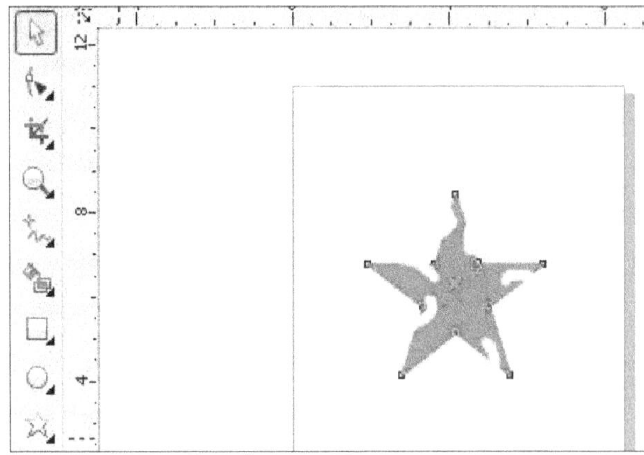

Picture 4.4

Using the Twirl Tool

The Twirl tool introduced in the CorelDRAW X6 application allows you to create spirals or round shapes along the outline of objects. You are required to just apply the tool directly on the object that results in numerous spiral patterns. It curls the outline by creating twirls (or spirals) around the shape. The number of twirls depends on how you hold down the tool over the selected object on the Drawing page. In this section, you learn to create twirls on an ellipse object. Let's perform the following steps to use the Twirl tool:

1. **Open** a new drawing, and then **create** an object on the Drawing page. In our case, we create an **ellipse** object by using the Ellipse tool, (picture 4.5).

Picture 4.5

Picture 4.6

2. **Click** the arrow on the right side of **Shape Edit tools** from Toolbox, and then select the **Twirl** tool from the flyout.

3. **Select** the desired location on the object where you want to apply the **Twirl** tool. In our case, we select the **top left** location of the ellipse.

4. **Hold** the click to on the specified location to modify the object with the help of **Twirl tool**. The twirls will be created automatically in a circular motion (picture 4.6). You can create the desired number of twirls on the object by using the Twirl tool.

Using the Attract Tool

In CorelDRAW X6, the new Attract tool allows you to appeal the edges or nodes of objects to the specified positions. By using this tool, you can attract the nodes (along its outline) of object to the desired position. In this section, you learn to apply the Attract tool on the Rectangle object created in the Drawing page. Let's perform the following steps to use the Attract tool:

1. **Open** a new drawing, and then **create** an object on the Drawing page. In our case, we create a **rectangle** object by using the Rectangle tool.

2. **Click** the arrow on the right side of **Shape Edit tools** from Toolbox, and then select the **Attract** tool from the flyout.

3. **Select** the desired location on the rectangle object where you want to apply the Attract tool. In our case, we select the **top right corner** of the rectangle.

4. **Drag** and **hold** the mouse pointer to apply the Attract tool. You can create the desired shape patterns of the object by using the Attract tool.

Using the Repel Tool

The newly-introduced Repel tool in the latest CorelDRAW X6 version allows you to reshape the object. This functioning of the tool is just opposite to the Attract tool learned in the previous section. The tool enables the object to be prevented from the area where you apply the tool. In this section, you learn to apply the Repel tool over the complex star object drawn on the Drawing page. Let's perform the following steps to use the Repel tool:

1. **Open** a new drawing, and then **create** an object on the Drawing page. In our case, we create the **complex star** object by using the Complex Star tool.

2. **Click** the arrow on the right side of **Shape Edit tools** from Toolbox, and then select the **Repel** tool from the flyout.

3. **Select** the desired location on the complex star object where you want to apply the Repel tool. In our case, we select the **top right corner** of the object.

4. **Hold** the selection from the specified location. As a result, the shape of the object will change with the help of the Repel tool. You can modify the shape into desired patterns by using the Repel tool.

Modifying Shapes and Lines

In CorelDRAW, the most complex and intricate shapes you create begin as simple shapes, such as square, rectangle, ellipse, polygon, and star. These shapes lay the foundation that you build on, bit by bit, by adding more shapes or modifying existing ones, so that you ultimately have the shape of your choice. The basic shapes are, therefore, the building blocks and fundamental to the process of creating the final shape. In this section, you learn to modify the basic shapes, as well as change one shape into another shape. In this section, you learn to apply the convert to curves command, convert an ellipse into a pie, crop a line, and split a line.

Applying the Convert to Curves Command on Objects

In CorelDRAW, converting an object into a curve object is one of the most common methods of changing the shape of the object. You can convert an object to a curve object by using the Convert to Curves command, located in the Arrange menu in the Menu bar. A curve object contains editable nodes and control handles, which appear along the outline of the object. You can use these nodes and handles to change the shape of the object. A curve object need not necessarily be curved. It can be a straight line as well. The Shape tool is usually used to edit curve objects. Let's perform the following steps to use the Convert to Curves command to convert an object into a curve object:

1. **Open** a new drawing in CorelDraw, and then draw an **ellipse** on the Drawing page using the Ellipse tool.

2. **Select** the ellipse object on the Drawing page, by using the Pick tool from Toolbar.

3. Select **Arrange> Convert to Curves** from the Menu bar.

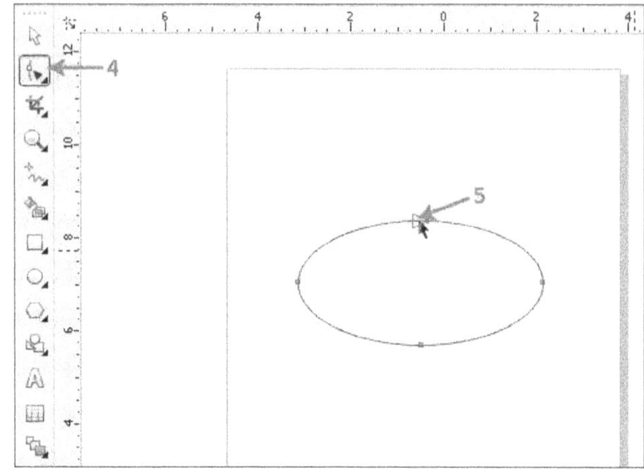

Picture 4.7

4. Select the **Shape tool** from Toolbar, as shown in picture 4.7. The selected ellipse is now a curve object and appears with editable nodes.

5. **Click** the ellipse on the Drawing page. As you move the nodes to change the shape of the curve object, the Bezier handle appears along the nodes.

You can also convert an object to a curve object by clicking the **Convert to Curves** button on the Property bar or pressing the **Ctrl+Q** keys in combination.

Converting an Ellipse into a Pie

You can convert one shape to another shape by modifying the geometry of objects with the help of tools, such as the Shape tool. In CorelDRAW, you can not only round shapes, such as squares and rectangles, but can also convert one shape to another shape. For example, ellipses can be made into pie shapes or arcs. You can make these special transformations by changing the properties of the shapes from the Property bar. In this section, you learn to change an ellipse to a pie. Let's perform the following steps to convert an ellipse into a pie:

1. **Open** a new drawing, and then draw an **ellipse** on the Drawing page using the Ellipse tool.

2. **Click** the arrow on the right side of the **Shape Edit Tools** from Toolbox.

3. Select the **Shape tool** from the flyout, as shown in picture 4.8.

4. **Select** the node that appears on the outline of the ellipse on the Drawing page by using the **Shape tool** (picture 4.8).

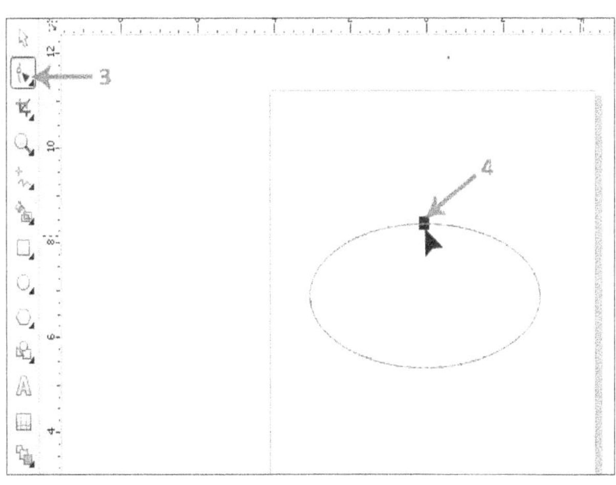

Picture 4.8

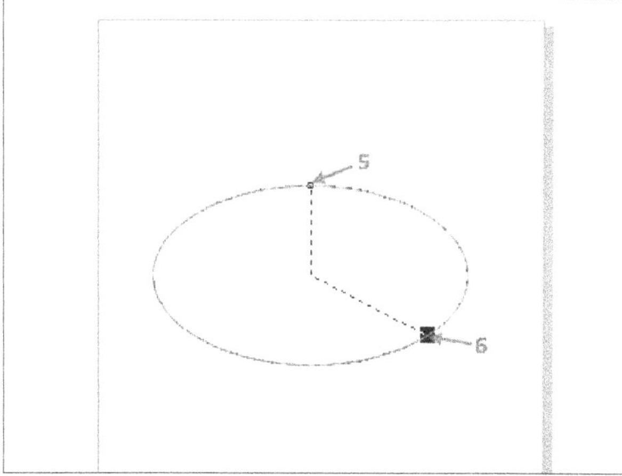

Picture 4.9

5. **Drag** the selected node till the shape of ellipse changes to a pie, which is the desired shape, as shown in picture 4.9.

6. **Release** the mouse button when you get the pie shape. As a result, the ellipse is converted into a pie on the Drawing area.

Cropping a Line

You can crop a line in CorelDRAW by using the Crop tool. Cropping is a process which essentially means removing unwanted areas or portions from the object. While cropping a line object, you need to define the cropping area. The cropping area is a rectangular area that encloses the required selection, which you want to retain from the object. In other words, the area outside the cropping area does not appear in the final cropped selection. Let's perform these steps to crop a line object:

1. **Open** a CorelDRAW document containing the line object you want to crop. In our case, we open a document containing a rectangle, an ellipse, a star, and a spiral drawn on the Drawing page (picture 5.0).

2. Click the arrow on the right side of the **Crop tools** from Toolbox.

3. Select the **Crop tool** from the flyout.

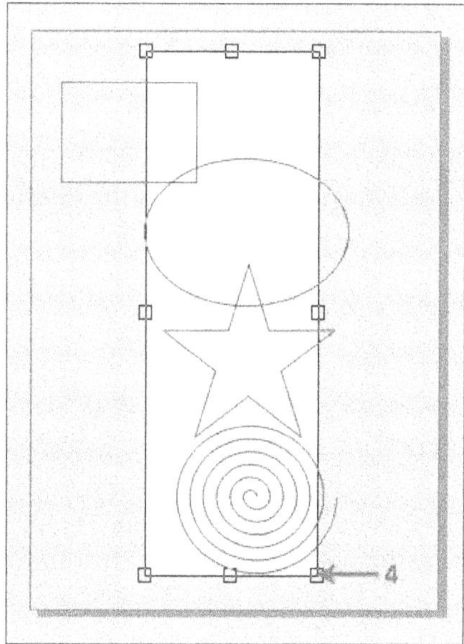

Picture 5.0

Keep in mind that if you do not select any object and apply the **Crop tool** option, all the objects on the Document window will be cropped.

4. **Click** and **drag** the mouse pointer to define the cropping area on the Drawing page. The entire **Document window**, excluding the cropping area, turns grey, as shown in picture 5.0.

5. Press the **Enter** key. The cropped line object appears on the Drawing page and the grey highlight disappears.

Keep in mind that you cannot crop Object Linked and Embedded (OLE) objects and Web graphics, rollovers, content of power clips objects, and locked or hidden objects.

Splitting a Line

In the CorelDRAW X6 application, you can split a line object into two parts by using the Knife tool. This tool can be used over an object by specifying the starting and ending points from where you want to apply the cur or break part of an object. In this section, you learn to split an object drawn on the Drawing page with the help of the Knife tool. Let's perform the following steps to split a line object:

1. **Open** a new drawing in CorelDRAW. In our case, we open the drawing having a <u>rectangle</u> and an <u>ellipse</u> drawn on the Drawing page (picture 5.1).

2. **Select** the **ellipse** object on the Drawing page by using the Pick tool.

3. **Click** the arrow on the right side of the **Crop tools** from the Toolbox. Then select the **Knife tool** from the flyout.

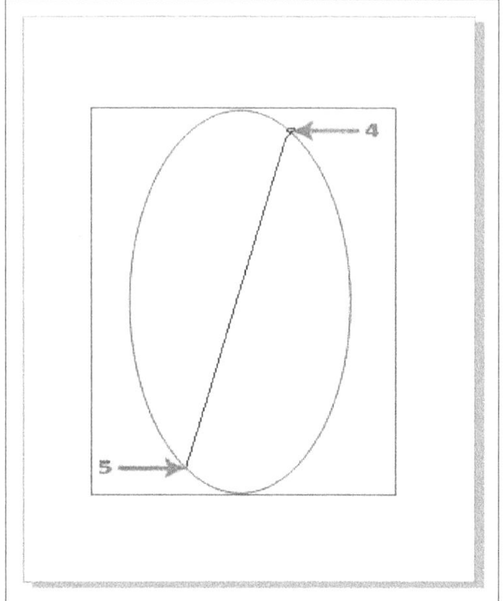

Picture 5.1

You need to keep in mind that splitting is always performed on a selected object. In our case, the ellipse is selected.

4. **Click** a point on the boundary of the circle from where you want it to be split, as shown in picture 5.1 with red arrow numbered 4.

5. **Click** the point where you want the splitting to end, as shown in picture 5.1 with red arrow numbered 5.

6. Select the **Pick tool** and **drag** the split portion on the Drawing page. The circle splits along a straight line defined by the starting and ending points, dividing the object into two parts, as shown in picture 5.2.

Keep in mind that using the Knife tool on a selected object converts the object into a curve object.

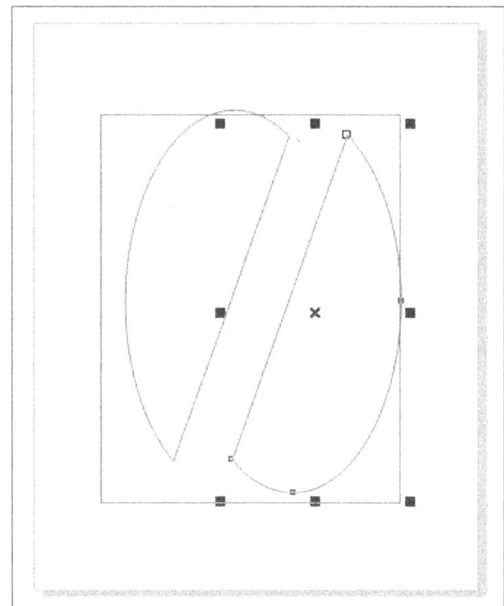

Picture 5.2

After learning the procedure to modify shapes and lines in this section, let's further learn to perform advanced operations with line objects in the following section.

Performing Advanced Operations with Line Objects

CorelDRAW X6 allows you to change the shape of a line object by using the Fillet, Scallop, and Chamfer tools on the corners of the object. These tools enable you to apply various changes and effects to the corners of vector drawings, which would otherwise be a difficult task. For example, you can use these tools to create the curved, reverse-curved, or beveled effects. Using the Fillet, Scallop, and Chamfer tools help save a lot of time and enable you to create a variety of complex effects on the corners of the line objects. You can apply the Fillet, Scallop, and Chamfer tools only on the undistorted curve objects. In addition to these tools, you can use the Envelope tool to edit the lines and shapes of objects. Moreover, CorelDRAW provides various mapping modes to edit shapes, which you will learn in this section. Let's begin this section by learning to use the Fillet tool to round the corners of an object in the following section.

Using the Fillet Tool to Round the Corners of an Object

In the CorelDRAW X6 application, you can use the Fillet tool on objects to modify the corners into a round shape. The tool creates corners of uniform roundness of a specific radius by just using the mouse pointer. Let's perform the following steps to round the corners of an object by using the Fillet tool:

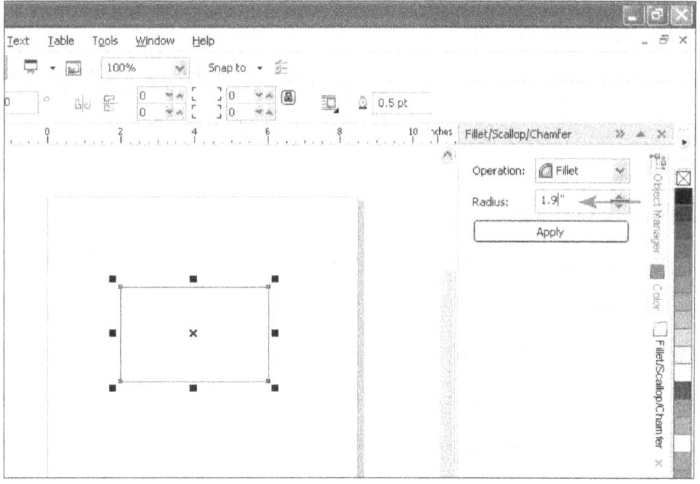

1. **Open** a drawing in CorelDRAW X6. In our case, we open the drawing having a <u>rectangle</u> drawn.

2. **Select** the rectangle object on the Drawing page by using the Pick tool.

Picture 5.3

3. Select **Window**> **Dockers**> **Fillet/Scallop/Chamfer** from the Menu bar. The Fillet/Scallop/Chamfer docker appears (picture 5.3).

4. Select the **Fillet** radio button under the Fillet/Scallop/Chamfer docker.

5. **Type** a value in the **Radius** spin box to specify the radius for the rounded corners to be applied to the selected rectangle. In our case, we type the value, **1.9"**.

6. Click the **Apply** button in the Fillet/Scallop/Chamfer docker. As a result, the corners of the selected rectangle are rounded, as shown in picture 5.4. Let's next learn to use the Scallop tool on the corners of an object.

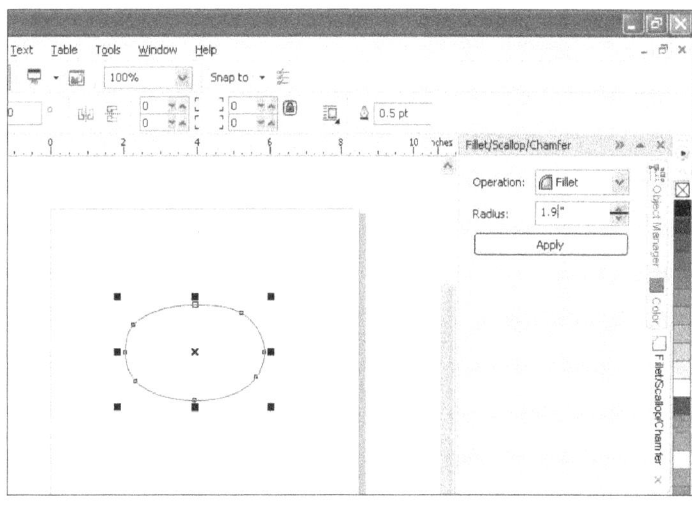

Picture 5.4

Using the Scallop Tool on the Corners of an Object

In the CorelDRAW X6 application, you can create scalloped or decorative objects with the help of the Scallop tool. The scalloped object appears with series of small curves along the edges. Scalloping instantly applies concentric reverse-rounded corners to the object and is opposite to the Fillet effect. This tool helps to create curves by rounding the corners of an object, and then inverting them. Let's perform the following steps to scallop the corners of an object:

1. **Open** a drawing in CorelDRAW. In our case, we open the drawing having a rectangle drawn.

2. **Select** the rectangle object on which you want to use the **Scallop** tool.

3. Select **Window> Dockers> Fillet/Scallop/Chamfer** from the Menu bar. The Fillet/Scallop/Chamfer docker appears.

4. Select the **Scallop** radio button under the docker.

5. **Type** a value in the **Radius** spin box to specify the radius for the round curves used to create scalloping in the selected rectangle. In our case, we type the value, **2.0"**.

6. Click the **Apply** button in the docker. You will see on your screen that the scalloping is applied to the corners of the rectangle.

Using the Chamfer Tool on the Corners of an Object

You can create flat corners, also known as chamfered corners, by using the Chamfer tool. By using this tool in CorelDRAW, you can convert the sharp corners of an object to uniform angled corners. Let's perform the following steps to use the Chamfer tool on the corners of an object:

1. **Open** a drawing in CorelDRAW. In our case, we open the drawing having a rectangle drawn.

2. **Select** the rectangle object on which you want to use the **Chamfer** tool.

3. Select **Window> Dockers> Fillet/Scallop/Chamfer** from the Menu bar. The Fillet/Scallop/Chamfer docker appears.

4. Select the **Chamfer** radio button under the docker.

5. **Type** a value in the **Distance** spin box to specify the amount for chamfering (flattening) required around the edges of the selected rectangle. In our case, we type the value, **1.3"**.

6. Click the **Apply** button in the docker. You will see on your screen that the corners of the selected rectangle are chamfered.

Using the Envelope Tool

By using the Envelope tool in the CorelDRAW X6 application, you can change the shape of an object. This tool creates multiple nodes on the object. By moving these nodes, you can change the shape of the object. You can also use envelope nodes on paragraph text to change the shape of the text. You can apply envelopes to any object either by selecting an envelope preset or by clicking the Add new envelope button from the Property bar. On selecting an envelope preset, the shape of the object changes according to the selected preset. However, to change the shape of the object manually, use an envelope mode. In CorelDRAW, the envelope modes available are briefly described in the following points, as follows:

Straight line mode: Allows you to create envelopes based on straight lines. This mode also adds perspective to an object.
Single-arc mode: Allows you to create envelopes with an arc shape on one side. Applying this mode on objects changes their appearance to concave or convex objects.
Double-arc mode: Allows you to create envelopes with the S shape on one or mode sides.
Unconstrained mode: Allows you to create freeform envelopes that let you change the properties of the nodes in the envelope. You can also add or delete a node in this mode.

You can also copy and remove envelopes in the CorelDRAW application. As stated earlier, you can edit an envelope applied on an object. You can change the shape of an object on which an envelope is applied, by dragging the nodes enabled on the envelope. In this case, the envelope contains the selected object, therefore, when you move the nodes on the envelope, the change is reflected simultaneously in the shape of the object to which the object is enveloped. Let's perform the following steps to use the Envelope tool:

1. **Open** a drawing in CorelDRAW. In our case, we open the drawing having a rectangle drawn.

2. **Select** the rectangle object on which you want to use the **Envelope tool**, by using the Pick tool.

3. **Click** the arrow on the right side of the **Interactive tools** from Toolbox. Then select the **Envelope tool** from the flyout, as shown in picture 5.5 with the red arrow numbered 3.

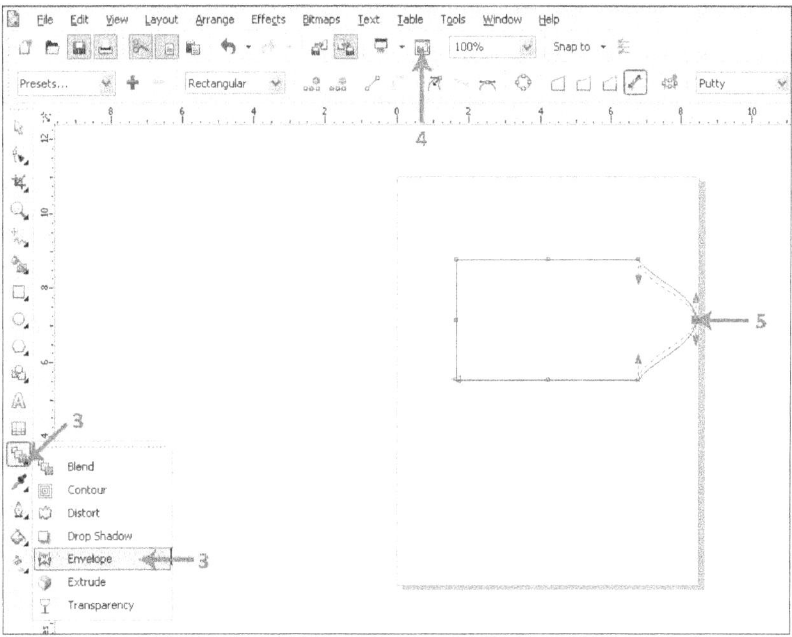

Picture 5.5

4. **Select** an envelope that you want to use on the rectangle, by clicking the respective button on the Property bar. In our case, we click the **Unconstrained Mode** button, as shown in picture 5.5 with the red arrow numbered 4. As a result, an envelope with nodes appears around the rectangle (picture 5.5).

5. **Click** the rectangle and **drag** its nodes to change the shape of the rectangle according to your requirements, as shown in picture 5.5 with the red arrow numbered 5. Finally, you will see on your screen that the object with the envelope appears on the Drawing page.

Copying an Envelope

In CorelDRAW, the Envelope effect applied on an object can be copied to another object on the Drawing page. By copying the envelope effect from one object to another, you are primarily imparting the settings and adjustments applied on the previous object to another object. In this section, you learn to copy the Envelope effect applied on a rectangle object onto another circle object drawn on the Drawing page. Let's perform the following steps to copy an envelope effect:

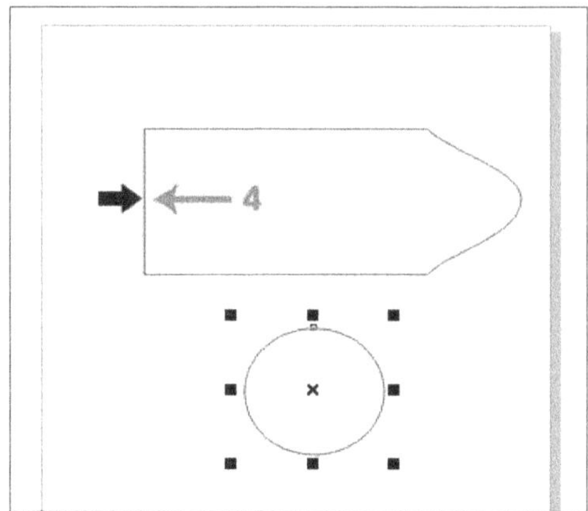

1. **Open** a drawing in CorelDRAW. In our case, we open a drawing having a circle object and an object with the Envelope effect drawn in the previous section of the lesson.

Picture 5.6

2. **Select** the object on the Drawing page on which you want to copy an envelope, by using the Pick tool. In our case, we select the circle (picture 5.6).

3. Choose **Effects> Copy Effects> Envelope From** from the Menu bar. The mouse pointer changes into an arrow appearing on the Drawing page, (picture 5.6).

The arrow points towards the objects on which the copied envelope effect can be applied.

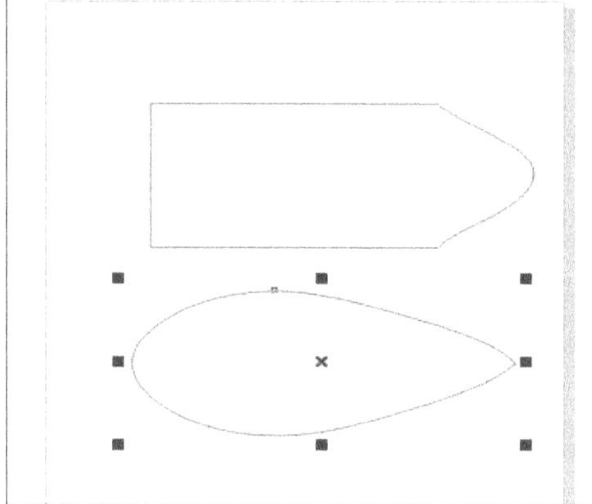

4. **Select** the object from which you want to copy the effect. In our case, we select the rectangle on which we have already applied the **Envelope effect**, as shown in picture 5.6 with the red arrow numbered 4.

As a result, the envelope effect is copied on the circle, as shown in picture 5.7.

Picture 5.7

Editing the Nodes and Segments of an Envelope

In CorelDRAW, the object with the Envelope effect applied comprises of editable segments and nodes. You can edit an envelope by changing the number of nodes it contains. These nodes are square shaped and can be increased or decreased depending on your requirements. Let's perform the following steps to edit the nodes and segments of an envelope:

1. **Open** a drawing in CorelDRAW. In our case, we open a drawing having a **star** object drawn on the Drawing page.

2. **Click** the arrow on the right side of the **Interactive tools** from Toolbox. Then select the **Envelope tool** from the flyout (already shown picture 5.5).

3. **Select** the node that you want to delete from the object having the Envelope effect.

In our case, we select the center node at the bottom line of the star object, as shown in picture 5.8.

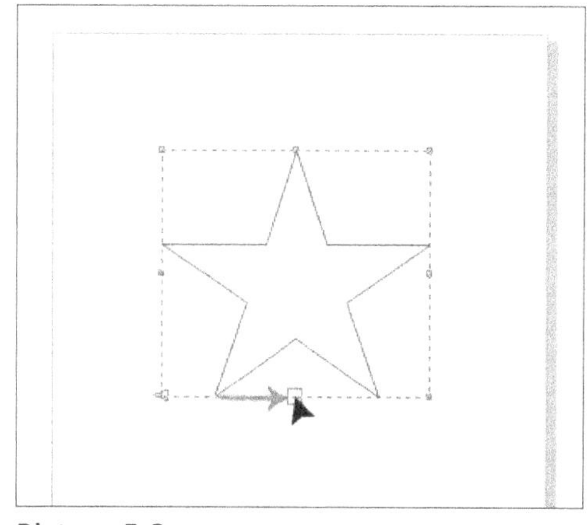

Picture 5.8

4. **Double-click** the selected node to delete it from the selected object. As a result, the node disappears (deleted) from the object on the Drawing page.

5. **Double-click** another point on the envelope to add a node. As a result, a new node appears on the envelope on that point.

Altering the Mapping Mode

You can define the Mapping mode as a space that determines the manner in which an object fits itself in an envelope. This mode appears as a dropdown list on the Property bar. There are four mapping modes in CorelDRAW X6: Horizontal, Original, Putty, and Vertical. The Putty mapping mode is selected by default. However, you can change this default selection to suit your requirements. Let's perform the following steps to alter the mapping mode:

1. **Open** a drawing in CorelDRAW. In our case, we open a drawing having an object with the **Envelope effect** applied on the Drawing page (picture 5.9).

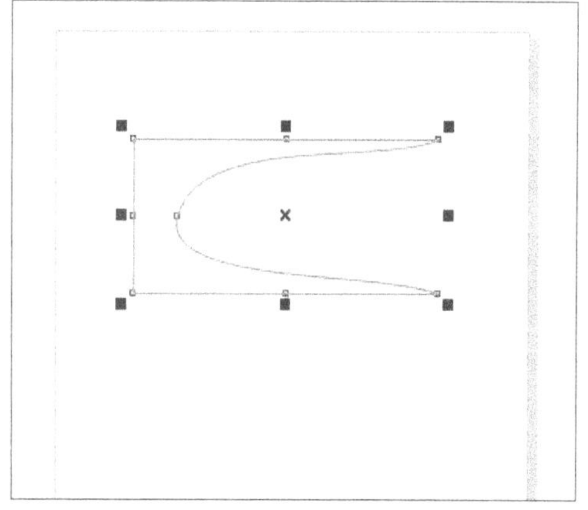

Picture 5.9

2. **Click** the arrow on the right side of the **Interactive tools** from Toolbox. Then select the **Envelope tool** from the flyout.

3. **Select** an object with an envelope effect on the Drawing page, as shown in picture 5.9.

4. Click the **Mapping Mode** list box on the Property bar (picture 6.0).

5. Select the **Vertical** mapping mode from the dropdown list, as shown in picture 6.0 with the arrow numbered 5.

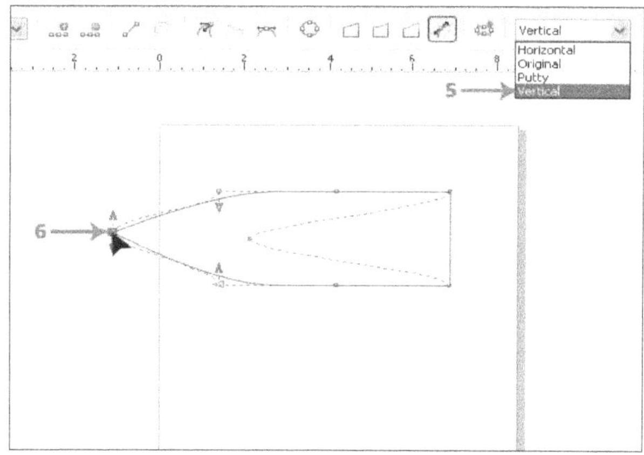

Picture 6.0

6. **Drag** the node of the object to apply the Vertical mapping mode to the object, as shown in picture 6.0 with the red arrow numbered 6.

As a result, you will see on your screen that the object having the Envelope effect is altered by using the mapping mode on the Drawing page. Let's next learn to create an outline around an object in the following section.

Creating an Outline Around an Object

You can define an object with the integration of its fill and outline. In CorelDRAW, the outline of an object describes the area engaged by the object on the Drawing page. The outline can be defined as a closed path around a selected object. An outline defines the extent and layout of the object. CorelDRAW provides a range of colors for creating outlines. You can select these colors as well as various other options related to outlines, such as width, size, style, from the Outline Pen dialog box. This dialog box opens when you select the Outline Pen tool from the Outline tools flyout on Toolbox. Let's perform the following steps to create an outline or boundary around an object and apply color to the outline:

1. **Open** a drawing in CorelDRAW. In our case, we open a drawing having an object on the Drawing page (picture 6.1).

2. **Select** the object that you want to surround with an outline by using the Pick tool from Toolbox.

3. Click the arrow on the right side of the **Outline tools** from the Toolbox, as shown in picture 6.1 with the red arrow numbered 3.

4. Select the **Outline Pen** tool from the flyout. The Outline Pen dialog box appears, as already shown in picture 3.9.

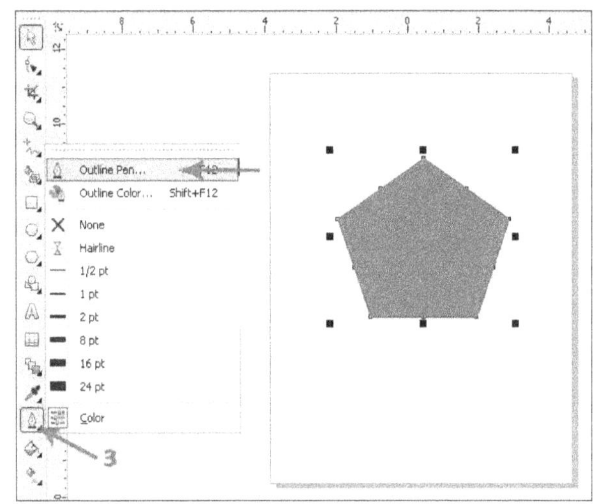

Picture 6.1

5. Click the **Color** down arrow button, and select <u>Red</u> color for the outline from the Color palette.

6. Type the value: **150.0 pt** in the <u>Width</u> combo box to specify the width of the outline.

7. Select the **Behind fill** check box, if you want the outline color behind the object.

8. Select the **Scale with object** check box, if you want the width of the outline to increase at the same rate as the shape itself.

9. Click the **OK** button to save the changes in the Outline Pen dialog box. As a result, the object appears with the outline according to the options selected in the Outline Pen dialog box.

By the way, you can also select an outline color for an object by simply right-clicking the color swatch in the Color palette, which you want to use as the outline color. The color will be applied to the outline of the object.

Working with Brush Strokes

Generally, in vector editing applications, the brush strokes play a significant role. The brush strokes are used to import a mark or impression in a design. In CorelDRAW, you can create designer patterns by using these brush strokes in a drawing. Each brush stroke leaves a mark that is unique to the brush used to create it. Brushes with firm bristles create textures in a drawing, which are different from the textures left by a soft-bristled brush. CorelDRAW X6 provides a wide range of built-in presets of brush strokes that you can use in your drawing. In case, these built-in preset brush strokes do not suit your requirements, you can also create your own custom brush strokes. In this section, you learn to use a preset brush stroke, and then learn to create a custom brush stroke. Let's begin this section by learning to use a preset brush stroke in CorelDRAW.

Using a Preset Brush Stroke

In CorelDRAW, you are enabled with various styles of preset brush strokes. You can use these brush strokes either with their default properties or their properties can be modified according to requirements. Some of the properties of a brush stroke, which you can modify, are brush width and stroke color. The modifications made to the properties of a brush stroke are temporary, and remain till you are using the brush stroke. When you switch to another brush stroke, the modifications made are restored to their default state. Let's perform the following steps to use a preset brush stroke in CorelDRAW:

1. **Open** a new drawing in CorelDRAW.

2. **Click** the arrow on the right side of the **Curve tools** from Toolbox.

3. Select the **Artistic Media tool** from the flyout, as shown in picture 6.2 with the red arrow numbered 3.

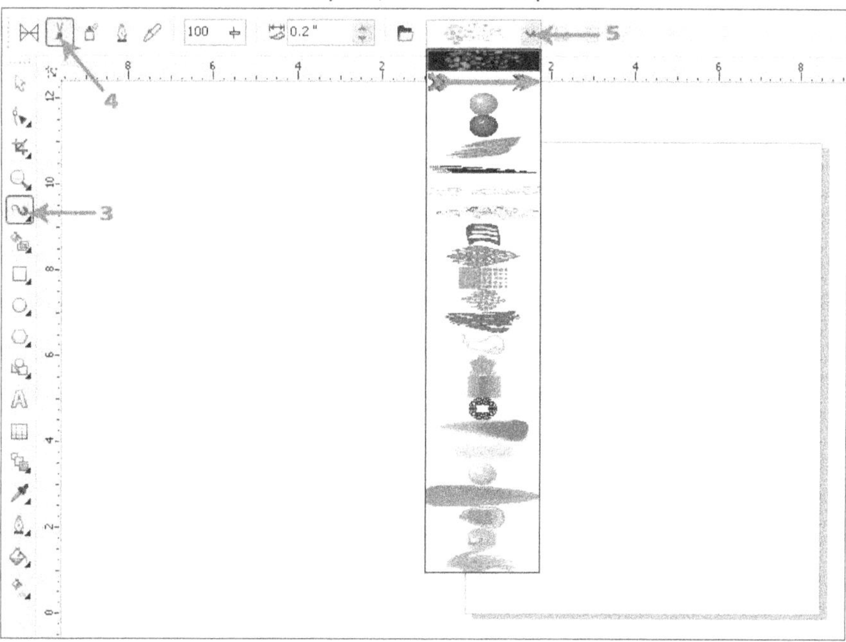

Picture 6.2

4. Click the **Brush** button on the Property bar, as shown in picture 6.2 with the red arrow numbered 4.

5. **Click** the down arrow of the Brush stroke list box on the Property bar. Then **select** a style from the list (picture 6.2). In our case, we select the **second** stroke style from the list.

6. **Click** on the Drawing page and then **drag** to create curves and shapes of the selected stroke style required.

By the way, you can make changes to the selected brush stroke style by typing a value for smoothness in the **Freehand smoothing** spin box and typing a value for the width of the stroke in the **Stroke width** spin box on the Property bar.

Creating a Custom Brush Stroke

In the CorelDRAW application, you can create custom brush stroke. Custom brush strokes can be created by drawing the desired pattern drawn by the user. In the application, the default preset brush strokes are already available. In case, the default brush strokes are not able to meet the requirements, you can create a pattern of brush stroke that exactly matches your specifications. Custom brush strokes can be created by forming a pattern from a single brush stroke or from a group of different brush strokes. The brush stroke patterns created in this way can be saved as preset brush strokes. Let's perform the following steps to create a custom brush stroke:

1. **Open** a new drawing in CorelDRAW application.

2. **Create** a shape that you want to use as a custom brush stroke by using the **Freehand tool** from Toolbox, as shown in picture 6.3.

3. **Select** the shape on the Drawing page by using the **Pick tool** from Toolbox.

4. **Click** the arrow on the right side of the **Curve tools** from Toolbox.

5. Select the **Artistic Media tool** from the flyout.

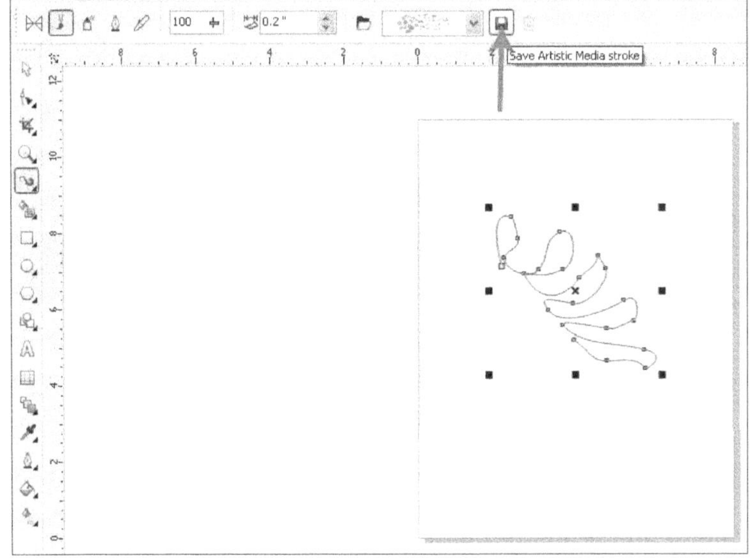

Picture 6.3

6. Click the **Save** button from the Property bar, as shown in picture 6.3 with the red arrow. It opens the **Save as** dialog box.

7. **Type** the name in which you want to save the shape as a custom brush stroke in the **File name** text box in the Save as dialog box. In our case, we type the name, **My Stroke**.

8. Click the **Save** button to save the custom brush stroke. As a result, the custom brush stroke is saved with the specified name. The default location where CorelDRAW saves the newly-created brush stroke is the Custom Media Strokes folder.

Working with Grids and Guidelines

You can align and position objects on the Drawing page with the help of grids in CorelDRAW. The grids can be defined as a pattern of lines on a plane, which represents the longitude and latitude distances. These distance help determine the absolute location of an object on the Drawing page. You can set the distance between grid lines.

On the other hand, a guideline can be defined as a colored dotted line that can be used to precisely position or align objects according to the rulers. You can create vertical and horizontal guidelines by simply clicking the vertical and horizontal rulers, respectively, and dragging the mouse pointer to position the guidelines onto the Drawing page. Apart from these two types of guidelines, you can also create a slanted guideline. Both grid lines and guidelines are used for precise drawing and placement of objects on the Drawing page. Let's begin this section by learning to set the distance of the lines in a grid in the following section.

Setting the Distance Between Grid Lines

You can modify the arrangements of grid lines by altering the number of grids and changing the space between adjacent grid lines in CorelDRAW X6. Grids are generally used to create precise and accurate drawings, ranging from technical illustrations to magazine layouts. Therefore, changing the distance and frequency of grid lines is often needed. In this section, you learn to set the distance between the lines in a grid. Let's perform the following steps to set the distance between grid lines:

1. **Open** a new drawing in CorelDRAW.

2. Select **View> Setup> Grid and Ruler Setup** from the Menu bar to open **Options** dialog box. The Grid subcategory under Document category is selected by default, with its options displayed on right pane, (picture 6.4).

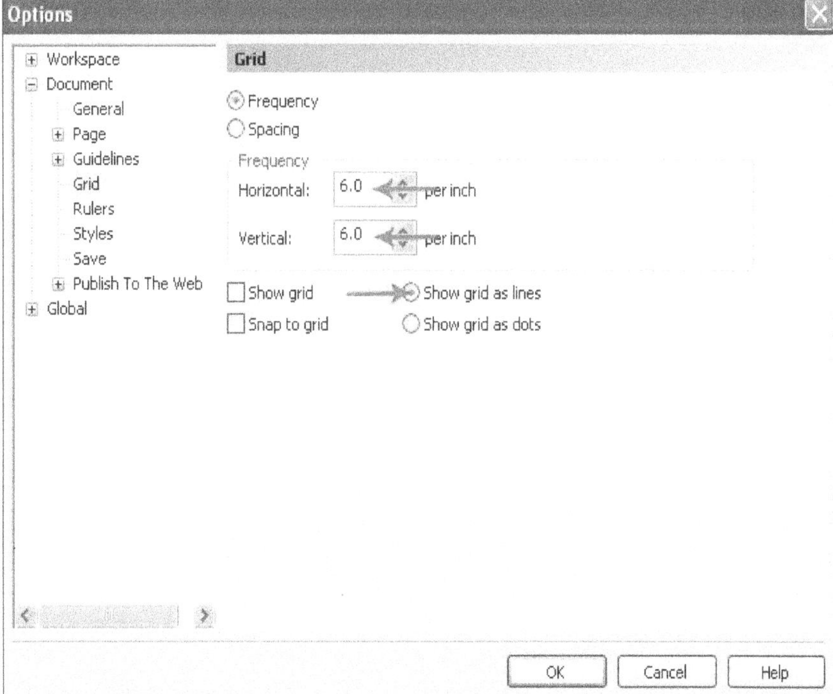

Picture 6.4

3. **Type** the value: **6.0** in the <u>Horizontal</u> spin box under the Custom grid section to specify the distance between the horizontal lines in the grid, as shown in picture 6.4.

4. **Type** the value: **6.0** in the <u>Vertical</u> spin box under the Custom grid section to specify the distance between the vertical lines in the grid, as shown in picture 6.4.

5. Select the **Show grid** check box, as shown in picture 6.4. Then click the **OK** button to save the changes. As you click the OK button, the grid appears on the drawing area of your screen (picture 6.5).

By the way, you can select the **Snap to grid** check box in the <u>Options</u> dialog box to position an object to the closest intersection of the grid.

Snapping Objects to the Grid

In CorelDRAW, you can snap object with the grid drawn on the Drawing page. Snapping can be referred as a manner of swift attachment (or attraction), which happens whenever you bring an object near a grid line. In this way, the object that you want to snap is automatically held by the grid line. This sudden capturing of the object by the grid line is called snapping. Snapping allows you to accurately align objects on the Drawing page. Let's perform the following steps to snap an object to the grid:

1. **Open** a drawing in CorelDRAW. In our case, we open the drawing created in the previous section.

2. Select **View> Snap to Grid** from the Menu bar.

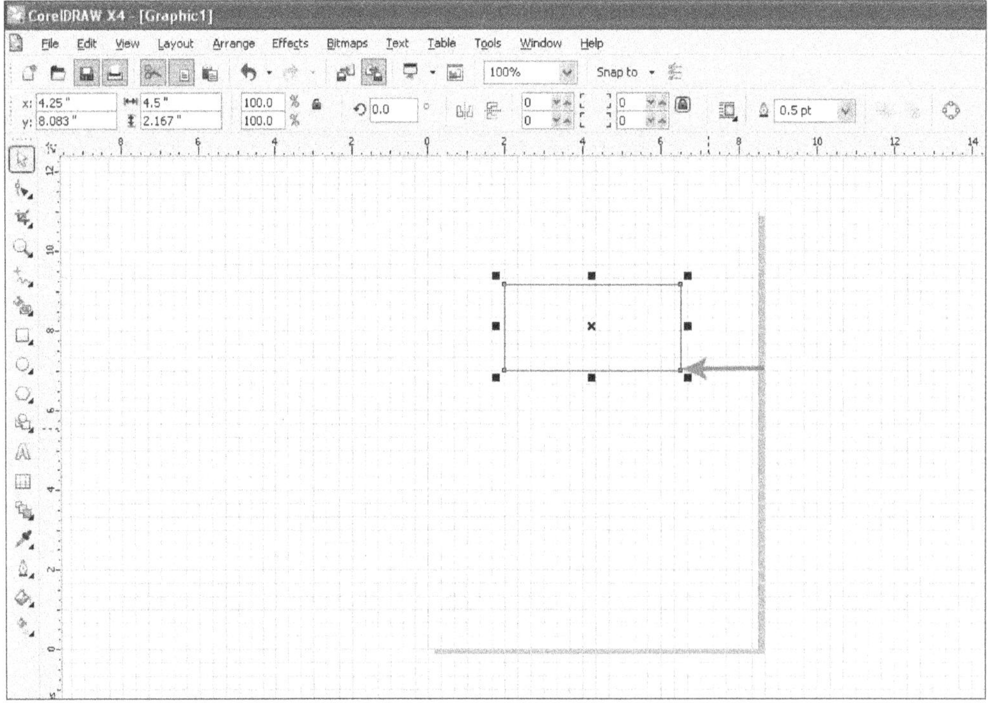

Picture 6.5

3. Select the **Rectangle tool** from Toolbox and **draw** a rectangle on the Drawing page. The mouse cursor will automatically snap to the grid pattern drawn on the Drawing window, as shown in picture 6.5.

4. Select the **Pick tool** from Toolbox.

5. **Select** the rectangle and **drag** it on the Drawing page. As soon as you release the mouse button, the rectangle aligns itself to the nearest grid on the Drawing page.

Snapping an Object with Guidelines

You can add guidelines in the CorelDRAW Document window, which help you to align and place the objects precisely and in the specified gaps. CorelDRAW lets you place these guidelines anywhere on the Document window. As stated earlier, you can create three types of guidelines: Horizontal, Vertical, and Slanted. Similar to grid lines, you can also snap objects with the guidelines. Let's perform the following steps to snap the distance between guidelines:

1. **Open** a new document in CorelDRAW.

2. **Click** the <u>ruler</u> aligned with Toolbox to create a vertical guideline, as exactly shown in picture 6.6 with the red arrow numbered 2.

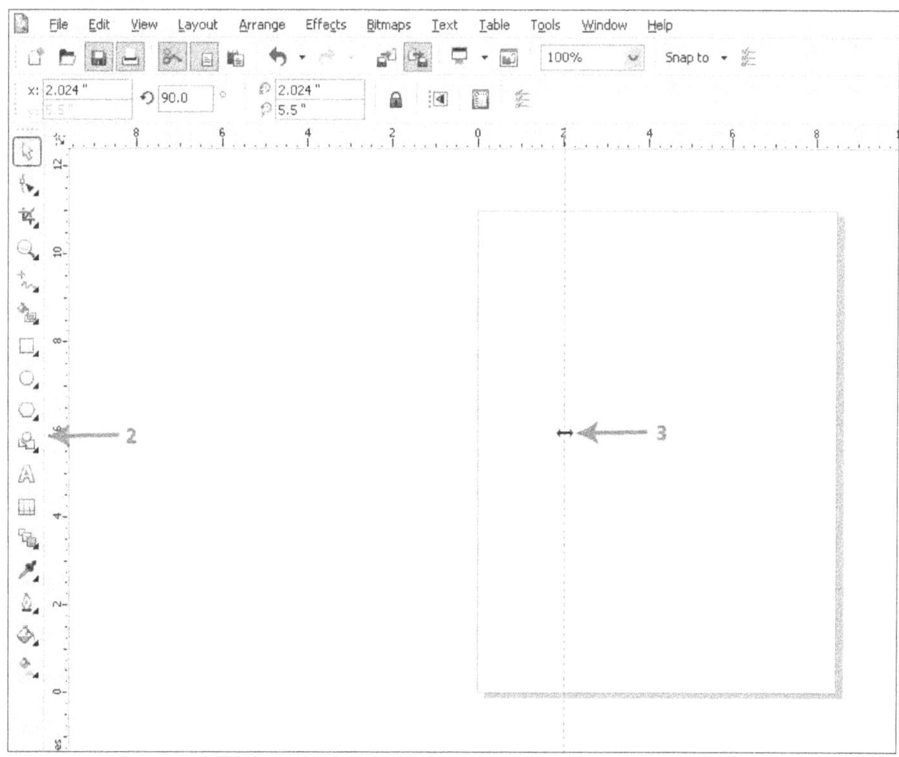

Picture 6.6

3. **Drag** onto the Drawing page to the desired location where you want to create a vertical guideline, as shown in picture 6.6 with the red arrow numbered 3.

4. **Click** the <u>ruler</u> aligned with the Property bar to create a horizontal guideline, as exactly shown in picture 6.7 with the red arrow numbered 4.

5. **Drag** onto the Drawing page to specify the location for the horizontal guideline, as shown in picture 6.7 with the red arrow numbered 5.

6. **Drag** to create a rectangle on the Drawing page by using the **Rectangle tool**.

7. Select **View> Snap to Guideline** from the Menu bar.

8. **Drag** the rectangle towards the guidelines by using the **Pick tool**. It will automatically snap with the specified guideline drawn on the Drawing window, as shown in picture 6.7 with red arrow numbered 8.

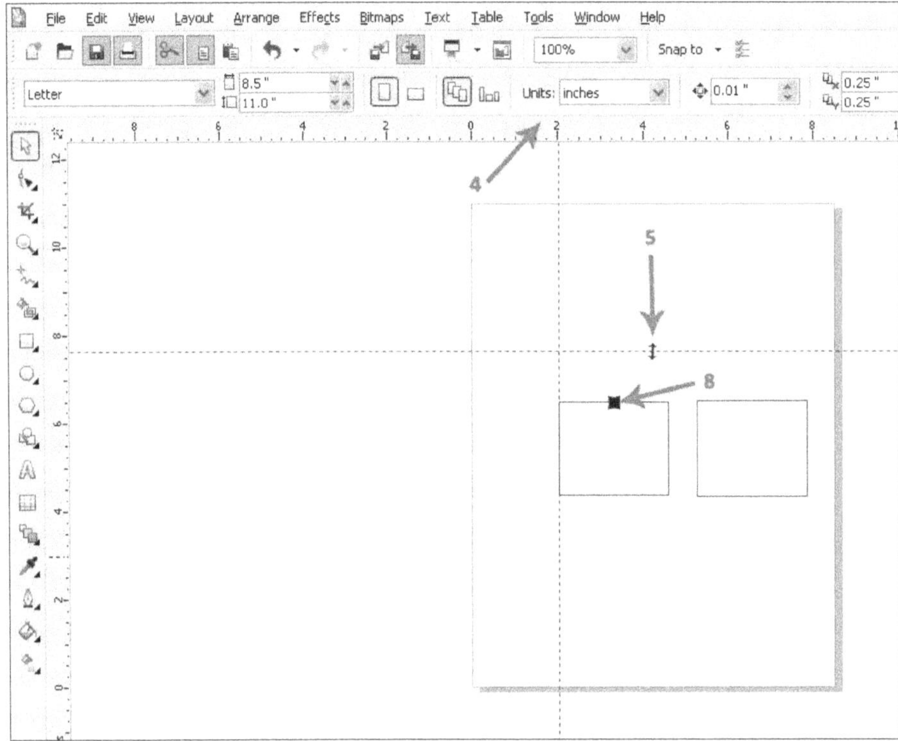

Picture 6.7

As the rectangle comes close to any of the guidelines, the edge of the rectangle aligns with that guideline. On your screen, the rectangle appears aligned with the guideline on the Drawing page.

Lesson 5
Working with Colors and Filling Objects

In any graphical and designing application, such as CorelDRAW and Illustrator, color imparts a noteworthy and significant impact. Attractive colors of graphics not only look prominent, but also seek attention of a user. The final results of graphical illustrations are awaited to experience the visual elements, such as color and texture, which are some of the first things that users notice in your work. The graphics having an interesting mix of colors bound the users to have an enduring glance, and if they find it appealing, they will look at other elements, such as text, and read the message you want to communicate through your work.

In the CorelDRAW application, you are enabled with numerous ways to add colors to images, objects, and text. However, the most common as well as the easiest method of adding color is by using the default color palette. The default color palette aligning to the right side of the Document window provides you with various color samples to use in your drawing. Apart from using the color palette, you can fill objects and graphics to create complex color combinations, such as gradient and textured patterns of your choice in a graphics, by using various tools. You can also adjust the color harmonies of multiple objects to create outstanding and reliable graphics. You can easily manage these colors by using the Document Palette docker, which keeps the record of all the colors used in the document.

In this chapter, you learn to select colors by using the color palette. You also learn to display and organize the default color document palette in CorelDRAW X6. Next, you learn to create a custom color palette by selecting colors manually from an object and a document. Further, you learn to edit a custom color palette by changing the colors to the required ones. In addition, you learn to use uniform fills on objects drawn on the Drawing page. This chapter also explains the procedure to use fountain fills, in which you learn to use a preset fountain fill and a custom fountain fill. Towards the end of the chapter, you learn to work with custom build color harmonies of CorelDRAW. Moreover, you learn to use pattern fill, wherein, you discuss the 2-color pattern fill and bitmap pattern fill. At the end of the chapter, you learn to apply texture fills, mesh fills, and fills to areas. Let's begin the chapter by learning the procedure to select colors by using the default color palette in the next section.

Selecting Colors by Using the Default Color Palette

In CorelDRAW, the color palette is referred to a collection of solid colors that allows you to select colors for fills and outlines or for highlighting text. You can select the fill and outline colors by using either the default color palette or a custom color palette. CorelDRAW X6 comes with the default color palette, which is available aligning to the right side in the Document window. This color palette contains a set of 99 predefined colors from the CMYK (Cyan, Magenta, Yellow, and Key or Black) model. A custom color palette, on the other hand, is the color palette in which the colors are defined by the user. You can fill an object with a color of the default color palette by simply selecting the object with the Pick tool, and then clicking the desired color swatch in the default color palette located on the right side of the Document window. The color you selected automatically gets applied to the object on which you desired to add the color. After selecting a color by using the default color palette, let's now learn to display and organize the default Document Palette in CorelDRAW X6.

Displaying and Organizing the Default Document Palette

As colors are essential parts of graphics, designing applications including CorelDRAW include a number of features for the easy and efficient management of colors. The application provides Palette Editor, which allows you to quickly access and display all the available colors in the default color palette, including Document Palette or Image Palette, and can keep a record of all the colors used in the drawing of the document. Now perform the following simple steps on your computer to display Document Palette:

1. **Launch** the CorelDRAW X6 application.

2. Select **Window**> **Color Palettes**> **Document Palette** from the Menu bar. It displays the Document Palette docker aligned at the right side of the Document window of your screen (picture 6.8).

3. **Click** at the top right corner of the Document Palette docker. Then **drag** it to organize it at another place on the Document window. The Document Palette docker can be adjusted anywhere on the Document window.

4. **Drop** the Document Palette docker at the desired location. In our case, we relocate the docker from the right side to the middle of the Drawing window.

In case, you want to place the docker back to its original place, you can double-left click at the top of the docker. After displaying and organizing the Document Palette docker in CorelDRAW, let's now learn to create a collection of desirable colors by creating a custom color palette in the next section.

Creating a Custom Color Palette

The custom color palette can be created by assimilating multiple of desired colors in a single location with a specified name. The customized color palettes are useful when you are required to frequently select the same color, or when you want to work with a specific set of colors.

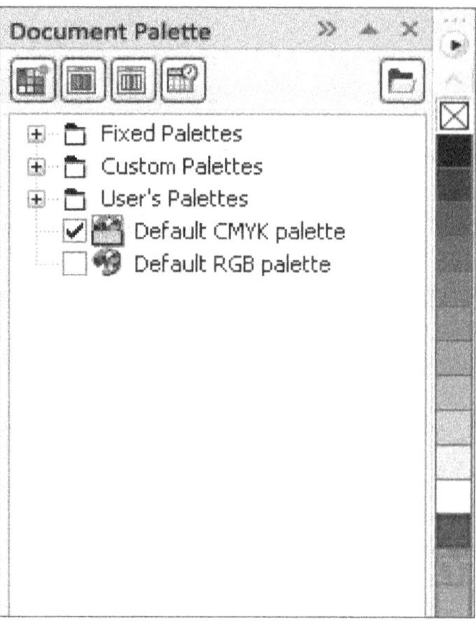

Picture 6.8

You can add colors in the customized color palette simply by selecting each color manually from the default colors available in the color palette, by using the colors in an object, or from Document Palette. In this section, you learn to create a custom color palette by selecting colors manually from the objects and from the document of CorelDRAW. Let's begin the procedure to create a custom color palette by selecting colors manually in the next section.

Creating a Custom Color Palette by Selecting Colors Manually

Custom color palette can be created manually by following a simple procedure, in which you are required to select each color manually. The colors can be added manually to a color palette by selecting a color model, such as RGB (Red, Green, and Blue) or CMYK, and then changing the color composition of the selected model. Perform these steps to create a custom color palette:

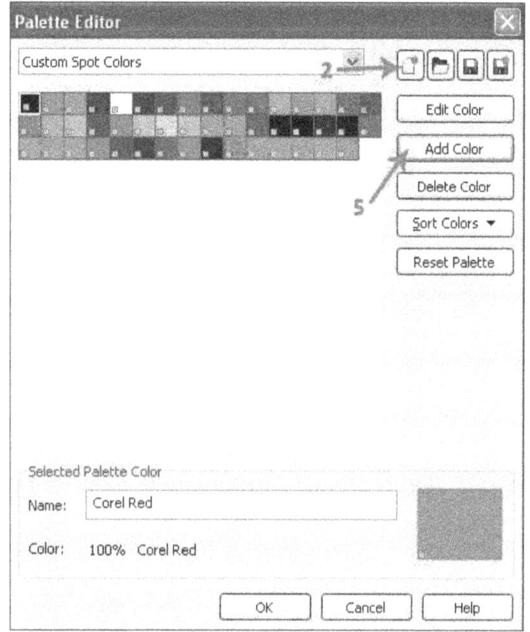

Picture 6.9

1. Select **Window> Color Palettes> Palette Editor** from the Menu bar. It opens the Palette Editor dialog box (picture 6.9).

2. Click the **New Palette** button in the Palette Editor dialog box, as shown in picture 6.9 with the arrow numbered 2.

The New Palette dialog box appears with the default **My Palette** folder location on your screen.

3. **Type** the name in the **File name** text box to specify a name for the custom color palette you want to create. In our case, we type **Color Palette01**.

4. Click the **Save** button in the New Palette dialog box. The **Palette Editor** dialog box again appears on your screen.

5. Click the **Add Color** button in the Palette Editor dialog box, as already shown in picture 6.9 with the red arrow numbered 5.

The **Select Color** dialog box appears on your screen, displaying the Palette tab selected by default, as shown in picture 7.0.

6. **Select** the color from the list that you want to add in the Custom palette, as shown in picture 7.0 with the red arrow numbered 6.

7. Click the **Add To Palette** button in the Select Color dialog box, as shown in picture 7.0 with the red arrow numbered 7. It will add the selected color in Color Palette01 you have created.

8. Click the **OK** button in the Select Color dialog box to save the changes.

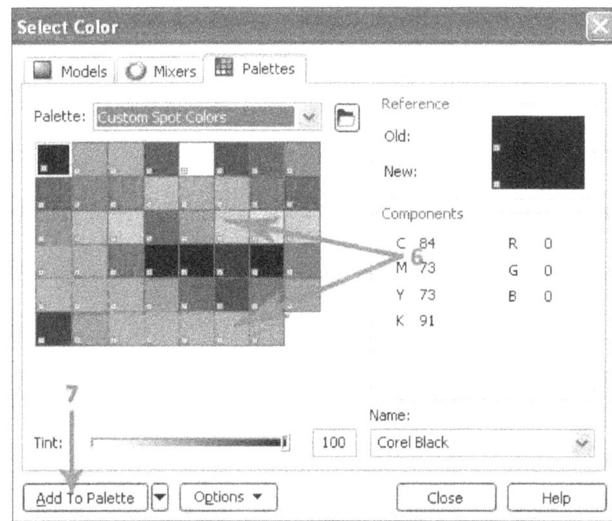

Picture 7.0

9. Click the **OK** button in the Palette Editor dialog box. The Specified color is automatically added in the palette, Color Palette01.

Now the file name, Color Palette01, will act as a color palette in which you can add custom colors of your choice. Apart from creating a color palette by specifying colors in the Select Color dialog box, you can also create a color palette from an object, as discussed in the next section.

Creating a Color Palette from an Object

You can collect all the colors present in an object into a color palette in CorelDRAW X6. For this you are required to select the object from the Drawing page with the requisite color, and then create a color palette from the object. This is helpful when you have to frequently select the same colors used in the object. The color palette created this way can be used for filling other objects in your drawing. Perform the following steps to create a color palette from an object:

1. **Open** a CorelDRAW document containing objects with various colors. It must be a CorelDRAW (.cdr) file. In our case, we open one which is shown in picture 7.1.

2. **Select** the object by using the Pick tool from Toolbox.

3. Choose **Window> Color Palettes> Create Palette From Selection** from the Menu bar. It opens the Save As dialog box on your screen.

4. **Type** a name for the custom color palette in the File name text box in the Save As dialog box. In our case, we type the name, **Color Palette02**.

5. Click the **Save** button in the dialog box. By default, the new custom color palette is saved in the My Palette folder, and the palette appears on the right side of the Document window, as shown in picture 7.1 with the red arrow.

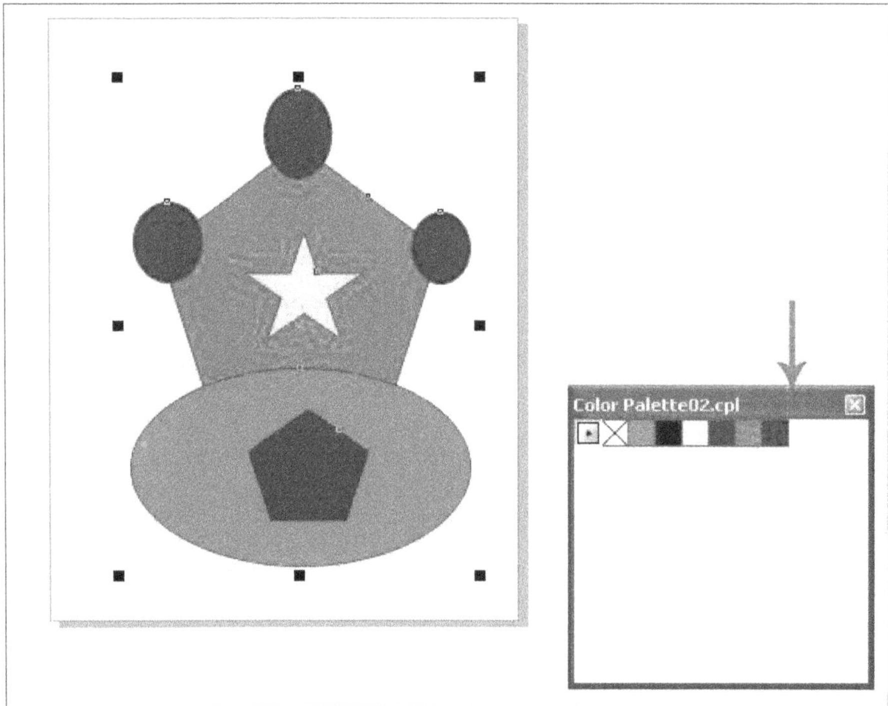

Picture 7.1

Creating a Color Palette from a Document

The colors used in a document can be extracted for further usage by creating a custom color palette from a document. In this way, the colors present in all the objects placed on the Drawing page are mutually integrated in a specified color palette. The created color palette will show all the colors that are being used on the objects in a document. Creating a custom color palette from an object requires you to select the desired objects from the Drawing page whose colors you want to keep in a separate specified color palette. On the other hand, creating a custom color palette from a document does not require any selection from the Drawing page. It automatically captures all the colors used in the document in the custom palette you create. Perform the following steps to create a custom color palette from a document:

1. **Open** a CorelDRAW document containing objects with various colors. It must be a CorelDRAW (.cdr) file.

2. Choose **Window> Color Palettes> Create Palette From Document** from the Menu bar. It opens the Save As dialog box on your screen.

3. **Type** a name for the custom color palette in the File name text box in the Save As dialog box. In our case, we type the name, **Color Palette of Document**.

4. Click the **Save** button in the Save As dialog box. The **Add Colors From Bitmap** dialog box appears on your screen.

5. **Enter** the desired number in the **How many colors do you wish to add to this color palette** spin box. In our case, we enter: **20**.

6. Click the **OK** button in the **Add Colors From Bitmap** dialog box.

As you click the OK button, a custom color palette named **Color Palette of Document** is created. The file created becomes a color palette, which appears beside the default color palette aligning to the right side of the Document window of CorelDRAW. The **Color Palette of Document** color palette contains all the colors used in the document.

Editing a Custom Color Palette

After creating a color palette, you can further edit it according to your requirements. In CorelDRAW X6, you can edit the custom color palette by performing various actions, such as adding new colors as well as deleting, sorting, and renaming the existing colors. In this section, you learn to edit a custom color palette by changing one of the colors from the color palette. Let's perform the following steps to edit a custom color palette:

1. **Open** a CorelDRAW document.

2. Select **Window> Color Palettes> Palette Editor** from the Menu bar. It opens the Palette Editor dialog box on your screen.

3. **Click** the combo box present at the top (in the middle) of the Palette Editor dialog box. A dropdown list appears from which you select the various color palettes that you want to edit. In our case, we select the color palette named **Color Palette02.xml**.

4. Click the **Edit Color** button on the right side in the Palette Editor dialog box. It opens the **Select Color** dialog box on your screen.

5. Click the **Models** tab in the Select Color dialog box.

6. **Type** the desired value in the **C, M, Y,** and **K** text boxes for the required colors. In our case, we type the values, 65, 3, 46 and 7, respectively in the four text boxes.

7. Click the **OK** button in the Select Color dialog box to save the changes.

8. Click the **OK** button in the Palette Editor dialog box to accept the edited color. The new color is saved in **Color Palette02.xml**. Now, you can create and edit the custom color palette in CorelDRAW.

Using Uniform Fills

In CorelDRAW, uniform fills are known as solid color fills, which you can select from the colors present in a color palette. Uniform fills allow you to fill the objects with one color, termed as the solid filling of an object. On the other hand, non-solid color filing can be done by selecting one or more colors for filling an object. Besides using the colors of the default color palette, you can create colors of your choice by specifying color values in the selected color model. Whenever a uniform fill is applied to an object, the object is filled with a solid color. You can apply a uniform fill to an object by using interactive fill tools and uniform fill tools on Toolbox, or by selecting a color from the default color palette. The interactive fill tool enables you to create your own selection of colors by applying different types of uniform, Fountain, pattern, and texture fills to an object. Let's briefly learn about the uniform fill and interactive fill tools in CorelDRAW:

Uniform Fill tool: Allows you to apply a solid color to an object.
Fountain Fill tool: Allows you to fill an object with a combination of two or more colors.
Pattern Fill tool: Allows you to apply a pattern of two or more colors to an object.
Texture Fill tool: Allows you to fill an object with a texture.
PostScript Fill tool: Allows you to apply an intricate pre-defined textures with an automatic preview to fill an object.
Interactive Fill tool: Allows you to fill an object with different types of fills, such as uniform, Fountain, pattern, and texture.
Mesh Fill tool: Allows you to apply gridlines inside the mesh of an object.
Smart Fill tool: Allows you to identify the enclosed area when one object overlaps another and fills that enclosed area. Now perform the following steps to apply uniform fills to an object:

1. **Open** a drawing in CorelDRAW, and **draw** a rectangle on the Drawing page (picture 7.2).

2. **Select** the rectangle by using the Pick tool.

3. **Click** the arrow on the right side of the **Fill tools** from Toolbox, as shown in picture 7.2.

4. Select the **Uniform Fill** tool from the flyout. It opens the Uniform Fill dialog box with the <u>Palettes</u> tab selected by default.

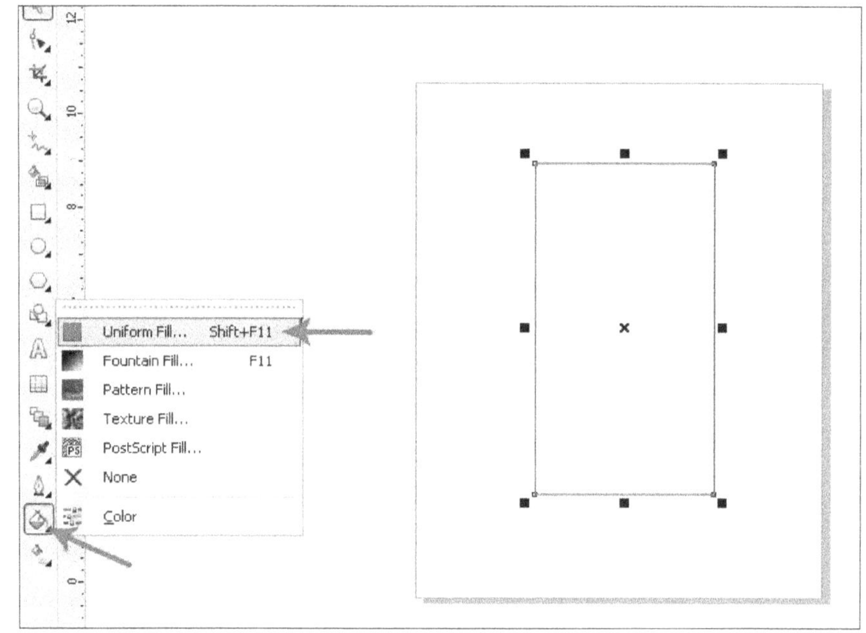

Picture 7.2

5. **Select** the desired color palette under the Palettes tab. In our case, we select the **Sky Blue** color palette with **100, 20, 0,** and **0** as its <u>CMYK</u> value.

6. Click the **OK** button in the Uniform Fill dialog box. As a result, the object is filled with the selected color.

As already learned, the Uniform Fill tool enables you to add a solid color to an object. This results in the object to be displayed in a single, desired color value. In CorelDRAW, apart from specifying values of colors, you can create your own colors and can fill a solid color impression on the selected objects by using the Uniform Fill tool.

Using Fountain Fills

In CorelDRAW X6, the fountain fill can be used to fill an object with a combination of two or more colors. The two color combination can be created in various ways, such as one color gradually fades into another and one color merges with another. The fountain fills are also known as gradient fills. You can apply the following four categories of fill types of the Fountain fill:

Linear: Refers to the fill type in which one color fades into another color in a straight line.
Radial: Refers to the fill type in which one color fades into another in the form of a circle.
Conical: Refers to the fill type in which one color fades into another color in a circular path that radiates from the center of the objects.
Square: Refers to the fill type in which one color fades into another in the form of a square.

You can apply fountain fills in many ways, such as by using a preset fountain fill, a 2-color fountain fill, or a custom fountain fill. In the following sections, you learn to apply preset fountain fills by using the Fountain Fill tool. You also learn to use custom fountain fills to objects. Let's first discuss to use preset fountain fill in the next section.

Using a Preset Fountain Fill

The preset fountain fills is referred to built-in texture patterns that can be directly applied on the objects on the Drawing page. In CorelDRAW, the advantage of these preset fountain fill is that they can be quickly applied to an object and do not have to be created from scratch, thereby, saving time. After selecting a preset fountain fill, you can specify various properties for it, such as the fill type, the angle of the fill, and the center point of the fill. Perform the following steps to apply a preset fountain fill to an object:

1. **Open** a CorelDRAW document having an object on the Drawing page.

2. **Select** the object by using the Pick tool. In our case, we select the **polygon** object.

3. **Click** the arrow on the right side of the **Fill tools** on Toolbox, and then select **Fountain Fill**. It opens the Fountain Fill dialog box (picture 7.3).

4. Select **Conical** option from Type drop down list, as shown in picture 7.3 with the red arrow numbered 4.

5. Select **Cylinder – 01** option from the list of Presets, which is at the bottom of the Fountain Fill dialog box (picture 7.3).

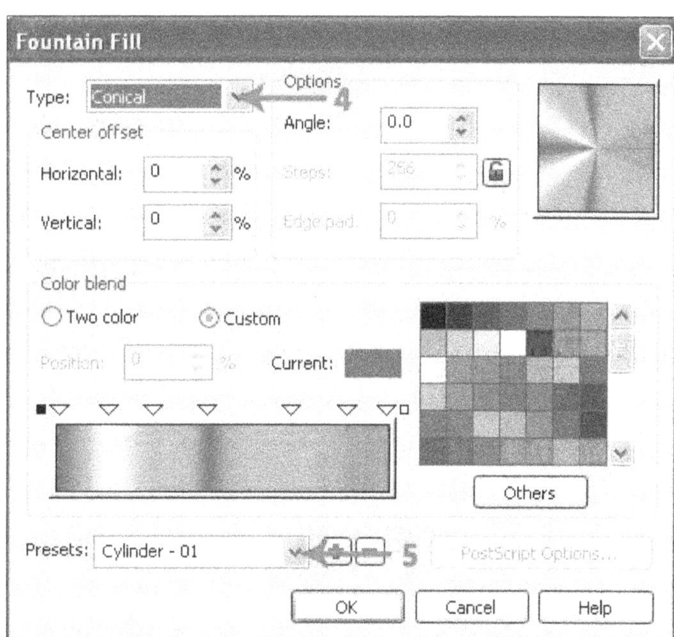

Picture 7.3

6. Click the **OK** button in the Fountain Fill dialog box to apply the select preset on the object. As a result, the polygon object on your drawing page appears with the preset fountain fill applied on it.

Using a Custom Fountain Fill

In CorelDRAW, you can apply custom fountain fills on an object that displays the combination of two or more colors. In a custom fountain fill, you are required to select the desired color manually by specifying the center point and the edge pad for the color fill. Moreover, the center point, from where the custom fountain fill imparts the center offset of the fill, can also be selected. The settings of the edge pad allow you to adjust the size of the outer edge fill color from inwards. After applying a custom fountain fill, you can also save it as a preset fountain fill. Perform the following steps to apply a custom fountain fill:

1. **Open** a CorelDRAW document having an object drawn on the Drawing page.

2. **Select** the object by using the Pick tool. In our case, we select the **ellipse** object.

3. **Click** the arrow on the right side of the **Fill tools** on Toolbox, and then select **Fountain Fill**. It opens the Fountain Fill dialog box.

4. Select **Square** option from Type dropdown list.

5. Select the **Custom** radio button under the Color blend section of Fountain Fill dialog box. A custom color blend appears with a black color at its left square box and white color at its right square box.

6. **Click** the white square box on the left side of the color band under the Color blend section in the Fountain Fill dialog box.

7. **Select** a color from the color swatch in the color palette. This color specifies the first fill color.

8. **Click** the right square box present on the right side of the color band under the Color blend section in the Fountain Fill dialog box.

9. **Select** a color of your choice from the color swatches in the color palette. This color specifies the second fill color.

10. Click the **OK** button in the Fountain Fill dialog box. As a result, the custom fountain fill is applied to the selected object.

Lesson 6
Working with Custom Build Color Harmonies

In CorelDRAW X6, the color styles docker allows you to create and edit colors and styles according to your requirements. The color harmony rule allows you to shift all the colors according to a predetermined logic and create various color arrangements. The color harmony selects the specified color as a base color and is used as a reference color for other colors on the color wheel. The color harmony by default comprises of seven colors, namely VIBGYOR (Violet, Indigo, Blue, Green, Yellow, Orange, and Red). You can rotate the color wheel over the required color to accomplish a harmony of colors in the selected object. Perform the following steps to create a new color harmony:

1. **Open** a drawing in CorelDRAW. In our case, we open a drawing having an object drawn on the Drawing page.

2. **Select** the object by using the Pick tool from Toolbar. In our case, we select the **polygon** with seven sides (picture 7.4).

3. Choose **Tools**> **Color Styles** from the Menu bar (picture 7.4). The **Color Styles** docker appears aligned to the right side of the Drawing window.

4. Click **New color harmony** button under the Color Styles docker, as shown in picture 7.5. It opens a dropdown list.

5. Select **New Color Harmony** option from the list. The new color harmony is created and the Color Styles docker allows you to adjust the color according to your requirements.

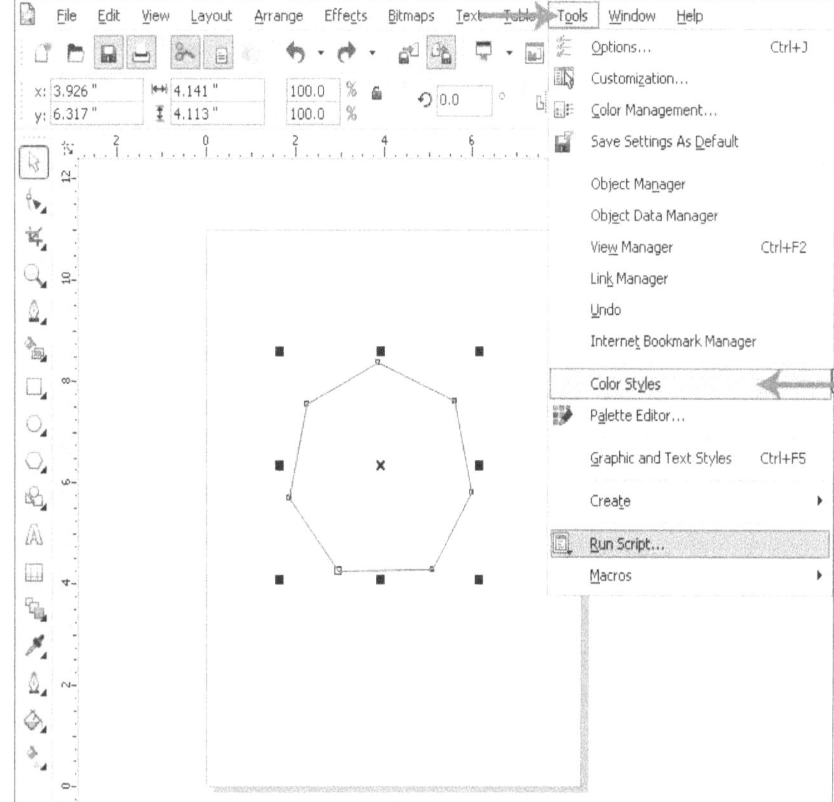

Picture 7.4

6. **Drag** the circle appearing inside the **Harmony Editor** section in the Color Styles docker to select the required color.

7. **Double-click** the color tab under the **Harmony Editor** section in the Color Styles docker. As a result, the color is applied to the selected object on the Drawing page.

Using Pattern Fills

You can apply a pattern of two or more colors to an object by using the pattern fills. In CorelDRAW, pattern fill enables you to fill the objects by using the 2-color, full color, or bitmap pattern fills. 2-color pattern fills consists of two colors, which you can select. Full color pattern fill are made of a complex vector graphics that can be composed of lines and fills. The bitmap pattern fill is created from the select bitmap image. You can also create your own pattern fills from objects you draw or from imported images. CorelDRAW application provides preset pattern fills that you can directly apply to objects.

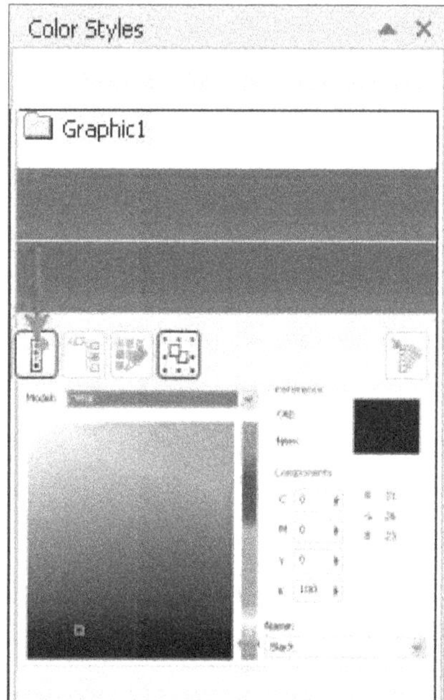

Picture 7.5

In this section, you learn to apply 2-color pattern fill and full color or bitmap pattern fills to an object. Let's begin by learning to use the 2-color pattern fill in the next section.

Using the 2-Color Pattern Fill

You can apply a pattern of two colors on an object by suing the 2-color Pattern Fill tool. As the name of the tool pattern fill indicates that it fills the objects with a pattern, whether it is from a preset or from selecting specific colors. The Pattern Fill tool enables the 2-color pattern fill mode, in which you can select the front color and the back color to fill the pattern. You can also change the file size of the pattern filled. Perform the following steps to apply a 2-color pattern fill to an object:

1. **Open** a CorelDRAW document having an object drawn on the Drawing page.

2. **Select** the object on the Drawing page by using the Pick tool. In our case, we select an **ellipse**.

3. **Click** the arrow on the right side of the **Interactive Fill tools** on Toolbox. Then select the **Interactive Fill tool** from the flyout, as shown in picture 7.6 with the red arrow numbered 3.

Now you can see on your screen that the Property bar appears with various options related to the interactive fill tool.

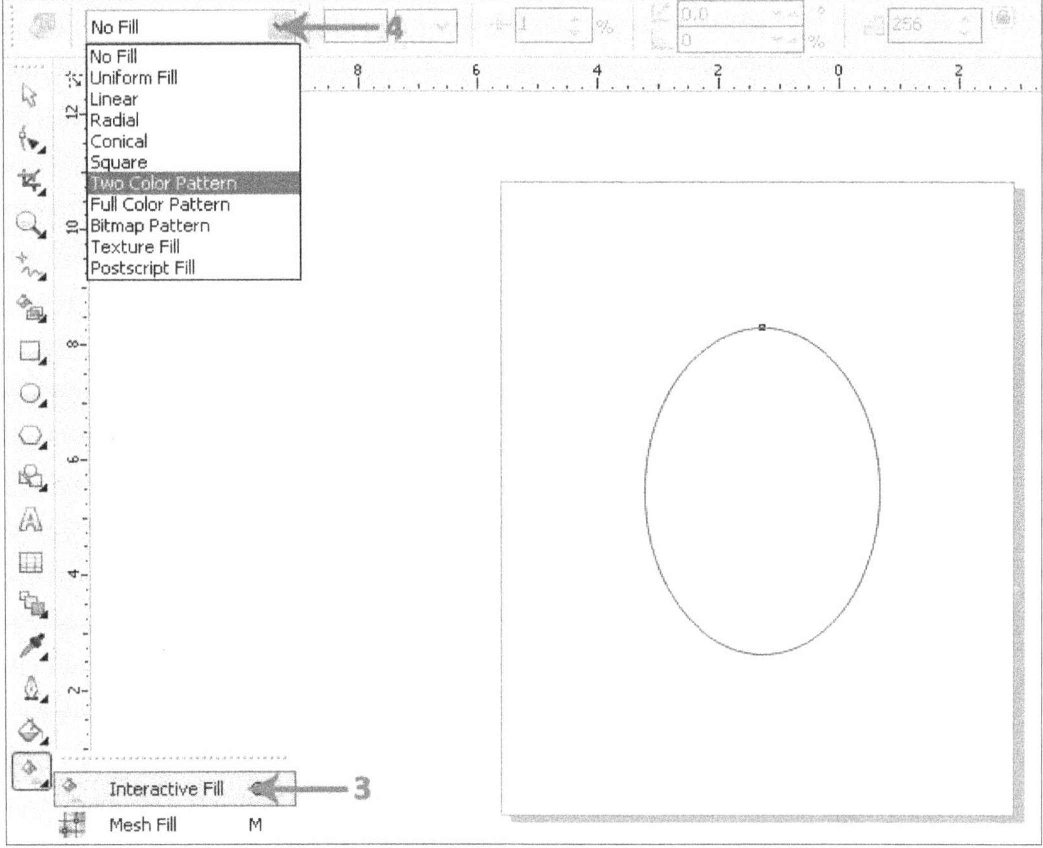

Picture 7.6

4. Click the **Fill type** list box from the Property bar. Then select the **Two Color Pattern** option from the dropdown list, as shown in picture 7.6 with the red arrow numbered 4.

Now you will see on your screen that the default pattern of the selected 2-color pattern fill is applied to the ellipse object on the Drawing page.

5. Click the **First fill color** list box on the Property bar. Then **select** an option from the dropdown list to fill the object with the required pattern. It is shown in picture 7.7 with the red arrow numbered 5.

6. Click the down arrow of the **Front color** button on the Property bar. Then **select** a desired color from the color palette flyout. It is shown in picture 7.7 with the red arrow numbered 6.

7. Click the down arrow of the **Back color** button on the Property bar. Then **select** a desired color from the color palette flyout. It is shown in picture 7.7 with the red arrow numbered 7.

By the way, you can also change the size of the tiles of the selected pattern by using the three buttons, **Small Tile for Pattern**, **Medium Tile for Pattern**, and **Large Tile for Pattern**, which are available on the Property bar.

The result of applying the 2-color pattern fill to the object will be shown on your drawing page.

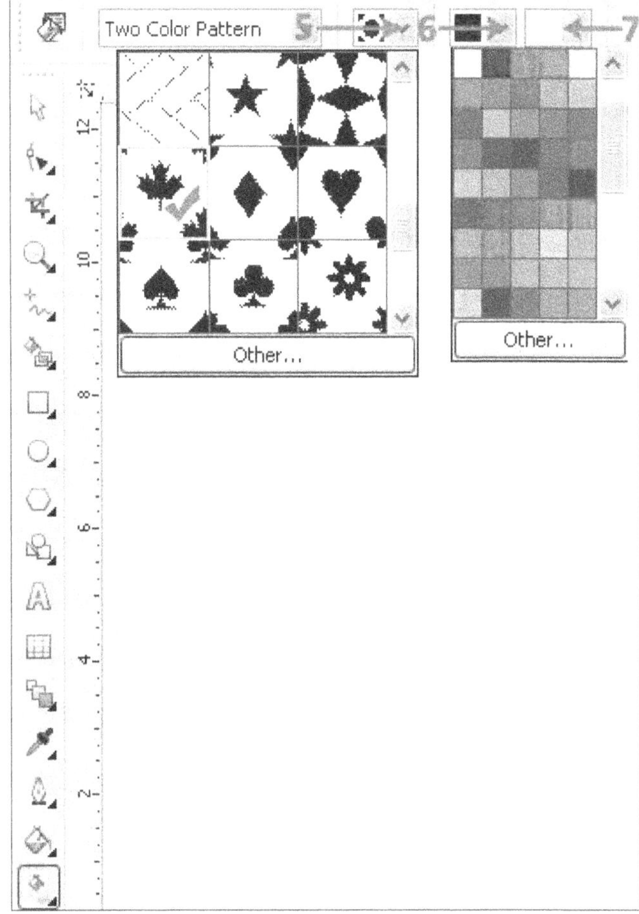

Picture 7.7

You can also change the size of the tiles used in the pattern from the **Edit Tiling for Pattern** spin box on the Property bar by typing the values as per your need for filling the drawing.

Using the Bitmap Pattern Fill

In CorelDRAW, the bitmap pattern fill can be created from a bitmap image. After selecting a bitmap image for the bitmap pattern fill, you can specify the tile size of the pattern fill. CorelDRAW provides various build-in patterns that can be applied to the objects by using the interactive fill tool enabling its Bitmap Pattern mode. The patterns applied can be further adjusted for scaling, tiling, and more as per your requirements. Perform the following steps to apply a bitmap pattern fill:

1. **Open** a CorelDRAW document having an object drawn on the Drawing page.

2. **Select** the object by using the Pick tool. In our case, we select an **ellipse** object.

3. **Click** the arrow on the right side of the **Interactive Fill tools** on Toolbox. Then select the **Interactive Fill tool** from the flyout. The Property bar now appears with various options.

4. Click the **Fill type** list box on the Property bar. Then select **Bitmap Pattern** from the dropdown list.

5. Click the **First fill color or pattern** list box on the Property bar. Then **select** an option from the dropdown list to fill the object with the required bitmap pattern. As a result, the selected bitmap pattern is applied to the object in your drawing page.

By the way, you can change the size of the tile used in the pattern on the Drawing page by using the three buttons, **Small Tile for Pattern**, **Medium Tile for Pattern**, and **Large Tile for Pattern**. In our case, we select the Medium Tile for Pattern button on the Property bar.

Using Texture Fills

In CorelDRAW, the texture fills are used to fill an object with a texture and enhance the appearance of the object. You can select the fill of an object from the libraries provided having various arrangement of textures. While selecting a texture, you can edit colors of the texture, set its resolution rate, preview, and save the modified texture fill, which you can overwrite as well. However, you cannot overwrite a preset of texture fill present in a texture. You have to save the texture fill with a unique name. One of the limitations or drawbacks of using a texture fill is that it only supports the RGB color model. However, other color models can be used as a reference to edit or create a color of your choice. Perform the following steps to apply a texture fill to the object:

1. **Open** a CorelDRAW document having an object drawn on the Drawing page. Then **select** the object by using the Pick Tool.

2. **Click** the arrow on the right side of the **Fill tools** on the Toolbox. Then select the **Texture Fill** tool from the flyout. It opens the Texture Fill dialog box, as shown in picture 7.8.

3. Click the down arrow of the **Texture library** button. Then select the texture fill **Sample 5** from the list, as shown in picture 7.8 with the red arrow numbered 3.

4. Select **O's** sample from the Texture list options to specify the texture style, as shown in picture 7.8 with the red arrow numbered 4.

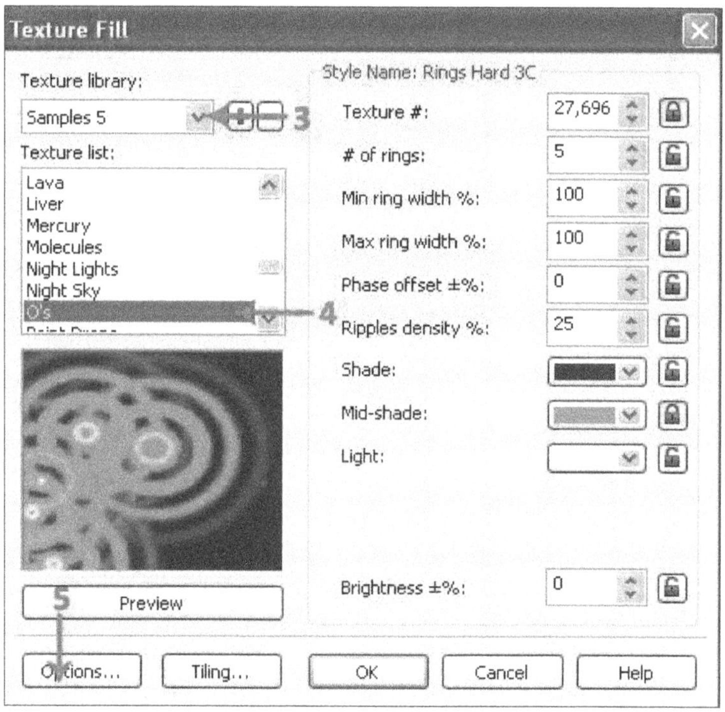

Picture 7.8

5. Click the **Options** button in the Texture Fill dialog box. It opens the Texture Options dialog box on your screen, as shown in picture 7.9.

6. Type a value in the **Bitmap resolution** text box to specify the resolution regarding the quality of the bitmap texture pattern. In our case, we type **380**.

7. Click the **OK** button to save the changes made in the Texture Options dialog box.

8. Click the **Tiling** button in the Texture Fill dialog box (picture 7.8). It opens the **Tiling** dialog box, as shown in picture 8.0.

9. Type values in the **Width** and **Height** combo boxes in the Size section. In our case, we type the width as **6.0** and the height as **7.0**.

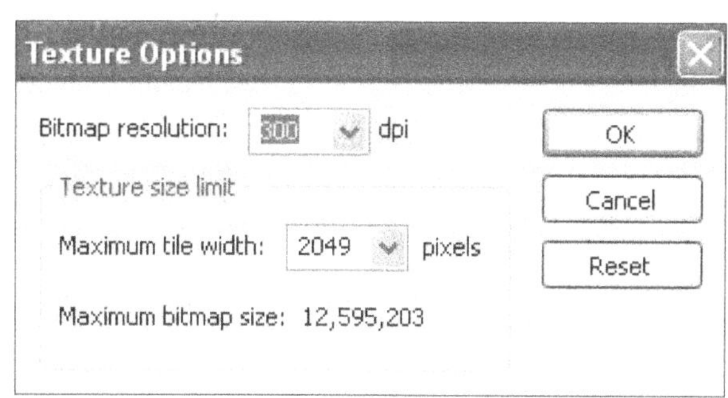

Picture 7.9

10. Select the **Column** radio button under the Row or column offset section to specify the bitmap pattern to be applied across the column of the selected object.

11. Type a value in the **Rotate** input box in the Transform section to specify the required amount of rotation. In our case, we type the value, **5.0**.

12. Click the **OK** button to accept the changes in the Tiling dialog box.

13. Click the **OK** button in the Texture Fill dialog box to save the changes.

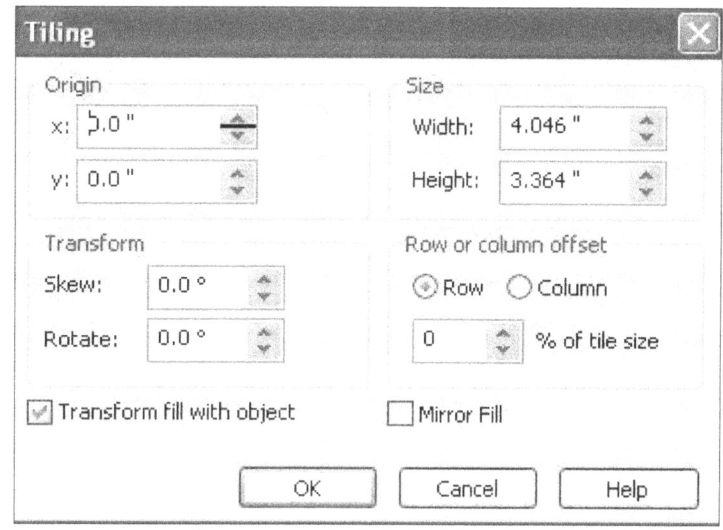

Picture 8.0

The texture fill of the specified settings is applied to the selected object on your Drawing page. Let's now discuss to apply the Mesh Fill tool to an objet in the next section.

Using Mesh Fills

The mesh fills are applied on an object to create unique effects, such as smooth color transitions in any direction, without having to create blends. The mesh fills first creates gridlines inside the object enabling to provide more smooth color transitions as the gridlines can be added or removed from an object. While applying a mesh fill, you need to specify the number of columns and rows in the grid, as well as the intersecting points or nodes of the grid. You can edit a mesh fill grid by adding, removing, and editing nodes or intersections by using the Mesh Fill tool. You can also remove the mesh fill, which is already applied on the object in CorelDRAW. In addition, the mesh fills can only be applied to closed objects drawn on the Drawing page. Perform the following steps to apply a mesh fill to an object:

1. **Open** a CorelDRAW document having an object drawn on the Drawing page.

2. **Select** the object by using the Pick tool. In our case, we select the **star** object.

3. Click the arrow on the right side of the **Interactive Fill tools** on Toolbox, and select **Mesh Fill tool**.

4. **Type** a value in the **Grid size** spin box on the Property bar to set the number of rows and columns of grid inside the selected object, as shown in picture 8.1 with the red arrow numbered 4. In our case, we type 4 and 6 in the spin boxes.

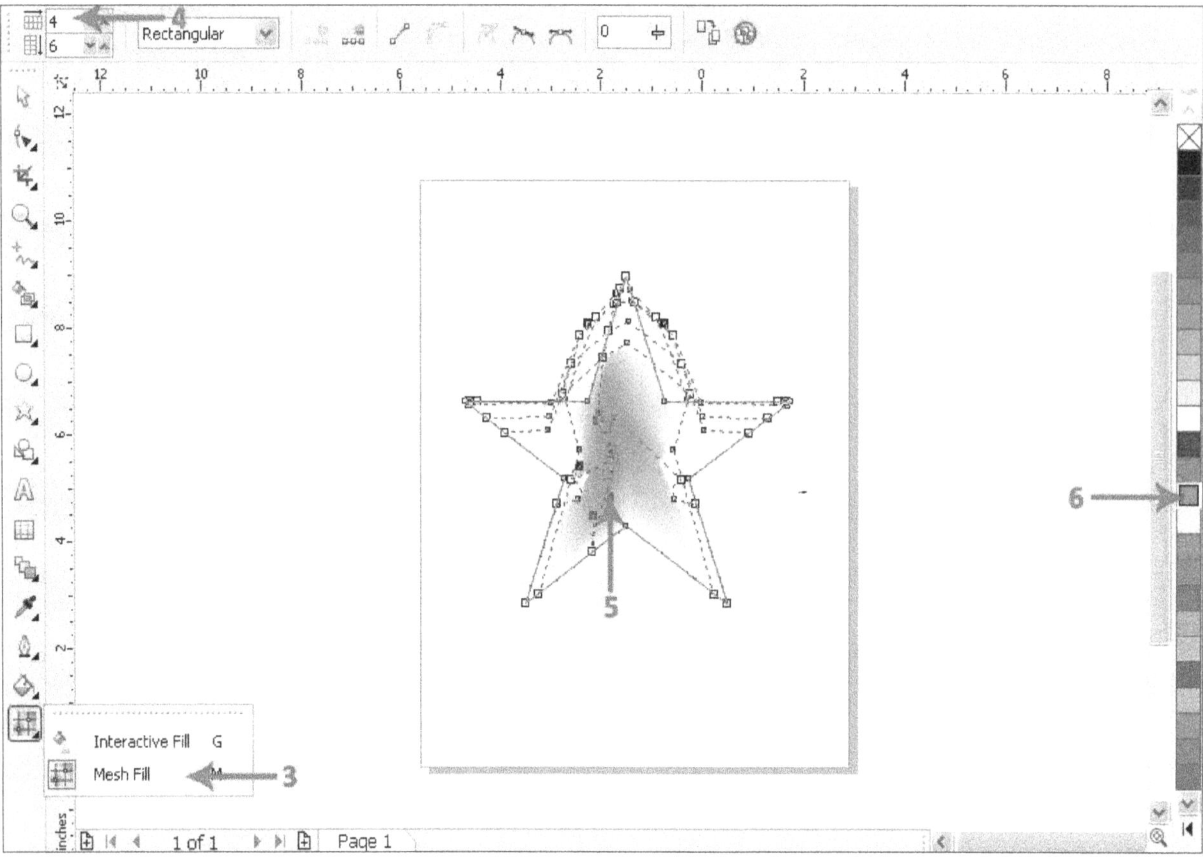

Picture 8.1

5. **Select** a node of the grid on the object that you want to select to fill with the desired color, as shown in picture 8.1 with the red arrow numbered 5.

6. **Click** the color on the default color palette aligning to the right side of the Document window to fill the color in the grid of an object (picture 8.1).

7. **Repeat** the steps **5** and **6**, to apply the mesh fill to the other nodes of grids in the object. As a result, the object with the mesh fill applied will be shown on your screen.

Using Fills to Areas

In CorelDRAW, the various fill tools that you used till now are useful to apply fills only to the larger areas of an object. However, the enclosed areas (the areas where one object overlaps the other) were left out. The smart fill tool helps you to apply a fill to an enclosed area by detecting the edges of an area and creating a closed path so that it can fill that area. In our case, the five spirals drawn on the Drawing area (picture 8.3) intersect each other at a number of points by creating enclosed areas. You can fill these enclosed areas by using the smart fill tool. Perform the following steps to fill the enclosed areas in a drawing by using the Smart Fill tool:

1. **Open** a CorelDRAW document having an object drawn on the Drawing page.

2. **Select** the object by using the Pick tool. In our case, we select **five spirals** (picture 8.2).

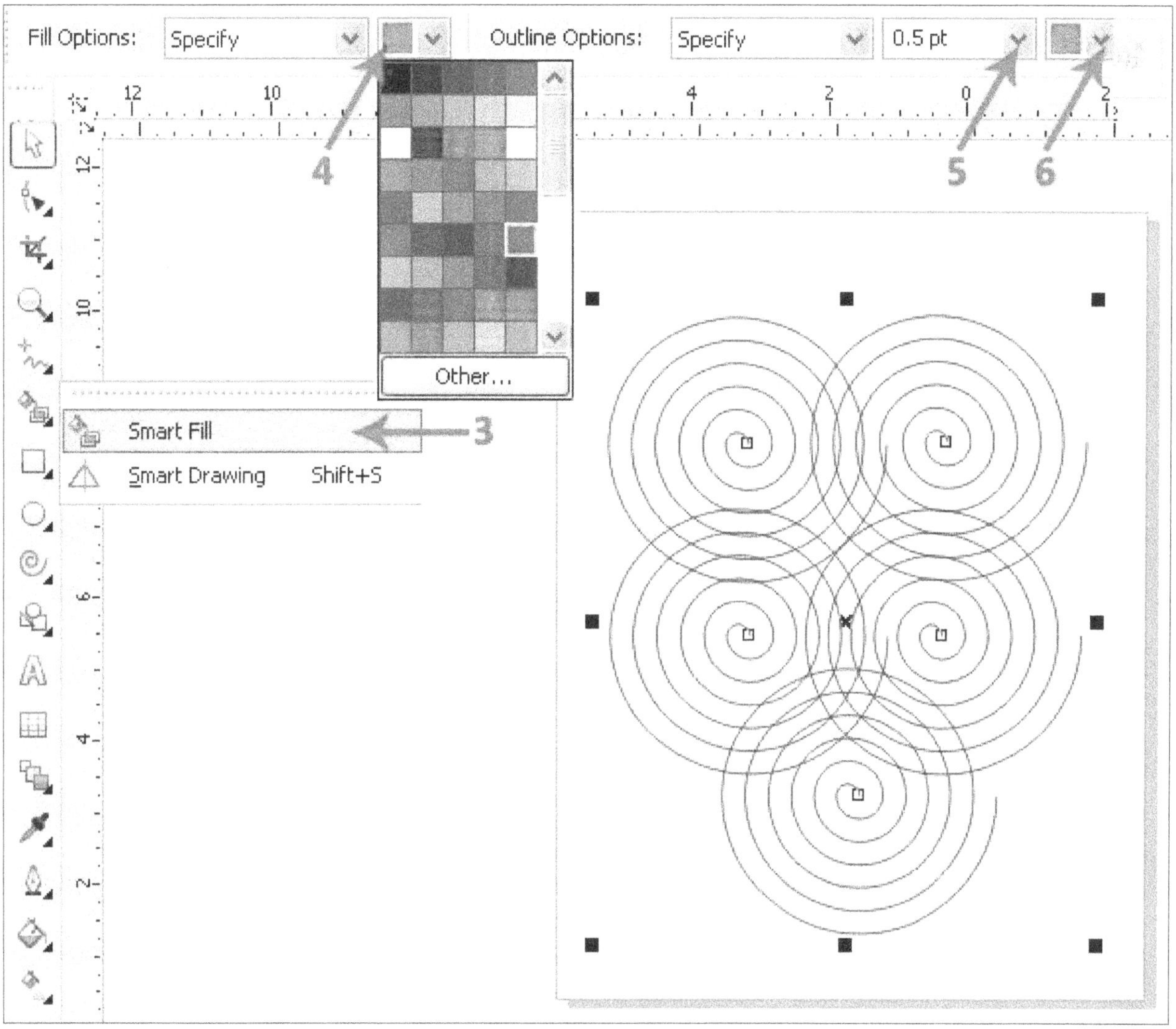

Picture 8.2

3. Click the arrow on the right side of the **Smart Fill tool** from Toolbox. Then select the **Smart Fill tool** from the flyout, as shown in picture 8.2 with the red arrow numbered 3.

4. Click the down arrow of the **Fill Color** list box on the <u>Property</u> bar. Then **select** the desired color from the color palette flyout, as shown in picture 8.2 with the red arrow numbered 4.

5. **Type** a value in the **Outline width** combo box in the <u>Property</u> bar to specify the width for the outline of selected object. In our case, we type the value **1 px**, as shown in picture 8.2 with the red arrow numbered 5.

6. Click the down arrow of the **Outline Color** list box in the Property bar. Then **select** a color from the color palette flyout, as shown in picture 8.2 with the red arrow numbered 6.

By the way, the Use Default option allows you to create the filling area with the default setting. If you select the third one, that is, No Fill, it applies no fill to the area. Here, Specify is activated by default.

7. **Click** the object where you want to fill color. The first click fills the object, as shown in picture 8.3 with the red arrow numbered 7.

8. **Click** the desired portions on the Drawing area to fill. In our case, we fill the area, as shown in picture 8.3.

As a result, the enclosed area of the object on your Drawing page is filled. In this section, you learnt the various fill tools that you used to apply fills only to the larger areas of an object. Using these tools, you can create several designs. In the next section, you are going to learn how to handle objects in CorelDraw.

Picture 8.3

Lesson 7
Handling Objects in CorelDRAW X6

In the CorelDRAW X6 application, objects play a basic elemental role. You can create as many objects as you need on the Drawing page of the application. Meanwhile, handling of objects for the required output is also necessary. You can modify the objects with specialized tools and commands in different ways to create the design of your choice. Toolbox provides various tools to not only create objects, but also make modifications in the properties of the objects. After selecting the object, you can apply various effects, such as moving, rotating, and scaling, on it and can turn the object into the desired shape you want. For example, you can draw a rectangle with the help of the Rectangle tool from Toolbox and also modify the properties, such as increasing or decreasing the thickness of the stroke used to draw the rectangle or changing the height and width or the fill color of the rectangle. While creating objects in CorelDRAW, you may not always get the preferred shape due to the default parameter settings of objects. For example, the oval object with shadow is not available as a single tool in CorelDRAW, if you want to apply shadow to the object, you are first required to create an object, and then apply the Drop Shadow effect on it.

The chapter begins by discussing different ways to work with objects in CorelDRAW by using the basic Cut, Copy, Paste, Duplicate, and Delete commands. You also explore the object styles docker introduced in CorelDRAW X6. Next, you learn to copy the properties, such as fill, size, and effects applied on an object, from one object to another. Towards the middle of the chapter, you learn the procedure to transform objects with the help of commands, such as Move, Scale, Rotate, and Mirror. Further, you learn the procedure to change the order of an object for transforming objects on the Drawing page. In addition, the chapter describes the ways to combine and break objects in CorelDRAW. Moreover, the chapter demonstrates the procedure to group objects, add an object to a group, remove an object from a group, edit a single object in group, and ungroup objects from the group. Getting towards the end of the chapter, you learn to create special effects on the drawn objects with the help of Envelope effect, Distort effect, Blend effect, Contour effect, Transparency tool, Drop Shadow tool, and Extrude tool. At the end of this chapter, you learn to align and distribute objects drawn on the Drawing page in CorelDRAW X6.

Working with Objects in CorelDRAW

Before performing any action on an object in CorelDRAW, you need to select the object. There are various actions that you can perform on the selected object, such as adding color, positioning objects, aligning the object, and distributing objects with respect to other objects on the Drawing page. The desired operations can be performed on objects by first selecting them with the help of Pick tool. After performing the desired actions on the selected object, you can deselect the object. Selecting and deselecting objects are probably the most frequent actions you perform while making any changes in an object.

Copying, Cutting, and Pasting Objects

In this chapter, you learn to perform various editing tasks, such as copying an object, creating a duplicate of the object, and deleting the object. In CorelDRAW, you can easily perform these tasks with the help of the Cut, Copy and Paste commands located in the CorelDRAW Menu bar. In case, when you are required to cut an object by using the Cut command, the object is removed from its location on the Drawing page and is placed in a temporary storage area called the clipboard. On the other hand, when you are required to copy an object by using the Copy command, the object is not removed from its location on the Drawing page, but it creates a copy of the object on the Drawing area. You can also retrieve the object from the clipboard when you paste the object on the desired location on the Drawing page.

By the way, clipboard is referred to a memory allocation unit in which you can temporarily store cut or copied data for later retrieval. While performing the cut, copy, and paste operations, the data can be anything from text to code to objects. Now perform the following steps to use the Copy and Paste commands:

1. **Open** a drawing in CorelDRAW X6. In our case, we open the drawing having a **star** object drawn on the Drawing page.

2. **Select** the object by using the Pick tool from the Toolbox. In our case, we select the star object from the Drawing page.

3. Select **Edit> Copy** from the Menu bar. The selected object is copied to the clipboard.

4. Select **Edit> Paste** from the Menu bar. As a result, the copied object is pasted on the same location on the Drawing page.

5. **Move** the copied object to another location by using the Pick tool. In our case, we move the object to new location.

Keep in mind that you can cut object by selecting Edit> Cut and paste them by selecting Edit> Paste from the Menu bar. The cut, copy, and paste operations can also be performed by clicking the Cut, Copy, and Paste buttons available on the Standard toolbar.

Duplicating an Object

In CorelDRAW X6, you can create duplicate objects by using the Duplicate command. Duplication is an important property while you work with complex object forms. Duplicate of objects can be created where you are required to have multiple copies of the same object, and you do not want to reflect any changes in the original object. Instead of creating a new object from scratch, you can create its duplicate. Duplication, unlike copying, where the copied object is first placed in the clipboard, and then pasted on the Drawing page, does not use the clipboard but places a copy of the object directly on the Drawing page. Duplication is much quicker than copying. Perform the following steps to create a duplicate object on the Drawing page:

1. **Open** a drawing in CorelDRAW X6. In our case, we open the drawing having a **rectangle** drawn on the Drawing page.

2. **Select** the object that you want to duplicate by using the Pick tool from Toolbox. In our case, we select the rectangle.

3. Select **Edit> Duplicate** from the Menu bar.

The **Duplicate Offset** dialog box appears, if you are duplicating an object for the first time. Type a value in the **Horizontal Offset** and **Vertical Offset** text boxes in this dialog box to specify the distance between the duplicate and original objects along the X and y axes. You can type any value depending on how you want the duplicate object to appear with respect the original object. Some guidelines to follow are as follows:

- Type the offset value 0, to place the duplicate object exactly on top of the original object.
- Type any positive offset value, to place the duplicate object above and to the right of the original object.
- Type any negative offset value, to place the duplicate object below and to the left of the original object.

4. **Enter** the value in the <u>Horizontal Offset</u> spin box. In our case, we enter **3.0"**, as shown in picture 8.4.

5. **Enter** the value in the <u>Vertical Offset</u> spin box. In our case, we enter **3.0"**, (picture 8.4).

6. Click the **OK** button in the Duplicate Offset dialog box. As a result, a duplicate of the object appears on the Drawing page. In the next section, you will learn to delete an object.

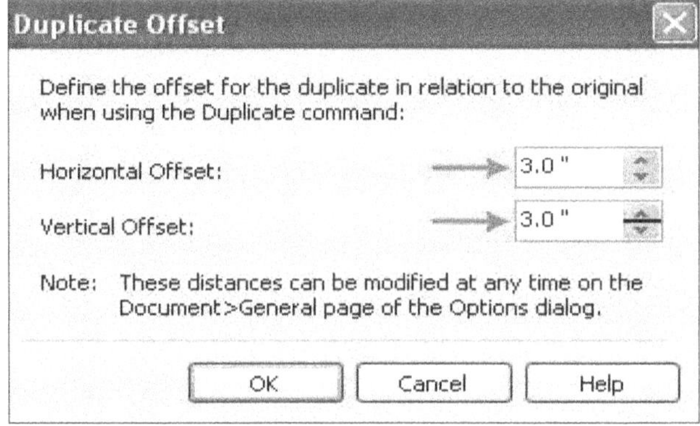

Picture 8.4

Deleting an Object

In CorelDRAW, you can use the Delete command to remove or erase an object. Deletion helps you to remove unwanted objects from the Document window. Unlike cutting, deletion does not necessarily leave the removed object in the clipboard from where it can be recovered. Perform the following steps to delete an object from the Drawing page:

1. **Open** a drawing in CorelDRAW X6. In our case, we open the drawing having **various objects** drawn on the Drawing page.

2. **Select** the object that you want to delete by using the Pick tool from Toolbox. In our case, we select the **star** object.

3. Select **Edit> Delete** from the Menu bar. As a result, the selected object is deleted from Drawing page.

Exploring the Object Styles Docker in CorelDRAW X6

In CorelDRAW, you can create styles based on the formatting of an object that you prefer and require. In other hand, you can also create a style from the basic setting of object attributes from the Object styles docker. In CorelDRAW X6, the new style docker named as Object Style docker is introduced that streamlines the features, such as creation, application, and management of styles. Styles in CorelDRAW can be referred as an agreement to the properties that specify the display and appearance of the objects drawn on the Drawing page. There are new style-sets introduced that enable you to group the styles by making them easier to implement same effects over multiple objects. In this way, the output generated can be iterative, creative, flexible, and consistent.

In the Object Style docker, you can apply styles and patterns on the graphic objects, artistic objects, text, callouts, dimensional objects, and objects created with the Artistic Media tools, in case, you want to specify the outline style of an object by changing the attributes, such as outline width, color, and line type. In addition, the text objects can be defined by specifying the attributes, such as font type, font style and size, text color, background color, and character position. Let's perform the following steps to work with the object styles docker:

1. **Open** a drawing in CorelDRAW X6. In our case, we have opened a drawing having the **ellipse**, **star**, and **rectangle** objects drawn on the Drawing page.

2. Select **Window> Dockers> Object Styles** from the Menu bar. The **Object Styles** docker appears aligned towards the right side of the Drawing window.

3. Click the down arrow of the **Default Object Properties** section in the Object Styles docker. The list of object properties that you can modify appears under the Default Object Properties section in the **Object Styles** docker.

4. Select the **Graphic** option from the list of object properties under the Default Object Properties section in the Object Styles docker.

5. **Select** the object by using the Pick tool from the Toolbox whose properties you want to change. In our case, we have selected the **ellipse** object.

6. Click the **Full-color pattern fill** button under the <u>Fill</u> group in the Object Styles docker.

7. Click the **Bitmap Pattern fill** button beside the <u>Type</u> option under the Fill group in the Object Styles docker.

8. **Click** the down arrow beside the pattern styles list box. A dropdown list of pattern styles appears.

9. **Select** the desired pattern style from the list. In our case, we select the **red and green** pattern style from the list.

10. Click the **Apply to Selected** button in the Object Styles docker. The specified bitmap pattern is applied on the ellipse.

11. **Select** the object by using the Pick tool whose properties you want to change. In our case, we select the **rectangle** object.

12. Click the **Full-color pattern fill** button under the <u>Fill</u> group in the Object Styles docker.

13. **Click** the down arrow beside the bitmap pattern styles list box. A dropdown list of pattern styles appears.

14. **Select** the desired pattern style from the list. In our case, we select the **grey and red** pattern style from the list.

15. Click the **Apply to Selected** button in the Object Styles docker.

16. Select the **star** object drawn on the <u>Drawing area</u> with the help of the Pick tool.

17. Click the **2-color pattern fill** button beside the <u>Type</u> option under the <u>Fill</u> group in the Object Styles docker.

18. Click the **Apply to Selected** button in the Object Styles docker. As a result, the star object appears with the specified 2-color pattern fill. Let's now learn to copy the properties of an object in the next section.

Copying the Properties of an Object

The objects drawn on the Drawing page possesses individual properties and attributes. CorelDRAW X6 provides a feature that you can use to copy the attributes and properties from one object to another. Using this feature, you can copy the properties, such as fill, outline, and effects, of an object and apply them to another object. This action is performed by using the Color Eyedropper and Attributes Eyedropper tools. The Color Eyedropper tool allows you to pick an effect, such as color, pattern, or texture, of an object, which you can then apply to other objects by using the Attributes Eyedropper tool. You can use the Attributes Eyedropper tool to copy multiple properties, transformations, and effects at a time to apply on the desired objects. In this section, you learn to copy the fill property, size of object, and effects from one object to another. Let's first learn to copy the fill property from one object to another in the next section.

Copying the Fill Property from one Object to Another

You can reproduce the color, outline, or text property of objects by copying the properties of specified object to paste it on another object. In this way, the properties blend with the general style of the document and impart exact features on another object. Before you can copy the properties of an object to another object, you have to create two objects, the first being the object whose properties you want to copy, and the second being the object to which the properties are copied. Perform the following steps to copy the fill property of one object to another:

1. **Open** a drawing in CorelDRAW X6. In our case, we open the drawing having the rectangle and polygon objects drawn on the Drawing page.

2. **Select** the object by using the Pick tool from Toolbox whose fill color you want to copy. In our case, we select the **polygon** object.

3. **Click** the arrow on the right side of the **Eyedropper tool** from Toolbox. A flyout appears on the screen.

4. Select the **Attributes Eyedropper** tool from the flyout. The shape of your mouse pointer changes into an eyedropper icon.

5. Click the **Properties** button on the Property bar. It opens a dropdown list.

6. Select the **Outline** and **Text** check box from the dropdown list to uncheck these check boxes, as all the options available in the dropdown list are checked by default.

By the way, you can also select all the Outline, Text, and Fill check box options simultaneously from the Properties dropdown list, to copy all the properties of an object to another object.

7. Click the **OK** button in the Properties dropdown list to save the changes.

8. **Select** the object on the Drawing page, whose fill color you want to copy, by using the **Attributes Eyedropper** tool. In our case, we select the polygon.

9. **Select** the object on which you want to apply the copied fill color. In our case, we select the rectangle object. As you click the rectangle, its fill color changes to match the fill color of the rectangle.

Keep in mind that to copy the property of one object to other object on the Drawing page, you need objects, such as source object and destination object. For copying the properties, first you have to right-click on the source object. Then, drag and drop the object to the destination object. A context menu appears on the destination object. From this context menu, select the Copy Fill Here option to copy the fill properties of the source object.

Copying the Size of One Object to Another

CorelDRAW X6 allows you to copy the physical attributes of an object to apply them on another object. By using the Transformations button on the Property bar, you can modify the size of an object with respect to another object. You can also copy the position as well as rotation properties of the object and apply them to another object. Here are the steps to copy the size of one object to another:

1. **Open** a drawing in CorelDRAW X6. In our case, we open the drawing having the ellipse and star objects drawn on the Drawing page.

2. **Select** the object whose size you want to copy by using the Pick tool from Toolbox. In our case, we select the star.

3. **Click** the arrow on the right side of the Eyedropper tools from Toolbox. It opens a flyout.

4. Select the **Attributes Eyedropper** tool from the flyout. The shape of the mouse pointer changes into an eyedropper icon.

5. Click the **Transformations** button on the Property bar. A dropdown list appears.

6. Select the **Size** check box from the dropdown list. Then click the **OK** button in the dropdown list to save the changes.

7. **Select** the object whose size you want to copy by using the **Attributes Eyedropper** tool. In our case, the object is a star. The size of the selected object is copied.

8. **Select** the object on which you want to apply the copied size of the object. In our case, the object is an ellipse. Depending on the size and angles of the source and destination objects, the size of ellipse object changes randomly.

By the way, you can also select the Rotation or Position check box from the Transformations dropdown list to copy the rotation or position of an object to another object. In addition, you can also copy all three transformations simultaneously.

Copying the Effects from One Object to Another

The effect can be termed as something that you can apply to an object to change its appearance, usually to make it more striking and attractive. Sometimes, you may want to copy one or more effects applied on an object to another object. In such cases, you can use the various tools available in CorelDRAW X6 to copy effects on objects. You can access these tools from the interactive tools flyout on Toolbox. Alternatively, you can click the Effects button on the Property bar. In this section, you learn how to apply the Perspective effect and copy it on another object. The Perspective effect provides the illusion of depth by extruding the object. In addition, nodes and control handles appear on the object, which you can use to modify the shape of object. Perform the following steps to apply the Perspective effect on an object, and then copy effect on another object:

1. **Open** a drawing in CorelDRAW X6. In our case, we open a drawing having an ellipse and a polygon drawn on the Drawing page.

2. **Select** an object from the Drawing page by using the Pick tool. In our case, we select a **polygon**.

Keep in mind that to copy an effect, you need to first apply the effect on an object from which you copy it on another object. In our case, we are using two objects, a polygon and a star. Add the Perspective effect on the polygon before copying the effect on the star.

3. Select **Effects> Add Perspective** from the Menu bar. The polygon now appears with a dotted grid pattern containing nodes, which you can use to edit the Perspective effect.

4. **Click** and **move** the nodes of the polygon to change the perspective (view) of the object.

5. **Click** the arrow on the right side of the **Eyedropper tool** from Toolbox. Then select the **Attributes Eyedropper tool** from the flyout.

6. Click the **Effects** button on the Property bar. Then select the **Perspective** check box from the dropdown list.

7. Click the **OK** button in the dropdown list.

You can also apply multiple effects to the selected object (which have already an effect applied on it) by selecting the check boxes that appear in the dropdown list. After this, click the **OK** button, which appears on the dropdown list to apply all the selected effects.

8. **Click** the object whose effect you want to copy by using the **Attributes Eyedropper tool**. In our case, we click the polygon that has the Perspective effect applied to it.

9. **Select** the object on which you want to apply the copied effect. In our case, we select the ellipse. As a result, the Perspective effect is applied on the ellipse.

Lesson 8
Transforming Objects
You can change the position of an object in different ways, such as by moving the object, nudging the object (that is, moving an object very slightly and precisely according to your requirement), and positioning the object according to the X and Y coordinates in the Drawing page. The proper positioning of objects if done appropriately enhances the visual appeal of the objet in a document. Using these options, you can move an object at a specified distance vertically and horizontally, or to a specific point in the document. In this lesson, you learn to move, scale, rotate, and mirror an object. You also learn to change the order of objects. Let's now learn to move an object in the next section.

Moving an Object
Movement of an object is considered as the most basic property, which is always required for creating designs in the application. You can position an object anywhere by moving it to the desired location. In CorelDRAW X6, you can move the object in the vertical (V) or horizontal (H) direction, or by specifying the distance on the Drawing page. While working in two-dimensional designing applications, such as CorelDRAW, the objects are moved with respect to its axis, namely x and y axis. In our case, we can either move the objects manually or can specify the dimensions in x and y axis for the desired location of an object. Perform the following simple steps to move an object to a desired location on the Drawing page:

1. **Open** a drawing in CorelDRAW X6. In our case, we open a drawing having a polygon drawn on the Drawing page.

2. **Select** the object by using the Pick tool. In our case, we select the polygon object.

3. **Drag** and **drop** the object at the location where you want to place it on the Drawing page. You will see on your screen that the object is placed at a new position on the Drawing page.

Scaling an Object

The process of scaling enables you to change the dimensions, such as width and height, of an object. You can also specify the required amount in percentage to scale the object. In CorelDRAW X6, the scaling enables you to change the dimensions of the object proportionally by maintaining the aspect ratio. Perform the following steps to scale an object:

1. **Open** a drawing in CorelDRAW X6. In our case, we open the drawing having a **complex star** drawn on the Drawing page, as shown in picture 8.5.

2. **Select** the object by using the Pick tool from Toolbox. In our case, we select the **complex star** object.

3. Select **Window> Dockers> Transformations> Scale and Mirror** from the Menu bar. It opens the **Transformations** docker on the right side of the Document window, as shown in picture 8.5.

4. **Clear** (uncheck) the <u>Proportional</u> check box, as shown in picture 8.5 with the red arrow numbered 4.

In the Transformation docker, the Proportional check box is checked by default, which increases or decreases the size of object proportionately while maintaining the aspect ratio of the object. In case you want to change the size object non-proportionally, that is, you do not want the object to retain the aspect ratio, clear the Proportional check box.

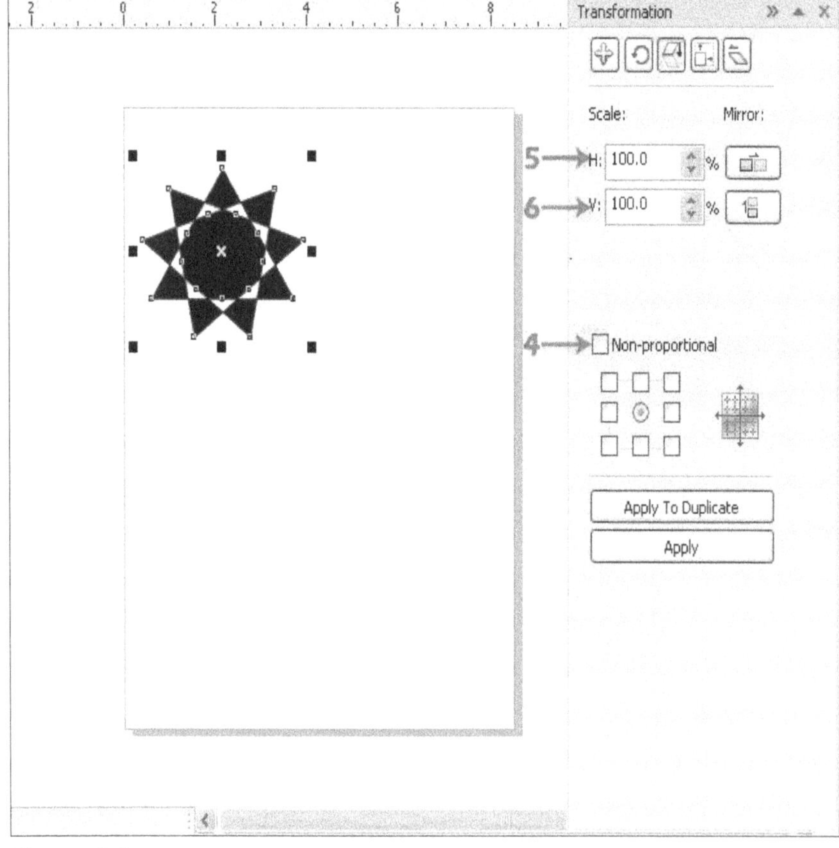

Picture 8.5

5. **Type** the value in the **H** spin box under the <u>Scale</u> section. In our case, we type the value: **350.0**.

6. **Type** the value in the **V** spin box under the <u>Scale</u> section. In our case, we type the value: **280.0**.

7. Click the **Apply** button to apply the changes. As a result, the complex star object is scaled to the specified value we entered in the Transformation docker.

Below the Proportional check box, you can also select a check box that corresponds to the anchor point that you want to change on the object and clear the Proportional check box to maintain the aspect ratio of the object. An anchor point is a point that remains stationary when you stretch, scale, or mirror an object. Anchor points correspond to the eight handles that are displayed when an object is selected. You can also scale an object by dragging a corner selection handle. Alternatively, you can type a value in the Scale factor boxes (the boxes with the % sings) on the Property bar to perform the same action.

Rotating an Object

The process of rotation performed on an object includes the motion of a rigid body around a fixed point. You can rotate an object along the horizontal and vertical coordinates. You can easily transform an object by rotating or by changing the orientation along the specified position (center). When you rotate an object drawn on the Drawing page, you are required to specify the angle of rotation and value for the centralized location from where the rotation occurs. Perform the following steps to rotate an object:

1. **Open** a drawing in CorelDRAW X6. In our case, we open the same **complex star** which we had created in the previous section.

2. **Select** the object by using the Pick tool from the Toolbox. In our case, we select the complex star.

3. Choose **Window> Dockers> Transformations> Rotate** from the Menu bar. It opens the Transformations docker on your screen.

4. **Type** a value in the **Angle of Rotation** spin box in the Rotation section to specify the angle by which you want to rotate the polygon. In our case, we type the value, **90.0**.

5. **Type** a value in the **Copies** spin box to specify the number of copies for the rotated object. In our case, we enter the value, **1**.

6. Click the **Apply** button to apply the changes. As a result, the object rotates by the specified angle. The rotated copy of the specified object is generated above the original object on the Drawing page.

7. **Move** the copied object by using the Pick tool. In our case, we move the object towards the right side of the Drawing page.

By the way, you can also rotate an object along the horizontal and vertical axes. For this, type the desired values in the H and V boxes in the Transformation docker. In addition, you can rotate an object by dragging the rotational handle of the object. You can change the angle of rotation by typing the desired value in the Angle of Rotation text box on the Property bar.

Creating a Mirror Object

Mirroring an object refers to the flipping of the object from left to right or from top to bottom on the Drawing page. The mirroring process lets you create the mirror image for an object to view the appearance of objects on the other half. By default, the anchor point of a mirrored object appears at the center of the object. In CorelDRAW X6, perform the following simple steps on your computer to mirror an object:

1. **Open** a drawing in CorelDRAW X6. In our case, we open a drawing having a spiral drawn on the Drawing page.

2. **Select** the object by using the Pick tool from Toolbox. In our case, we select the spiral object.

3. Select **Window**> **Dockers**> **Transformations**> **Scale** from the Menu bar. It opens the Transformation docker on your screen.

4. Click the **Vertical** mirror button in the Mirror category. Then click the **Apply** button to apply the changes. The object, with the mirror effect appears on your screen.

By the way, you can also mirror a selected object by clicking the mirror buttons, namely, Mirror horizontally and Mirror vertically on the Property bar. In addition, you can mirror the object by holding down the Ctrl key and dragging any of its handles in a direction opposite to that of the object. Depending on the shape of the object, you can drag the handles in the top, bottom, left, right, and even diagonal directions, to apply the mirror effect.

Changing the Order of an Object

While working with multiple objects on the Drawing page in CorelDRAW X6, the most recently-created objects appear above those that have been created earlier on the Drawing page. However you can change this default arrangement and can also determine which object appears in front and which object remains at the back on the Drawing page. An object is sent back or brought forward in relation to a selected object. In case, you want to change the arrangement order of an oval shape to put it behind the rectangle shape. For this, the rectangle shape appears in front and the oval shape appears behind the rectangle shape. In universal practice, the designers prefer to arrange the important objects in the front, while the other objects are placed at the back. In this section, you learn how to change the arrangement order of objects in CorelDRAW X6. Perform the following steps to change the order of objects on the Document page:

1. **Open** a drawing in CorelDRAW X6. In our case, we open a drawing having a **star** and a **rectangle** object drawn on the Drawing page.

2. **Select** an object by using the Pick tool from Toolbox. In our case, we select the star object on the Drawing page.

3. Go to **Arrange**> **Order**> **To Back Of Page** from the Menu bar. As you select the To Back Of Page option, the star goes to the back of the rectangle.

Similarly, you can select any object from the Drawing page and move it below or above the other objects according to your requirements. After learning the procedure to transform objects by moving, scaling, rotating, creating mirror, and changing order of objects in the above sections, let's now learn to combine and break objects in the next section.

Combining and Breaking Objects

Combining objects transforms them so that the action results in the common fill and outline attributes for the objects. In CorelDRAW X6, you can combine two or more objects drawn on the Drawing page. You can also break a combination to change the attributes of the individual objects in the combination. The combination can include different types of objects, such as rectangle, ellipse, polygon, star, spiral, or even text. The combined objects are selected as a single entity by using the Pick tool. In this section, you learn to combine as well as break apart objects in CorelDRAW X6. Let's now first learn to combine objects in the next section.

Combining Objects

You can combine multiple objects created on the Drawing page that possess same and identical properties on all the combined objects. In CorelDRAW X6, you can combine two or more objects so that they have common fill and outline attributes. While combining objects, the attributes of the initial object are reflected on the other objects in the combination. Perform the following steps to combine objects:

1. **Open** a drawing in CorelDRAW X6. In our case, we open a drawing having numerous objects drawn on the Drawing page, as shown in picture 8.6.

2. **Select** the objects that you want to combine by using the Pick tool from Toolbox. In our case, we select all the **four objects** holding the <u>Shift</u> key down on the keyboard.

Picture 8.6

Picture 8.7

3. Choose **Arrange> Combine** from the Menu bar. As a result, the selected objects combine so that they have the common fill color and outline attributes, as shown in picture 8.7.

Keep in mind that the objects, after combination, inherit the attributes of the object that you had selected or drawn on the Drawing page first. As a result, all the objects inherited the fill color and outline attributes of the ellipse object, and the overlapping portion between the shapes appears white. You can also combine objects by using the Combine button on the Property bar or by pressing the Ctrl+L keys together.

Breaking Apart Combined Objects

In CorelDRAW X6, you can separate or break apart an object from a combination. However, breaking apart objects from a combination results in the objects retaining the color and outline of the object with which they were initially combined. After breaking apart objects from a combination, you can modify the attributes of the individual objects. Perform the following steps to break apart the combined objects:

1. **Open** a drawing in CorelDRAW X6. In our case, we open the same drawing with objects which are shown in previous section in picture 8.7.

2. Choose **Arrange**> **Break Curve Apart** from the Menu bar. As a result, the combined objects break apart into individual objects, each having its own attributes.

The objects can now be selected individually by using the Pick tool. After they are separated or broken apart, the objects inherit the color and outline properties that they had when they were in combined state.

Grouping in CorelDRAW

Grouping is the procedure that allows you to collect multiple objects created on the Drawing page in a single entity. In CorelDRAW X6, you can group two or more objects into a single entity. In a group, all the objects are treated as a single unit, but each object retains its default properties, such as outline, fill color, outline style, and text, until these attributes are changed by the user. If you apply a property, formatting effect, or any other changes on the group, the changes are reflected on all the objects simultaneously in the group.

Keep in mind that a major difference between combining and grouping objects is that while combining results in a common fill color and outline attributes for the objects, in grouping, the objects retain their default attributes.

In this section, you first learn to group objects, add an object to a group, remove an object from the group, edit individual object of a group without affecting other objects in the group, and ungroup objects.

Grouping Objects

In the process of grouping multiple objects together prevents you from accidentally changing the position of an object in relation to other objects on the Drawing page. In addition, after the objects are grouped, they can be located easily as you do not have to search for the objects individually on the Drawing page. As a safe practice, you can pick commonly-used or important objects, group them, and keep them aside on the Drawing page. Doing this helps you to pick the objects easily from a single location when required. Perform the following steps to group multiple objects:

1. **Open** a drawing in CorelDRAW X6. In our case, we open a drawing having six objects drawn on the Drawing page, as shown in picture 8.8.

2. **Select** the objects by using the Pick tool from Toolbox. In our case, we select all the six objects drawn.

3. Choose **Arrange> Group** from the Menu bar. As a result, the selected objects form a group on Layer 1, (picture 8.8).

This is confirmed by the text, Group of 6 Objects on Layer 1, which appears on the Status bar. Let's now learn to add an object to a group in the next section of this lesson.

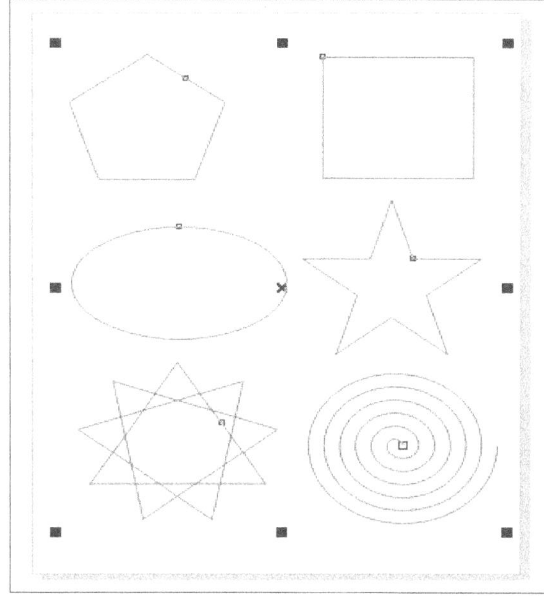

Picture 8.8

Adding an Object to a Group

You can add a new object in a group of objects already placed on the Drawing page. CorelDRAW X6 allows you to add a new object into a group of objects by using the Object Manager docker. In this way, a new object can be added after you have created a group, thereby, increasing the number of objects in the group. The added object becomes a part of the group. Perform the following steps to add an object to a group:

1. **Open** a drawing in CorelDRAW X6. In our case, we open the same drawing which we created in the previous section.

2. Create an **ellipse** on the Drawing page by using the Ellipse tool, as shown in picture 8.9.

3. **Select** the object that you want to add in a group, by using the Pick tool from Toolbox. In our case, we select the **ellipse**.

4. Choose **Window> Dockers> Object Manager** from the Menu bar. The Object Manager docker appears on the left side of the Document window, (picture 9.0).

5. Drag and drop the **Ellipse** layer downward under **Layer 1** into the **Group of 6 Objects** layer below **Layer 1** in the Object Manager docker, as shown in picture 9.0.

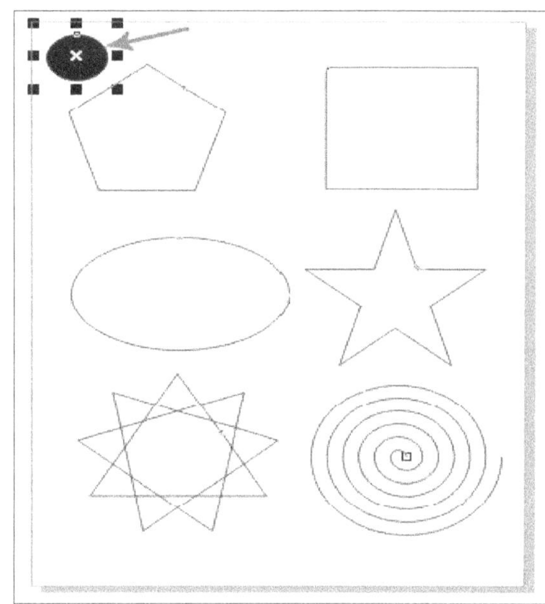

Picture 8.9

As a result, the object (ellipse) is added to the group. This is confirmed by the text, **Group of 7 Objects on Layer 1**, which appears on the Status bar.

Removing an Object from a Group

The group comprises of multiple objects that differs in their shape, size, color, and strength. You can transform the objects under a group according to your requirements. Sometimes, you are requested to remove one of the objects from the group. This can happen if you think that an object does not match a group or is not necessary in the group, you can easily remove the object with the help of the tools available in CorelDRAW X6. Perform the following steps to remove an object from a group:

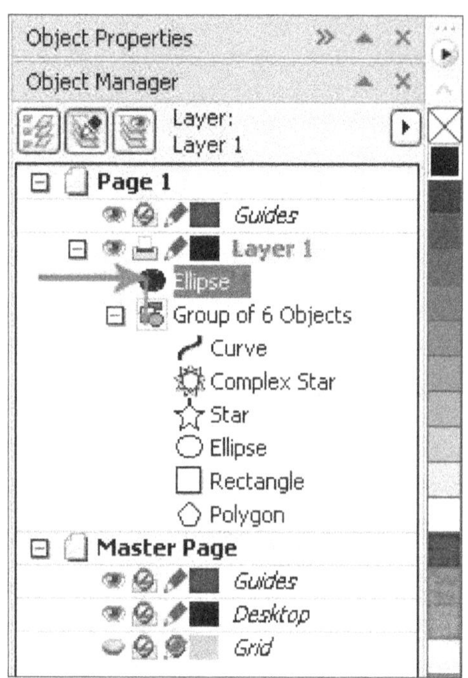
Picture 9.0

1. **Open** a drawing in CorelDRAW X6. In our case, we open the same drawing created in the previous section.

2. **Select** the group of objects by using the Pick tool from Toolbox. In our case, we select the group of seven objects from the Drawing page.

3. Go to **Window**> **Dockers**> **Object Manager** from the Menu bar. The Object Manager docker appears on your screen.

4. **Click** the (+) sign beside the **Group of 7 Objects** group under Layer 1 in the Object Manager docker. The Group of 7 Objects group expands to display a list of objects in the group.

5. **Select** the desired objects that you want to remove from the **Group of 7 Objects** group under Layer 1. In our case, we select the **Star** and **Rectangle** objects.

6. **Drag** and **drop** the selected Star and Rectangle objects from the **Group of 7 Objects** group to the Layer 1. As a result, the name of the layer changes from Group of 7 Objects to **Group of 5 Objects** as two objects are removed from the layer.

Editing a Single Object in a Group

The collection of objects in a group does not allow editing the property of a single object. In CorelDRAW X6, you are enabled with a feature that allows you to edit a single object in a group of objects. Using this feature, you can modify that object without disturbing the configuration of the other objects in the group. Now, you are going to perform the following simple steps on your computer to edit a single object in a group:

1. **Open** a drawing in CorelDRAW X6. In our case, we open the same drawing having a group of objects drawn on the Drawing page.

2. **Select** the group of objects from the Drawing page by using the Pick tool from Toolbox. The objects under the group are mutually selected.

3. Press the **Ctrl key** from the keyboard and select the object that you want to edit. In our case, we select the **spiral** object.

As a result, the spiral appears with editable nodes around the selected object. You can use these nodes to edit the object without an effect on the other objects in the group in any way. After knowing how to edit individual objects in a group, let's now learn to ungroup the objects of a group in the next section.

Ungrouping Objects

The term ungrouping objects refers to the removal of objects from a group. In CorelDRAW X6, you can ungroup the collection of multiple objects into particular objects. In this way, the objects under the group can be selected and edited individually. It may involve breaking a group into individual objects or a nested group into multiple groups. You can ungroup a single group as well as multiple groups into individual objects. Perform the following steps to ungroup objects in CorelDRAW X6:

1. **Open** a drawing in CorelDRAW X6. In our case, we open the drawing created in the previous section.

2. **Select** the group of objects by using the Pick tool from Toolbox.

3. Choose **Arrange**> **Ungroup** from the Menu bar. As a result, the objects in the group break apart into individual objects.

This way, you know that the selected object has been removed from the group when you compare the Status bar shown at the bottom of your screen.

Lesson 9
Creating Special Effects

In designing applications, the graphics are referred to as the images that can communicate the idea and the motive visually. The special effects applied on the objects make them more elaborate and communicative. In CorelDRAW X6, you can produce special effects on objects and use them in your graphics. CorelDRAW provides a wide range of tools to create these special effects. A special effect helps you to capture the interest of users so that they can read and understand the message being conveyed by the graphics. Therefore, special effects are a way of communicating with users, which at once attracts by the novelty of approach. CorelDRAW X6 provides various special effects that can be applied not only to objects, such as rectangle and polygon, but to text as well. Examples of these effects are the Envelope, Distortion Effect, Blends and Contours, Lens, Transparency, and Shadows effects. In this section, you learn about these effects. Let's first learn to use the Envelope tool.

Using the Envelope Effect

The Envelope command in CorelDRAW X6 allows you to change the shape of an object by using the Envelope tool. The envelope, which is created on the object, consists of multiple nodes. By moving the nodes in the envelope, you can change the shape of the object. Perform the following steps to apply the Envelope effect to an object:

1. **Open** a drawing in CorelDRAW X6. In our case, we open a drawing having a **star** object drawn on the Drawing page, as shown in picture 9.1.

2. **Select** the object by using the Pick tool from Toolbox. In our case, we select the **star**.

3. **Click** the arrow on the right side of the **Interactive tools** from Toolbox. It opens a flyout on your screen, as shown in picture 9.1.

4. Select **Envelope tool** from the flyout. This is the fifth tool in the flyout list.

Now the selected star object on your Drawing page appears with modifiable nodes around the boundary of it. You can select any of these nodes to edit the shape of the object.

5. **Select** the node of star object and drag it according to your requirements.

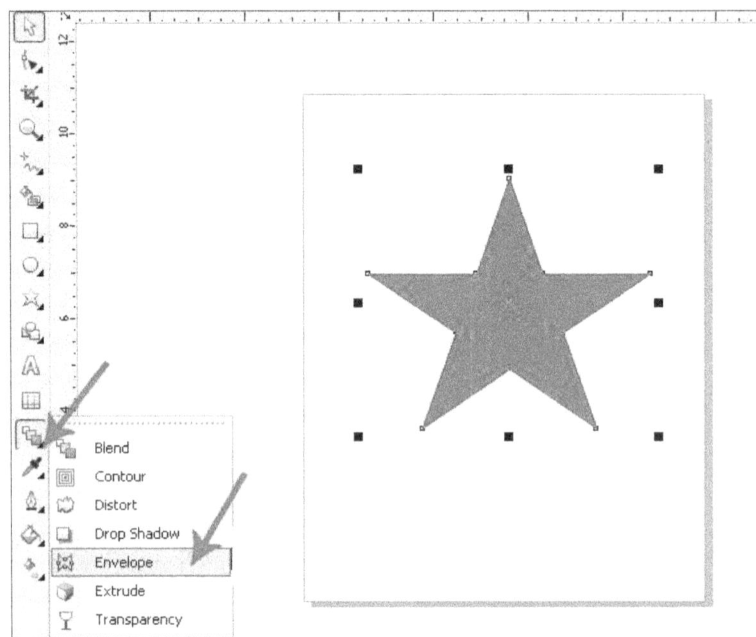
Picture 9.1

6. **Release** the mouse pointer when the desired shape is obtained, as shown in picture 9.2. Let's now learn to use the Distort tool in the next section.

Using the Distort Effect

The Distort command in CorelDRAW X6 allows you to twist a regular shape of an object into a new shape. The Distortion effect completely changes the shape of the original object. In our case, we are distorting the shape of a star object by dragging the object from inward to outward. Perform the following simple steps on your computer to apply the Distort effect:

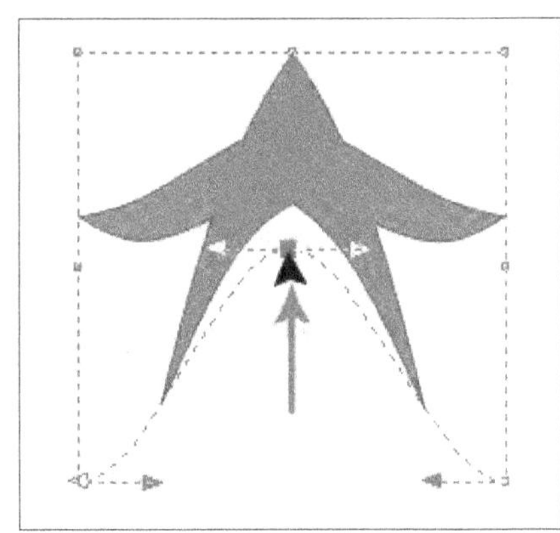
Picture 9.2

1. **Open** a drawing in CorelDRAW X6. In our case, we open a drawing having a **star** object drawn on the Drawing page, same as shown in picture 9.1.

2. **Select** the object that you want to distort by using the Pick tool from Toolbox. In our case, we select a **star**.

3. **Click** the arrow on the right side of the **Interactive tools** from Toolbox. It opens a flyout.

4. Select the **Distort tool** from the flyout. The star appears with editable nodes, using which you can distort (twist) the shape.

5. **Select** the polygon and **drag** to shape it according to your requirements.

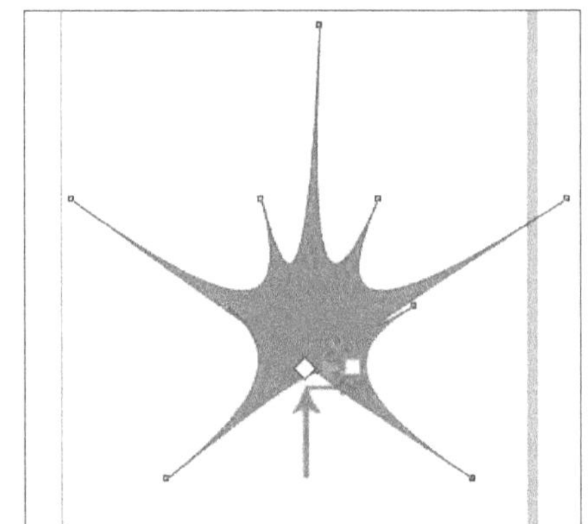
Picture 9.3

In our case, we have started from the **center of the star** and dragged in the **right direction**, as shown in picture 9.3. The star object, after applying the Distort effect appears on the Drawing page having an irregular (or distorted) shape.

Using the Blend Effect

The Blend effect in CorelDRAW X6 allows you to create the intermediate shapes between two different shapes in steps that show how one shape changes or blends to the other shape. Along with the change in the shape, the color of the shape also changes. In this section, you learn to use the Blend effect on the polygon and star shaped objects. Perform the following steps to apply the Blend effect:

1. **Open** a drawing in CorelDRAW X6. In our case, we open the drawing having the **polygon** and **star** objects drawn on the Drawing page, as shown in picture 9.4.

Picture 9.4

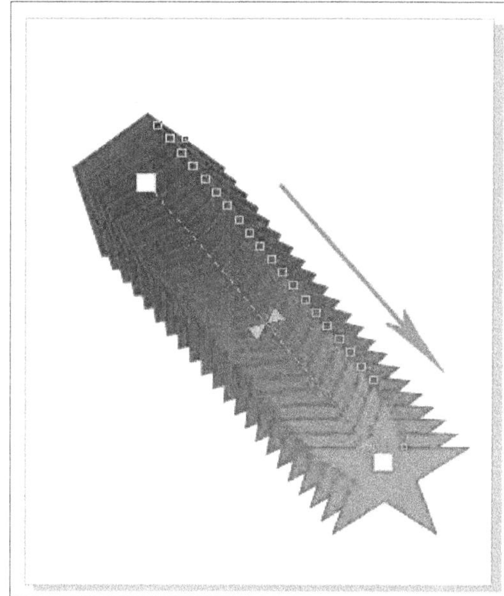

Picture 9.5

2. **Click** the arrow on the right side of the **Interactive tools** from Toolbox. Then select the **Blend tool** from the flyout.

3. Click the <u>polygon</u> and **drag** the mouse pointer towards the <u>star</u> object. As you drag the mouse pointer towards the star, a wire frame is created between the two objects, providing a preview of the Blend effect on the Drawing page.

4. **Click** the star to finalize the Blend effect. The result is shown in picture 9.5. Let's now learn to use the Contour tool in the next section.

Using the Contour Effect

The Contour tool in CorelDRAW X6 allows you to create multiple copies of an object, but unlike the Blend effect, in which two objects are used, the Contour effect uses only one object. In this type of effect, the object is surrounded by the same shape radiating outward or inward in a concentric pattern, similar to a wave created when a stone is thrown in still water. In this section, we are going to apply the Contour effect on a polygon. Perform the following simple steps on your computer to apply the Contour effect:

1. **Open** a drawing in CorelDRAW X6. In our case, we open the drawing having the **polygon** object drawn on the Drawing page.

2. **Select** the object by using the Pick tool from Toolbox. In our case, we select the polygon.

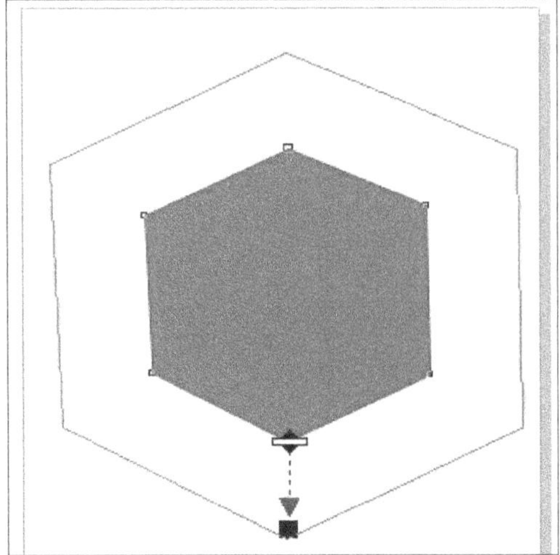

Picture 9.6

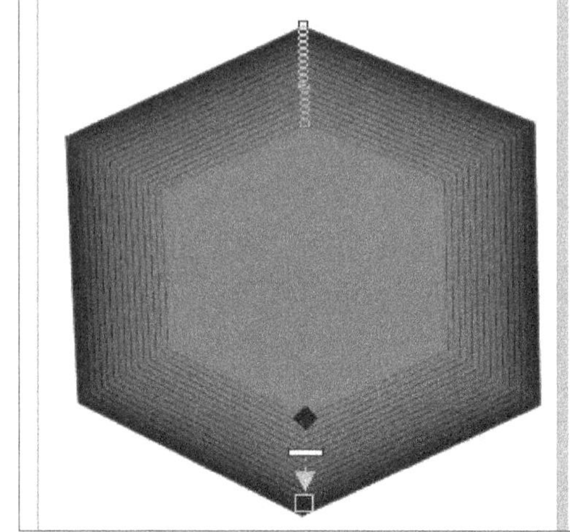

Picture 9.7

3. **Click** the arrow on the right side of the **Interactive tools** from Toolbox. Then select the **Contour tool** from the flyout.

4. **Click** the polygon and **drag** in the outward or inward direction, according to your requirement, to create the Contour effect. In our case, we drag it **outwards**, as shown in picture 9.6.

5. **Move** the slider to adjust the number of steps and the degree of offset in the contour. In our case, we have moved the slider towards the bottom. The Contour effect is applied on the polygon, (picture 9.7).

Applying the Transparency Effect
The Transparency command in CorelDRAW X6 enables you to increase or decrease the opacity levels of the objects on the Drawing page. The graphical illusion produced by this effect helps you to create realistic glossy effects with a translucent look. The transparency also adds luster to the objects. Perform the following steps to apply the Transparency effect on an object:

1. **Open** a drawing in CorelDRAW X6. In our case, we open a drawing having a **complex star** drawn on the Drawing page.

2. **Select** the object by using the Pick tool from Toolbox. In our case, we select the **complex star**.

3. **Click** the arrow on the right side of the **Interactive tools** from Toolbox. Then select the **Transparency tool** from the flyout.

4. **Click** the object and **drag** in the outward direction on the Drawing page.

The Transparency effect applied on the object varies in accordance to the location you click first and the specified direction where you drag along with the expansion of the location. You can set the transparency by dragging the start handle, which appears white by default. In addition, the progression of the transparency can also be adjusted by moving the slider.

5. **Move** the slider in either direction to adjust the transparency according to your requirements. In our case, we have moved the slider in the **downward** direction, as shown in picture 9.8.

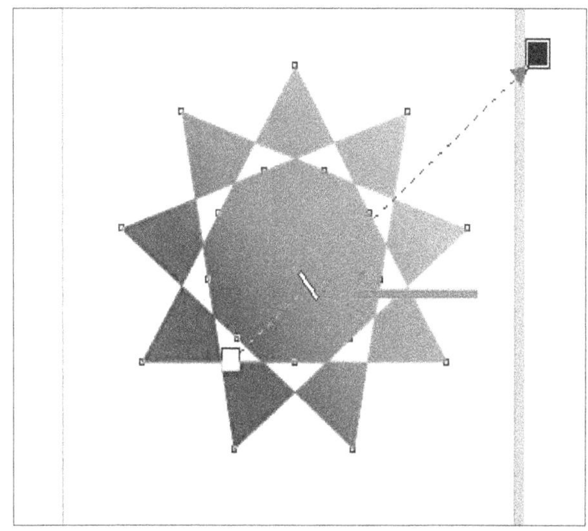

Picture 9.8

The Transparency effect is applied on the object. The object appears to fade in the direction you have dragged the mouse pointer, giving it a transparent look.

Keep in mind that the point where you start is white, while the end point is black by default. You can adjust the level of transparency by specifying the distance using the slider or change the color used to display the Transparency effect by dragging a color from the default color palette that appears on the left side of the Document window and dropping it to the end point on the slider. The lighter the color, the more opaque the resulting transparency will be.

Using the Drop Shadow Effect

The Drop Shadow command in CorelDRAW X6 allows you to create the shadow of an object by stimulating light falling on the object from the right, left, bottom, or top perspectives (views). In addition, the shadow you create can be easily modified by editing its color and brightness. You can modify the shadow of the object on the Drawing page by dragging the handles that appear when the effect is applied on the object. Perform the following steps to apply the Shadow effect:

1. **Open** a drawing in CorelDRAW X6. In our case, we open a drawing having an **ellipse** object drawn on the Drawing page.

2. **Select** an object by using the Pick tool from Toolbox. In our case, we select the **ellipse** object.

3. Click the arrow on the right side of the **Interactive tools** from Toolbox. Then select the **Drop Shadow** tool.

4. **Click** the object and **drag** in the outward direction on the Drawing page. The ellipse appears with the Drop Shadow effect, as shown in picture 9.9.

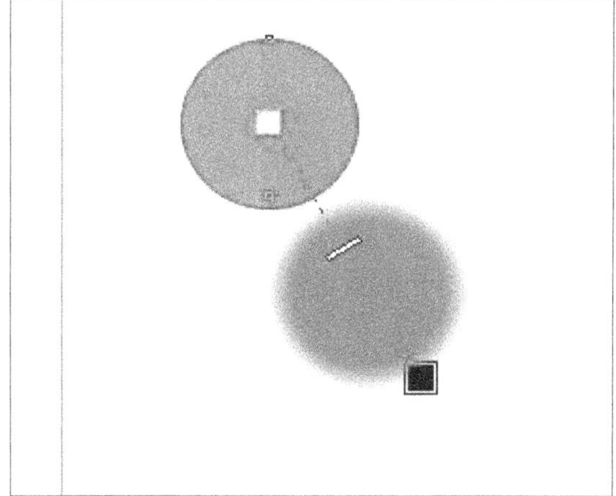

Picture 9.9

Using the Extrude Effect

The Extrude command in CorelDRAW X6 allows you to create an object in three-dimensional display. The extrusion can be developed either inward or outward of the object. In other words, you can extrude the object surface by providing it depth or height. The extruded object can be further rotated and rounded as desired by adjusting the nodes on the object. Perform the following steps to apply the Extrude effect:

1. **Open** a drawing in CorelDRAW X6. In our case, we open a drawing having a **star** object drawn on the Drawing page.

2. **Select** an object by using the Pick tool from Toolbox. In our case, we select the **star** object on the Drawing page.

3. Click the arrow on the right side of the **Interactive tools** from Toolbox. Then select the **Extrude tool** from the flyout.

4. **Click** the object and **drag** it in the outward direction. The object appears, displaying the Extrude effect, as shown in picture 10.0.

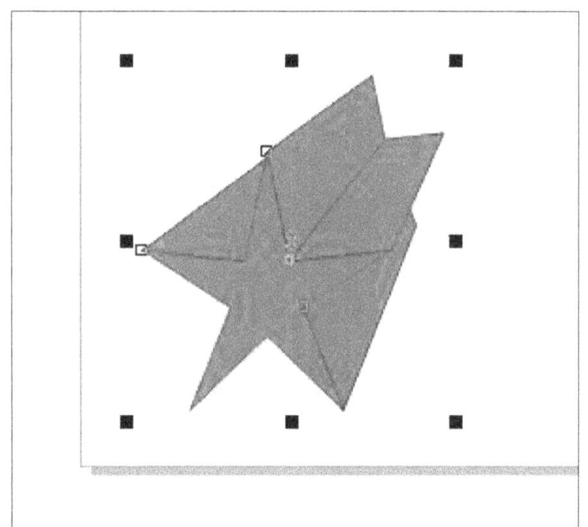

Picture 10.0

Aligning and Distributing Objects

You can use the positioning properties to decorate the objects drawn on the Drawing page. Positioning objects also enables you to organize the content of your document according to your requirements. In CorelDRAW X6, you can position objects by aligning them either with each other or in relation to the Drawing page. Depending on your need, you can position the elements to the left, center, or right of the Drawing page. CorelDRAW considers the center and edges of the objects while aligning them. Distributing objects refers to the positioning of objects in the given space, based on the center point, height, and width of the objects. In a distributed drawing, objects appear evenly distributed on the Drawing page. In this section, you learn to align objects with other objects, align object with the center of page, and distribute objects. Let's first learn to align an object with other objects drawn on the Drawing area in the next section.

Aligning an Object with Other Objects

You can align one object with another object drawn on the Drawing page. CorelDRAW X6 enables you to align objects by specifying certain properties, such as center, edges, and grid, of the Drawing page. You can align objects or group objects in various positions, such as left, right, top, bottom, center horizontally, and center vertically.

Grids are intersecting lines that are used to precisely align and position objects on the Document window. Now perform the following steps to align an object with another object in a CorelDRAW drawing:

1. **Open** a drawing in CorelDRAW X6. In our case, we open a drawing having the **ellipse**, **polygon**, **rectangle**, and **star** objects drawn on the Drawing page, as shown in picture 10.1.

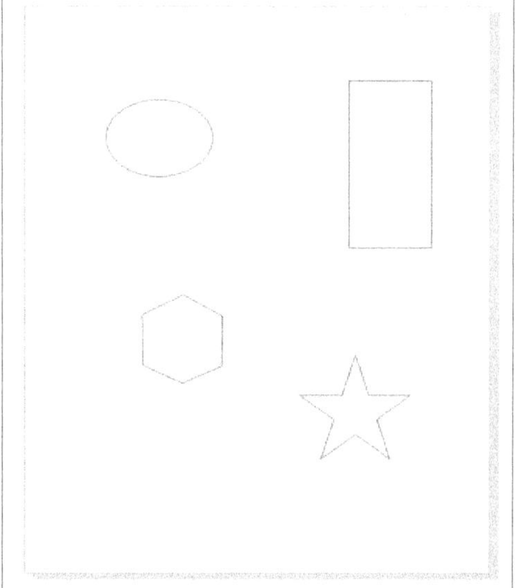

Picture 10.1

2. **Click** the arrow on the right side of the **Pick tools** from Toolbox, as shown in picture 10.2 with the red arrow. It opens a flyout.

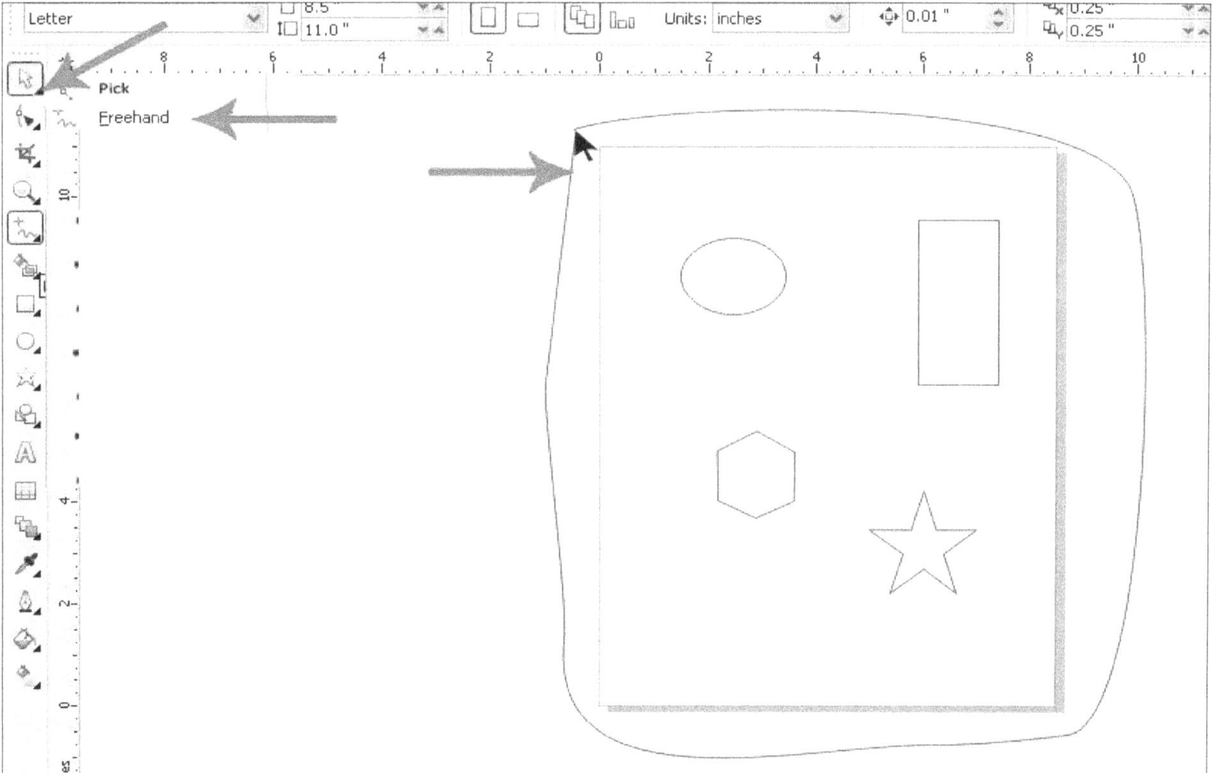

Picture 10.2

3. Select the **Freehand Pick tool** from the flyout, as shown in picture 10.2 with the red arrow.

4. **Drag** over the objects that you want to select by using the **Freehand Pick** tool. In our case, we have dragged over the area on the Drawing page, as shown in picture 10.2.

5. Choose **Arrange> Align and Distribute> Align and Distribute** from the Menu bar. It opens the Align and Distribute docker on your screen.

6. Select the **Align center horizontally** button under the <u>Align</u> section. As a result, the objects automatically align themselves at the center of the Drawing page horizontally, as shown in picture 10.3.

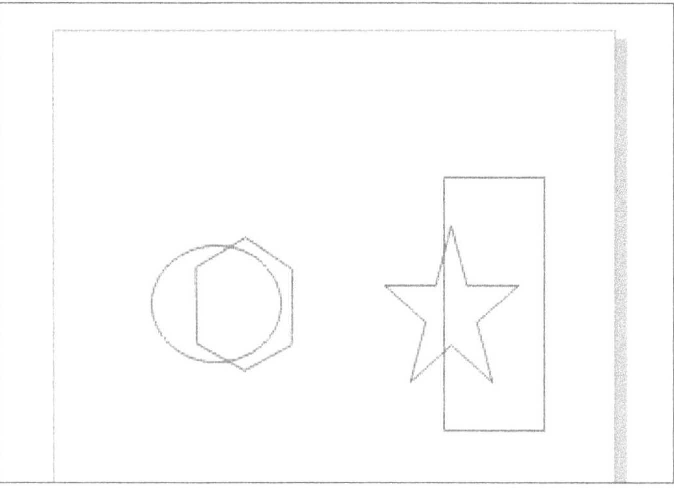

Picture 10.3

7. Now, on the right side of your screen, select the **Page center** button under the <u>Align objects to</u> section in the <u>Align and Distribute</u> docker. It automatically aligns objects on the center of the Drawing page.

Alternatively, you can align an object by selecting Arrange> Align and Distribute from the Menu bar, and then selecting the Align Left, Align Right, Align Top, Align Bottom, Align Centers Horizontally, or Align Centers Vertically commands from the Menu bar. You can also align objects by first selecting them from the Drawing page, and then clicking the Align and Distribute button on the Property bar.

Distributing Objects

You can distribute objects either horizontally or vertically by specifying the spacing with respect to their center points, widths, and heights. The process of distribution and alignment of objects allows you to move an object with respect to other objects according to the space available on the Drawing page. You can distribute objects in various positions, such as left, right, top, bottom, center horizontally, center vertically, space horizontally, and space vertically. In this way, the distributing and aligning properties lets you make optimum use of the available space. Perform the following steps to distribute objects:

1. **Open** a drawing in CorelDRAW X6. In our case, we open the drawing created in the previous section.

2. **Select** the objects you want to distribute on the Drawing page by using the Pick tool from Toolbox. In our case, we select **all** the objects.

3. Choose **Arrange> Align and Distribute> Align and Distribute** from the Menu bar. It opens the Align and Distribute docker on the right side of your screen.

4. Click the **Distribute left** button under the <u>Distribute</u> section in the Align and Distribute docker.

5. Click the **Distribute top** button under the <u>Distribute</u> section in the Align and Distribute docker.

6. Click **Extent of page** button under the <u>Distribute objects to</u> section in the Align and Distribute docker. The selected objects get distributed towards the top in the left side extended on your drawing page.

Lesson 10
Working with Text in CorelDRAW X6
The purpose of text is to communicate information, characters, or symbols in different languages, such as English, French, Chinese, and many more. In any graphical and layout designing application, text exhibits an important role in expressing the idea of the layout or drawing. Therefore, these applications have built-in features that support the use of text. Similarly, in the CorelDRAW X6 application, you are enabled with the Text tool, which can be used to work with text. After you have added text in your drawing by using this tool, you can apply various formatting options to the text, such as changing the font type, font size, and font style, or aligning and spacing of text in the Drawing page according to your requirements. In addition to this, you can also apply effects, such as fitting text to a path, using the Drop Cap effect to enlarge the initial letter and inserting it into the body of text.

This lesson begins by exploring the working of text types of CorelDRAW X6: artistic and paragraph. You also learn to convert text of one type to another type. Then, you learn the procedure to change the appearance of the text by using certain ways, such as changing font style, size, color, alignment, and text spacing. In addition, this lesson discusses the procedure to use the Find Text and Replace Text options, which allows you to find and replace specific text quickly and efficiently. After this, you learn about the various types of effects that you can apply to your text, such as Drop Cap, Outline, and Mirror. Moreover, you also learn about a feature that allows you to add text along a specified path, such as a curve or a circle. Towards the middle of this lesson, you learn to fit the text to an object path. In addition, you learn to work with the Asian and Middle Eastern script types in CorelDRAW X6. At the end of this lesson, you learn to convert text into an object, wherein you learn to break apart text and convert a table into text. Let's begin the lesson and first learn to work with different types of text of CorelDRAW X6 in the next section.

Working with Text Types in CorelDRAW X6
CorelDRAW X6 is available with two types of text: artistic and paragraph. You can create these types of text with the help of the Text tool from Toolbox. While creating an artistic text, you are simply required to type text on the Drawing page by specifying the location with a single click. However, on the other hand, when you create paragraph text, you have to first create a text frame, and then type the text within the frame. The two types of text can be briefly explained as follows:

- **Artistic Text:** Refers to the text type that can be created with the help of short lines of text, such as titles, to apply graphics effects, such as fitting the text to a path. You can also use this type of text in artistically versatile and easy-to-handle work. Moreover, artistic text type can be used to create a variety of special effects. The procedure to create this text is easy, as you are just required to click at the point where you want to insert the text and start typing. Artistic text is generally used to type single lines of text, for example, titles and headings. You can also use it to add special effects, such as Mirroring and Drop Cap.

- **Paragraph Text:** Refers to the text type that can be created in text-intensive projects, such as advertisements and brochures. In the paragraph type of text, the text is created in frames, and you can use various paragraph formatting features, such as Bullet Lists, Tabs, Indents, and Drop Cap.

In this section, after a brief discussion of the two types of text that you can create in CorelDRAW X6, let's quickly move ahead to the next section. In the next section, we learn to create text, starting with artistic text.

Creating Artistic Text

You have already discussed in brief about the artistic text type in CorelDRAW X6. You can create artistic text where you need to add titles, headings, or any other short lines of text. You can add artistic text along on open or closed path. In CorelDRAW X6, the artistic text type can contain up to 32,000 characters. You can add the text simply by clicking the initial point on the Drawing page, and then typing the text. Perform the following simple steps to create artistic text on the Drawing page:

1. **Open** a drawing in CorelDRAW X6. In our case, we open a new drawing, **Untitled- 1**.

2. Click the **Text tool** on Toolbox to select it.

3. **Click** at the location from where you want to start typing the text in the Drawing page.

4. **Type** the text from the keyboard on the Drawing page. The typed text on your Drawing page appears in the **Arial** font having **24 pt** size by default. CorelDRAW allows you to change the settings of typed text.

Creating Paragraph Text

In CorelDRAW X6, the paragraph text can be created when large blocks of texts are required on the Drawing page. The procedure to create paragraph text is contradictory to artistic text. For creating paragraph text, you are required to first create a frame for the text, and then type the text within the frame. In addition, you are required to select the location in the frame from where you want the text to start before beginning to type. Perform these steps to create paragraph text on the Drawing page:

1. **Open** a drawing in CorelDRAW X6. In our case, we open the drawing created in the previous section.

2. Select the **Text tool** on Toolbox of your screen.

3. **Click** and **drag** the mouse-pointer on the Drawing page to specify the location of the paragraph frame.

4. Click the down-arrow button of the **Font size** combo box on the <u>Property bar</u> to specify the font size of the text you want to enter in the paragraph frame. It opens a dropdown list.

5. **Select** the required font size from the dropdown list.

6. **Type** the required text in the paragraph frame on the Drawing page.

By the way, a small black down arrow appears on your screen below the frame, which indicates that the frame contains additional text or the length of your text is more than the size of the frame. For resolving this problem, you can drag this arrow for resizing the size of the frame. In this way, the entire text is visible. To make all the text visible, drag any one of the handles that surround the frame to increase the size of the frame.

Converting the Text from One Type to Another

In CorelDRAW X6 application, the types of text on the Drawing page area can be converted from one form to another. You have already learnt the procedure to create both types of texts, artistic and paragraph, available in CorelDRAW. If you want to convert artistic text typed on the Drawing page into paragraph text or vice versa, you can do with the Convert To command available in the Menu bar. In this way, you can save the time and trouble of typing again and again the entire text into another mode. Perform the following steps to convert paragraph text to artistic text:

1. **Open** a drawing in CorelDRAW X6. In our case, we open a drawing having artistic text and paragraph text typed on the Drawing page.

2. **Select** the text frame of paragraph text typed on the Drawing page by using the Pick tool on Toolbox.

3. Choose **Text> Convert To Artistic Text** from the Menu bar.

As a result, the paragraph text is automatically converted into artistic text. You can confirm this conversion of text by noticing the absence of frame (that is only available in paragraph texts) on the Drawing page.

The procedure to convert artistic text to paragraph text is equivalent. You can select the Pick tool from Toolbox, and then select the artistic text that you want to convert into paragraph text. Next, select Text> Convert To Paragraph Text from the Menu bar to convert the artistic text to paragraph text.

Changing the Appearance of Text

In designing applications, such as CorelDRAW, the designs and layouts are deliberated to influence a significant impact on the output. In the same way, the texts used in a drawing can also be deliberated with various features, such as font style, size, color, alignment, and text spacing. In CorelDRAW X6, number of features are enabled that help to change the appearance of text in a drawing. You can align the text and can also change the spacing of the text on the Drawing page.

In this section, you learn to change the text properties, such as font style, font size, font color, font alignment, and text spacing. Let's begin this section by learning to change the font style and font size of the text in the next section.

Changing the Font Style and Font Size of Text

The font styles can be added in a drawing to make it more appealing. In CorelDRAW X6, a huge variety of font styles are available that can be applied directly to the text written on the Drawing page. In addition, you can also import the desired font style to prepare specific layouts for special purposes, such as a magazine, which has a defined space for defined content. Perform the following steps to change the font style of text in a CorelDRAW drawing:

1. **Open** a drawing in CorelDRAW X6. In our case, we open a drawing having an artistic text on the Drawing page.

2. **Double-click** the text whose font style you want to change by using the Pick tool.

3. Click the down arrow of the **Font list** combo box on the <u>Property bar</u>. A dropdown list appears.

4. **Select** a font type for the selected text from the dropdown list. In our case, we select the **Parchment**. The font of the text changes to the selected font.

5. Click the down arrow of **Font size** combo box on the Property bar. A dropdown list with various options appears.

6. **Select** a font size for your text from the dropdown list to specify the font size you require on the selected text. In our case, we select **200 pt**. The size of the text changes to the selected font size.

Changing the Font Color of the Text

The CorelDRAW X6 application allows you to change the font color of the text in your drawing. This color of font helps you to make the drawing look more presentable. The text typed on the Drawing area has default color as black. You can change and apply the desired color from the wide range of colors available in the color palette of CorelDRAW. Perform the following steps to change the color of text in a CorelDRAW drawing:

1. **Open** a drawing in CorelDRAW X6. In our case, we open the drawing created in the previous section.

2. **Double-click** the text whose font color you want to change by using the Pick tool.

3. **Click** a color for the text from the default **Color palette** located to the left of the Drawing window. In our case, we select the **red** color.

Changing the Alignment

CorelDRAW X6 enables you to align both artistic and paragraph text according to your requirements on the space available in the Drawing page. In case of paragraph text, you can align the text vertically in the top, bottom, or center of the text frame. While aligning the text, you can also specify the required amount of height and width of the text frame. A paragraph block, on the other hand, can be aligned horizontally or to some other direction. Text is horizontally aligned in the left direction by default, but you can change this and have the text aligned to the center or right directions. Alignment of text is always specified according to the bounding frame of the typed text. Perform the following steps to change the alignment of text:

1. **Open** a drawing in CorelDRAW X6. In our case, we open a drawing having an artistic text and a paragraph text on the Drawing page.

2. **Click** your text frame in the Drawing page by using the Text tool.

3. **Type** some text in the text box, which you want to align to the existing text.

4. **Double-click** the text that you want to align.

5. Click the **Text alignment** button on the Property bar. A dropdown list appears.

6. **Select** an alignment option from the dropdown list. In our case, we select the **Force Justify** option. As a result, the text aligns itself to justify itself inside the text frame.

7. Select the **Text tool** on Toolbox.

8. **Click** and **drag** the mouse-pointer on the Drawing page to specify the location of the frame to write paragraph text.

9. **Type** a text in the frame.

10. Choose **Text**> **Text Properties** from the Menu bar. The Text Properties docker appears on the right side of the Drawing window.

11. Enter the value in the **First line indent** spin box under the Paragraph section in the Text Properties docker. In our case, we enter **0.6"**.

12. Enter the value in the **Left line indent** spin box under the Paragraph section in the Text Properties docker. In our case, we enter **3.1"**.

As a result, the paragraph text is changed according to the values specified in the Text Properties docker. After learning about text alignment, let's now discuss about text spacing in the next section.

Changing the Text Spacing

You can change the spacing between the words or characters typed in either artistic or paragraph text types. CorelDRAW X6 provides you with the feature to change the spacing between two lines in selected paragraphs, in an entire paragraph text frame, or in artistic text. In case of paragraph text, when you change the spacing between lines of text, the spacing is applied only to lines of text in the same paragraph. You can also change the spacing between paragraphs in paragraph text. Perform the following steps to manage the text spacing of text in CorelDRAW:

1. **Open** a drawing in CorelDRAW X6. In our case, we open a drawing created in the previous section.

2. **Double-click** the text that you want to select by using the **Text tool**. In our case, we select the paragraph text typed on the Drawing page.

3. Choose **Text**> **Text Properties** from the Menu bar. The Text Properties docker appears aligning to the right side of the Drawing window.

4. Enter the value in the **Character spacing** spin box under the Paragraph section in the Text Properties docker. In our case, we enter **30.0%**.

5. Enter the value in the **Word spacing** spin box under the Paragraph section in the Text Properties docker. In our case, we enter **220.0%**.

As a result, the selected paragraph text changes according to the specified values for character spacing and word spacing. Let's now learn about the Find Text and Replace Text features in the next section.

Finding and Replacing Text

In CorelDRAW X6, you are provided with interesting features known as Find and Replace. These features let you search for and replace specific text respectively in the currently active drawing. You can use these features to perform the find and replace operations quickly, thereby saving time. In addition, these features are useful in extended drawings, where manual searching and replacing would be a tedious and time consuming process. Let's begin this section by learning to find specific text in a CorelDRAW drawing in the next section.

Finding Text

In CorelDRAW, you can find a particular keyword or letter from a drawing having an extended text typed on the Drawing page. For this, you can use the find feature to search a particular letter from the drawing. You can also use the find feature where you have to find a word or phrase in the drawing in which you are working continuously, as it becomes difficult to search numerous keywords again and again manually in long text drawings. Using the find feature, you can begin searching for the specific text from the current cursor position. For this, you just simply click the point in the drawing from where you want to start your search and use the feature to find the text. Perform the following steps to find a text in a CorelDRAW drawing:

1. **Open** a drawing in CorelDRAW X6. In our case, we open the drawing created in the previous section.

2. Select the **Text tool** from Toolbox.

3. **Select** the frame containing the text in which you want to find the specific text. In our case, we have selected the paragraph text typed on the **top** of the Drawing page.

4. Choose **Text> Edit Text** from the Menu bar. It opens the Edit Text dialog box on your screen.

5. Click the **Options** button. It opens a dropdown list of various options.

6. **Select** the option from the dropdown list. In our case, we select the **Find Text** option. It opens the Find Text dialog box.

7. **Type** the word you want to search, in the <u>Find</u> combo box.

To make your search case-specific, select the Match case checkbox in the Find Text dialog box, and select the Find whole words only check box to find the text from the selected text.

8. Click the **Find Next** button in the <u>Find Text</u> dialog box to find the typed word.

In case, if you want to find the specified text in another location within the paragraph, click the Find Next button in the Find Text dialog box. Otherwise, the CorelDRAW X6 message box appears displaying that the Find feature has reached the end of the selected text; do you want to continue the search from the beginning of the text again. You can select Yes, if you want to repeat the Find feature again, else select No.

9. Click the **Yes** button in the message box to continue the search from the beginning of the text.

10. Click the **Close** button in the Find Text dialog box. The specified text you want to search gets highlighted in the Edit Text dialog box.

11. Click the **OK** button to close the Edit Text dialog box.

Replacing Text

In CorelDRAW X6, the Replace Text option allows you to replace text with some other text in a drawing. The replace option is generally used along with the Find option as you first need to find the text, and then replace it with the text of your choice. Perform the following steps to replace text in CorelDRAW:

1. **Open** a drawing in CorelDRAW X6. In our case, we open the drawing created in the previous section.

2. **Select** the frame containing the text that you want to replace by using the **Text tool**.

3. Choose **Text> Edit Text** from the Menu bar. The Edit Text dialog box appears on your screen.

4. Click the **Options** button to open a dropdown list.

5. Select the **Replace Text** option from the dropdown list. It opens the Replace Text dialog box.

6. **Type** the text you want to search in the Find combo box. In our case, we type **copies**.

7. **Type** the text with which you want to replace the **copies** keyword in the Replace With combo box. In our case, we type **duplicates**.

By the way, you can select the checkbox besides Find whole words only in the Replace Text dialog box to find the text from the selected text.

8. Click the **Replace** button in the Replace Text dialog box. The CorelDRAW X6 message box appears.

When you are required to replace every occurrence of the text typed, you can replace it by clicking the Replace All button in the Replace Text dialog box.

9. Click the **No** button in the CorelDRAW X6 message box.

10. Click the **Close** button in the Replace Text dialog box. The Edit Text dialog box appears again.

11. Click the **OK** button in the Edit Text dialog box. The dialog box closes and the text you typed to replace gets accomplished (replaced) on the Drawing page.

Applying Effects to Text

In CorelDRAW X6, you are provided to modify the text appearance with the help of various effects, such as Drop Cap, Outline, and Mirroring. When you apply the Drop Cap effect to paragraph text, the initial letter of the paragraph is enlarged. You can also manage various properties to apply the effects on texts. The mirroring effect allows you to flips the text either horizontally or vertically on the Drawing page. You can find the mirror options easily on the Property bar of the application. The effects can be applied to both artistic and paragraph types of texts available on CorelDRAW X6. In this section, you learn to apply these effects. Let's now learn to apply the Drop Cap effect in the next section.

Applying the Drop Cap Effect

The Drop Cap effect can be applied to specific paragraph text in which you want to highlight or differentiate the starting alphabet. You can apply the Drop Cap effect to the starting paragraph of new chapters, novels, articles, and many more.

In addition, you can customize the settings of the effect, such as specifying the number of lines next to the drop cap and the distance between the drop cap and the body of the text. Perform the following steps to apply the Drop Cap effect to text in CorelDRAW:

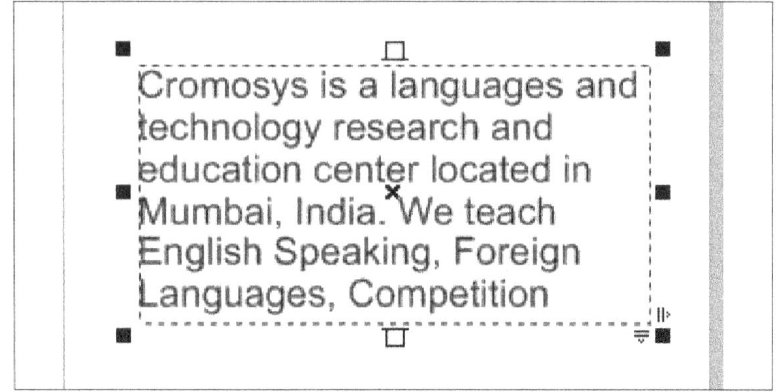

Picture 10.4

1. **Open** a drawing in CorelDRAW X6. In our case, we open the drawing created in the previous section.

2. **Select** the text in the frame of the drawing in which you want to apply the Drop Cap effect by using the **Text tool**, as shown in picture 10.4.

3. **Click and select** the starting alphabet of the selected paragraph text where you want to apply the Drop Cap effect. In our case, we select the **C** alphabet.

4. Choose **Text> Drop Cap** from the Menu bar to open its dialog box, as shown in picture 10.5.

5. Select the **Use drop cap** check box in the Drop Cap dialog box.

6. **Type** a value in the **Number of lines dropped** spin box to specify the number of lines you want to cover by the first alphabet under the Appearance section. In our case, we type: **3**, (picture 10.5).

Picture 10.5

7. **Type** a value in the **Space after drop cap** spin box to set the spacing between the drop cap and the next character in the paragraph, in the Appearance section. In our case, we type: **0.3"**.

By the way, you can also select the Use hanging style for drop cap check box if you want no text aligning below the drop cap text, whereas the Preview checkbox appears checked in by default in the Drop Cap dialog box.

8. Click the **OK** button in the Drop Cap dialog box. The selected paragraph text with the Drop Cap effect applied appears on your screen, as shown in picture 10.6.

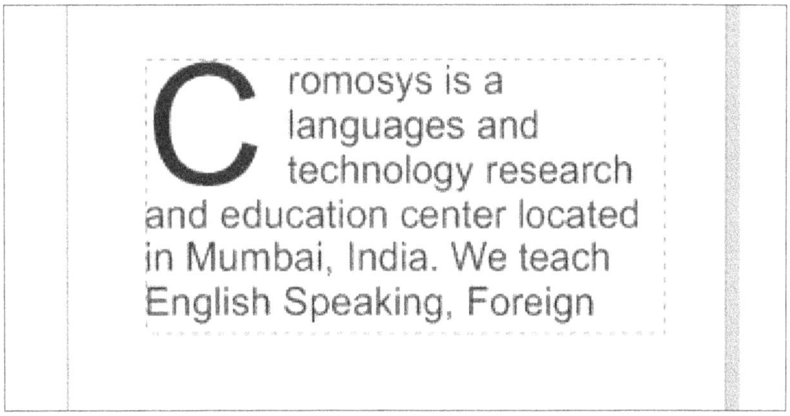

Picture 10.6

Applying the Outline of Text

In CorelDRAW X6, another effect that you can apply on text is the outline. While applying an outline, you can specify the color, width, and style of the outline. You can also create calligraphic outlines by specifying their thickness. The thickness of calligraphic outlines depends on the width and angle of the nib of pen used. You can also set the corners and end points of the outline. In CorelDRAW, the outline is applied on the top of the fill of the text by default, but you can also apply the outline behind the text fill. You can link the outline thickness to the size of the text so that when you increase or decrease the text size, the size of the outline changes with the same proportion. CorelDRAW provides the Outline Pen tool to apply an outline to text. Perform the following steps to apply an outline to text in CorelDRAW:

1. **Open** a drawing in CorelDRAW X6. In our case, we open the drawing created in the previous section.

2. **Select** the text in which you want to apply an outline by using the Text tool.

3. Click the **Outline Pen tool** from Toolbox. Then select the **Outline Pen** tool from the flyout.

The Outline Pen dialog box appears on your screen. All the options in the Outline Pen dialog box are disabled, except for the Width combo box, which displays the None option selected by default.

4. **Click** the down arrow button of the **Width** combo box in the Outline Pen dialog box.

5. **Select** a value for the width you want to apply to the outline of the selected text, from the dropdown list. In our case, we select **1.0 pt**.

As you make a selection from dropdown list, all the options in the Outline Pen dialog box are activated. Now, you can select and set values for other properties, such as color and corner styles of the outline.

6. Click the down arrow of the **Style** option to specify the style you want for the outline. In our case, we retain the default style.

7. Select a radio button in the **Corners** section to specify the style for the corners of the outline. In our case, we select the **second** radio button.

8. Type a value in the **Stretch** spin box in the Calligraphy section to specify the stretchiness level across the outline of the text. In our case, we type **82**.

9. Type a value for the angle of the outline in the **Angle** spin box of the Calligraphy section. In our case, we type **35.0**.

10. Select the **Scale with object** checkbox. Then click the **OK** button in the Outline Pen dialog box. Now, the text appears with a modified outline, enabling the settings specified in the Outline Pen dialog box.

Applying the Mirror Effect

The Mirror effect allows you to produce interesting outputs under the special effects category. Mirroring allows you to flip your text vertically or horizontally in such a way that the text appears as though it is being viewed in a mirror. As stated earlier, you can use this effect in two ways, by flipping the text horizontally or vertically and consequently. CorelDRAW provides two buttons, namely Mirror horizontally and Mirror vertically, to perform the mirroring effect operation. These buttons are located on the Property bar. Now, let's learn to use both these buttons. Perform these steps to mirror text:

1. **Open** a drawing in CorelDRAW X6. In our case, we open a drawing having a paragraph text typed: **Cromosys** on the Drawing page, as shown in picture 10.7.

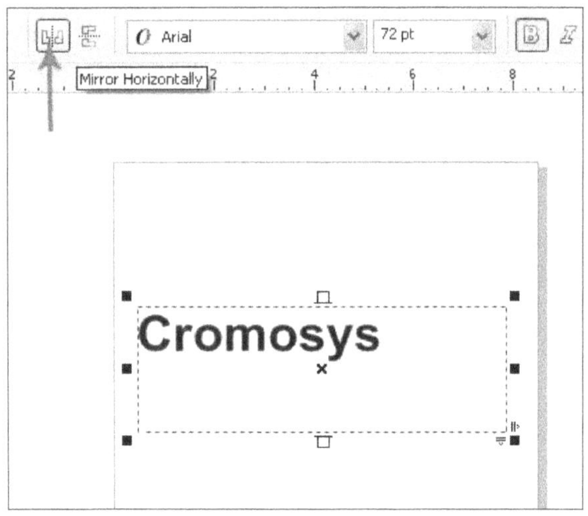

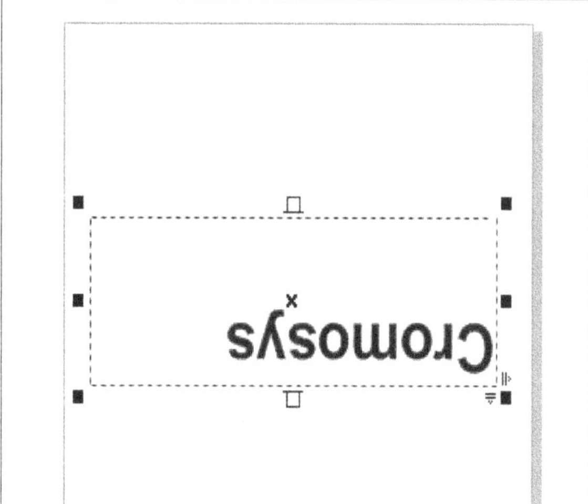

Picture 10.7   Picture 10.8

2. **Select** the text from a frame on which you want to apply a mirror effect by using the Text tool. In our case, we select the paragraph text: **Cromosys**.

3. Click the **Mirror horizontally** button on the Property bar to specify the text for horizontal mirror, as shown in picture 10.7 with the red arrow. The horizontal mirror effect is applied to the selected text.

4. Click the **Mirror vertically** button in the Property bar to specify the text for vertical mirror. The text, after the vertical mirror effect, appears on the Drawing page, as shown in picture 10.8.

Let's now move ahead and learn about another important feature that allows you to wrap text around an object in the next section.

Wrapping Paragraph Text around Objects

In CorelDRAW X6, you can apply various ways to display and adjust the text with objects. You can wrap text around your object, which allows you to save space. Wrapping text property is an interesting way to demonstrate the textual content on the Drawing page. There are two categories for wrapping text in CorelDRAW, contour wrapping and square wrapping. The contour wrapping follows the curve of the object while the square wrapping follows the boundary box of the object. While applying text wrapping, you can also set the space between the object and the text. Perform the following steps to wrap text around an object in CorelDRAW:

1. **Open** a drawing in CorelDRAW X6. In our case, we open the drawing having **paragraph text** on the Drawing page.

2. Create an **ellipse** by using the **Ellipse tool** from Toolbox on the Drawing page, as shown in picture 10.9 below.

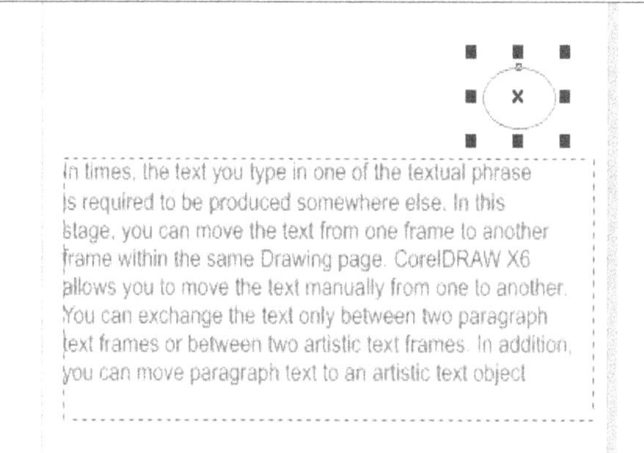

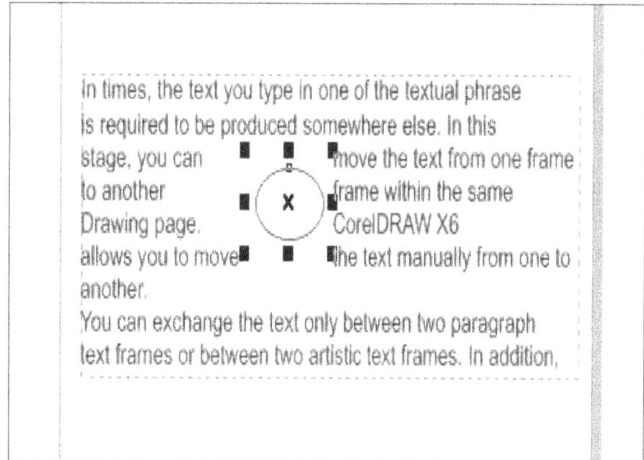

Picture 10.9   Picture 11.0

3. **Select** the ellipse drawn on the Drawing page by using the Pick tool on Toolbox.

4. Click the **Wrap text** button on the Property bar. It opens a dropdown list on your screen.

5. Select the **Straddle Text** option under the Square section in the dropdown list to specify the position of text for wrapping.

6. **Type** a value in the **Text wrap offset** spin box in the dropdown list to specify the offset value for wrapping text. In our case, we type **0.17**.

7. Press the **Enter key** on the keyboard to apply the values you typed in the Wrap text dropdown list.

8. **Drag** the ellipse between the selected paragraph texts on the Drawing page.

9. **Release** the mouse button to place the ellipse at the desired location in between the text on the Drawing page, as shown in picture 11.0.

As you place the ellipse at the desired location between the texts, the values you set in the Wrap text dropdown list are applied, and the text aligns to the right of the ellipse.

Fitting Text to an Object Path

CorelDRAW provides you a feature to add text along the path of an object with help of the fit text to path command. You can apply this command to either open or close paths. An open path is a path whose starting and ending points are not connected, and a close path is a path whose starting and ending points are connected. You can fit artistic text to an open or close path, but you can add paragraph text to an open path only. After fitting text to a path, you can set the position of the text relative to that path. Suppose you draw a close path, say an ellipse, and want to fit text along the drawn ellipse, let's learn how you will add text along the path. Perform the following steps to add text along the path of an object:

1. **Open** a new drawing in CorelDRAW X6.

2. Create a **polygon** by using the **Polygon tool** from Toolbox. In our case, we create a polygon on the Drawing page, as shown in picture 11.1.

3. **Select** the polygon drawn on the Drawing page by using the Pick tool. Then choose **Text> Fit Text To Path** from the Menu bar.

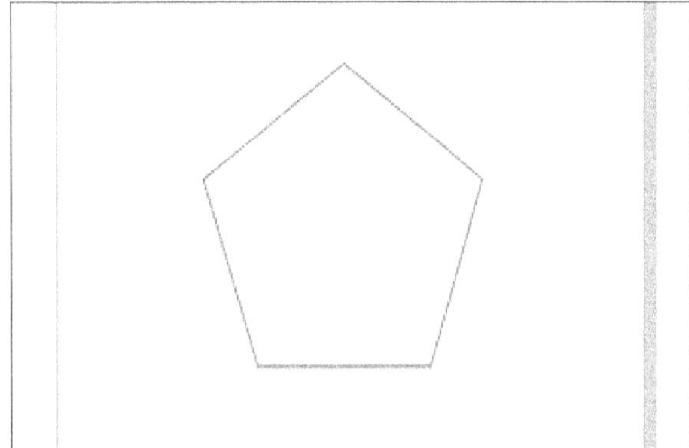

Picture 11.1

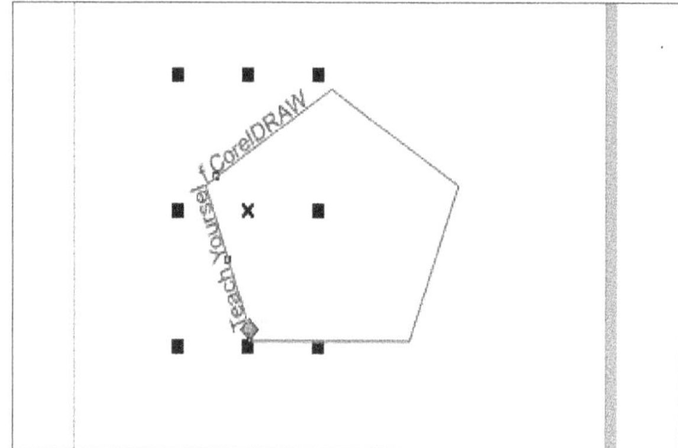

Picture 11.2

4. Click the down button of **Text orientation** on the Property bar.

5. **Select** an option to specify how you want the text orientation to be around the polygon. In our case, we select the **fourth** option from the list.

6. **Type** the required text from the point where a blinking cursor appears on the outer boundary of the polygon. In our case, we type the text, **Teach Yourself CorelDRAW**, as shown in picture 11.2.

7. **Type** a value in the **Distance from path** spin box in the Property bar to specify distance between the text and path. In our case, we type **0.15**.

8. **Type** a value in the **Offset** spin box on the Property bar to specify the distance you want to keep between the typed text and the outline of the polygon. In our case, we type **14.719**.

Now, you have learnt to fit text to an object path by setting various options, such as orientation, distance from path, and offset margin in CorelDRAW. Let's now learn to move the text between two frames in the next section.

Moving Text Between Frames or Text Objects

In times, the text you type in one of the textual phrase is required to be produced somewhere else. In this stage, you can move the text from one frame to another frame within the same Drawing page. CorelDRAW X6 allows you to move the text manually from one to another. You can exchange the text only between two paragraph text frames or between two artistic text frames. In addition, you can move the paragraph text to an artistic text object or artistic text to a paragraph text frame. Moving text between frames or text objects saves times, as you do not have to type the text again.

In case, if a paragraph text frame comprises of certain texts that you want to add in the other paragraph text frame, instead of rewriting the entire text again, you can just move the text between the frames to save time. In picture 11.3, there are two paragraph text frames in the Drawing page. In this section, we use the text of one paragraph frame to move into another paragraph frame. Perform the following steps to learn how to move text between two text frames:

1. **Open** a drawing in CorelDRAW X6. In our case, we open a drawing having two paragraph text frames, as shown in picture 11.3.

2. **Select** the text from first frame, which you want to move to the other frame by using the **Text tool**.

3. **Click** and **drag** the selected text to the second frame where you want to place the text.

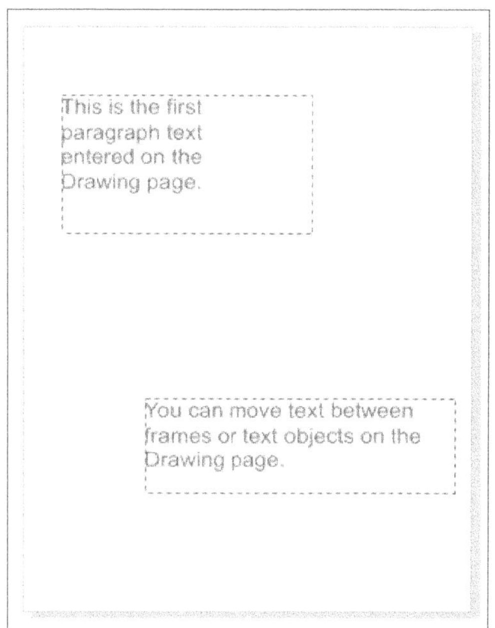

Picture 11.3

4. **Drop** the selected text at the desired location in the second frame. As a result, the selected text on your screen is moved from its original location in the first frame to the location of your choice in the second frame.

Working with Complex Script Types in CorelDRAW X6

You have already learnt the impact and role of text in a designing application. Now, CorelDRAW X6 supports various Asian and Middle Eastern languages, such as Arabic, Chinese, Japanese, Persian, Sanskrit, Tamil, Urdu, and Hindi. You can apply, install, and work with these script types easily in the same manner you work with the OpenType fonts available by default in the application. In addition, you can modify and manage the individual characters of these Asian and Middle Eastern languages according to your requirements by giving them a relative accuracy. In CorelDRAW, you can type the text for the required Asian languages in an exact and a well-addressed manner. The support enhanced for Middle Eastern and Asian languages in CorelDRAW X6 makes it worthy for customizing the characters to provide correctness and preciseness of regional characters. Perform the following steps to work with complex script types in CorelDRAW X6:

1. **Open** a new drawing in CorelDRAW X6. Then select the **Text tool** from Toolbox.

2. **Click** the down arrow of the **Font list** combo box on the Property bar. It opens a dropdown list.

3. **Select** a font type for the selected text from the dropdown list. In our case, we select **Walkman Chanakya-905**.

4. Click the down arrow of the **Font size** combo box on the Property bar. Then **select** a font size from the dropdown list. In our case, we select **60 pt**.

5. **Type** the desired text on the Drawing page.

Keep in mind that for enabling complex script types in CorelDRAW X6, you are first required to install the script, and then you are capable to use them in the application. In this section, we have worked with the regional Hindi language script. The way of way of writing different scripts varies from script to script.

After learning to work with complex script types, let's now discuss the utility of converting text into an object. And also learn to perform this task by using the Convert To Curve command in the next section.

Converting Text into an Object Using the Convert To Curve Command

You have already learnt the procedure to convert paragraph text to artistic text and vice versa. You can also convert artistic text or paragraph text into a curve by using the Convert To Curve command. In CorelDRAW X6, the text can be converted into a curved object that can be easily customized and reshaped according to your requirements. When text is converted to curve object, you can edit the shape of the individual characters of the text by using the Shape tool from Toolbox. Perform the following steps to convert text to a curve object:

1. **Open** a drawing in CorelDRAW X6 and **type** a sentence.

2. **Select** the text from the Drawing page by using the Pick tool on Toolbox.

3. Choose **Arrange**> **Convert To Curve** from the Menu bar.

As a result, the selected text is converted to a curve object in which you can treat the text as an object. It means you can edit the text with Shape tool, and the text can be further modified along its shape to create various patterns, which you can never edit with a normal typed text.

Breaking Apart Text

When the text is already converted into a curved object, you can treat all the text as a single object and make changes to its shape as a whole. However, if you want to edit a particular character in the object, you need to break the text apart. When you break apart text, each character of the text behaves similar to an individual and separate object. After breaking apart the text, you can edit the character individually. Perform the following simple steps on your computer to break apart artistic text on the Drawing page:

1. **Open** a new drawing in CorelDRAW X6.

2. **Type** artistic text on the Drawing page by using the Text tool. In our case, we type: **Cromosys Corporation**, as shown in picture 11.4.

3. Choose **Arrange> Break Artistic Text: Arial (Normal) (ENU) Apart** from the Menu bar.

As a result, the selected text breaks apart by enabling selection of each character of the text individually, as shown in picture 11.5.

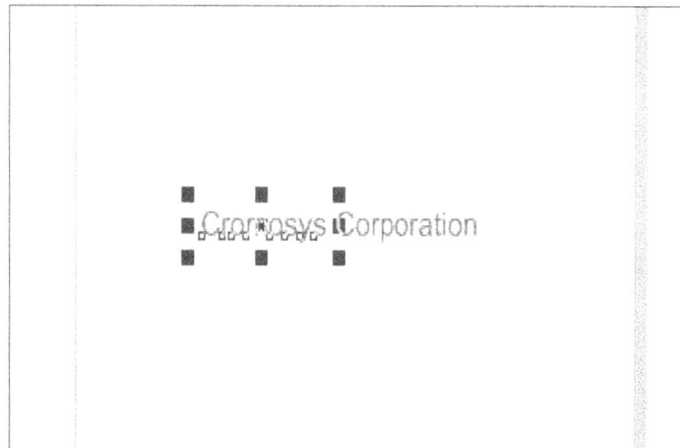

Picture 11.4   Picture 11.5

You can apply the same command from the Menu bar to further break apart the text. In our case, we have broken apart the text so that you can select the first word individually. If you break it further again, you can select individual character or characters and change their shapes. In addition, you can use the Shape tool from Toolbox to change the shape of the characters by dragging the editable nodes enabled after selecting the Shape tool.

In CorelDRAW, you can also convert a table with textual data into the paragraph text format on the Drawing page, as discussed in the next section.

Converting a Table to Text
In CorelDRAW X6, you can convert the text of table into normal text. For this, you are required to select the table having text typed in the respective rows and columns, and then select the Convert Table to Text command from the Menu bar. In this way, the text of table automatically appears in the paragraph text format. CorelDRAW provides the following options to separate the text in cells of the table when a table is converted to text:

- **Commas:** Allows you to substitute each column with a comma and each row with a paragraph marker.
- **Tabs:** Allows you to substitute each column with a tab and each row with a paragraph marker.
- **Paragraphs:** Allows you to substitute each column with a paragraph marker.
- **User defined:** Allows you to substitute each column with a character defined by the user and each row with a paragraph marker. Perform the following steps to convert a table to text:

1. **Open** a new drawing in CorelDRAW X6.

2. Select the **Table tool** on Toolbox.

3. **Click** and **drag** the mouse-pointer on the Drawing page to draw a table, as shown in picture 11.6 on the next page.

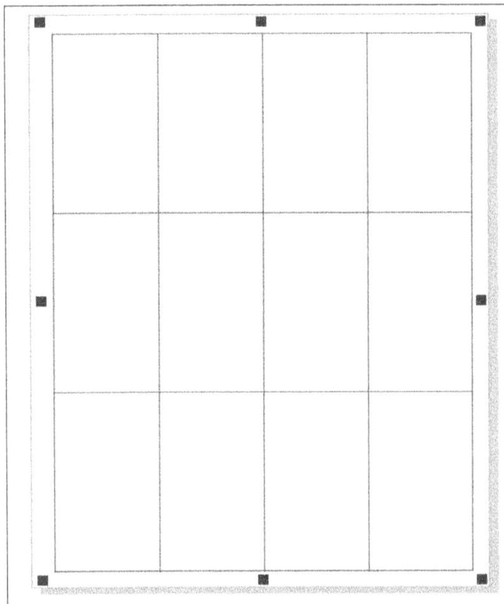

Picture 11.6

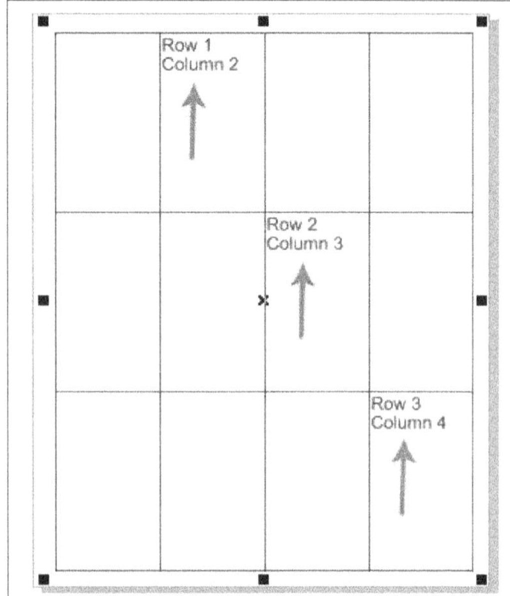

Picture 11.7

4. **Type** some text in the cells of the table, as shown in picture 11.7 with the red arrows.

By the way, for elaborated information on creating tables and adding text to them, you can refer to the next chapter of this book.

5. Choose **Table> Convert Table to Text** from the Menu bar. It opens the **Convert Table to Text** dialog box on your screen.

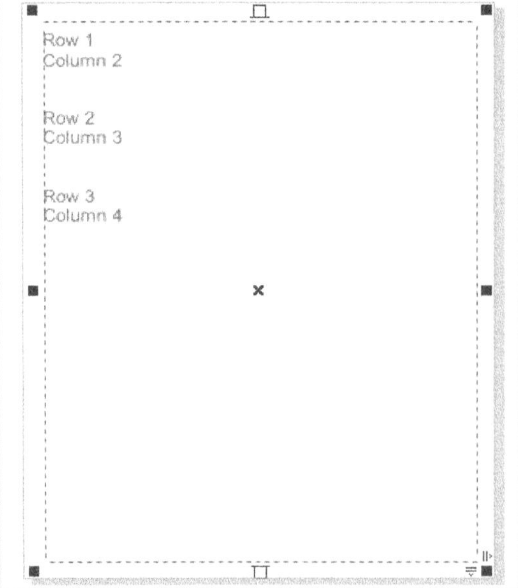

Picture 11.8

6. Select the **Paragraph** radio button under the <u>Separate cell text with</u> section to specify how you want to separate the text in cells of the table after they are converted into normal text.

7. Click the **OK** button in the Convert Table to Text dialog box. As a result, the table is converted to text, as shown in picture 11.8.

Lesson 11
Working with Tables in CorelDRAW X6

The table can be referred as an organized group of fields in the form of rows and columns. You can use tables to store data permanently or to frequently update within the demarcated space. Moreover, the tables represent an organized way to record a complete set of instructions and information in a finite manner. You can organize the information by differentiating them into distinct rows and columns. Sometimes, the table comprises the business information in the form of identity numbers, account numbers, addresses, and telephone numbers. On the other hand, sometimes, the table comprises the combination of graphical and informational data. You can place individual information source inside specific cells of the table. A table provides a structured layout to present text and graphics.

In CorelDRAW X6, you can create, modify, format, and decorate tables according to your requirements. CorelDRAW X6 provides an interactive tool named the Table tool that you can use the create tables. A cell in a table refers to the area enclosed, where a row intersects a column. Tables provide a convenient and an efficient way to display a large amount of data, which can be understood at a glance. You can use both textual data and graphics in a table. In addition, you can apply borders to a table and fill colors in it to make it eye-catching and attractive.

This chapter begins by discussing the procedure to work with tables, in which you first learn to create a table, specify required number of rows and columns, and add data in tables. Next, this chapter discusses the procedure to format data in table by changing the font size, color, and alignment. Further, you learn to modify table rows and columns, in which you discuss the procedure to insert and delete rows and columns of a table. Towards the end of this chapter, you learn to format tables by changing the borders outline, filling colors in cells, merging table cells, splitting table cells, and setting margins for text in table cells. Let's begin the chapter by learning to work with tables in the next section.

Working with Tables

A table can be referred as a collection of data in the form of text, numbers, or graphics, which can be arranged in the form of vertical columns and horizontal rows. In CorelDRAW, you can create a table from scratch on a Drawing page or import a table from other applications, such as Adobe Illustrator and Adobe Photoshop. When you create a table from scratch, CorelDRAW provides a table with three rows and four columns by default. You can modify the table and specify the number of rows and columns you want in it, according to the data you want to insert. If required, you can insert new columns or rows at a later stage, according to your requirements. Perform the following steps to add a table on a Drawing page in CorelDRAW:

1. **Open** a new drawing in CorelDRAW X6.

2. Select the **Table tool** on Toolbox.

3. **Click** and **drag** the mouse-pointer on the Drawing page to draw a table, as already shown in picture 11.6 above.

In the picture 11.6, the table is drawn with the help of the Table tool and appears in its default configuration, such as three rows and four columns. After learning to add a table in CorelDRAW X6, in this section, you learn to specify the number of rows and columns, add data in tables, and format data in tables by changing font properties and aligning data. Let's now learn to specify the number of rows and columns in the next section.

Specifying Number of Rows and Columns

Tables can be created on a Drawing page having minimum of two rows and two columns. You can create table with desired numbers of rows and columns by specifying the requirement. In CorelDRAW X6, you can create a table by using the Table tool, which creates table having three rows and four columns by default. You can easily modify the table by specifying the number of rows and columns you want in the table. By modifying your table in this way, you can arrange the data you want to include in it in the best possible way. The Property bar provides various options through which you can specify the desired number of rows and columns for the table. Perform the following steps to specify the number of rows and columns in a table:

1. **Open** a drawing in CorelDRAW X6. In our case, we open the same drawing which was created in the previous section having three rows and four columns of a table drawn.

2. **Select** the table on the Drawing page, by using the Pick tool.

3. **Type** a value in the **Rows and columns** spin box on the <u>Property bar</u>, to specify the number of rows for the table. In our case, we type: **2**, and press **Enter**, as shown in picture 11.9 with the red arrow.

4. **Type** a value in the **Rows and columns** spin box on the Property bar, to specify the number of columns for the table. In our case, we type: **8**, and press **Enter**, as shown in picture 11.9 with the red arrow.

Picture 11.9

Now, the table appears on your Drawing page with the specified value you entered in the Property bar. You can resize the table simply by dragging the handles that appear on its border or outline. Alternatively, you can also modify the thickness of the table border as well as the background of the table. Moreover, the tables can also be created by converting text to a table.

Adding Data in Table

When the table is created on the Drawing page with the specified number of rows and columns, you are required to add data to the table. In CorelDRAW X6, you can add any type of data, such as text, graphics, as well as other tables inside the cells of your table. You are also provided with the features to adjust the height and width of rows and columns to accommodate additional data. Commonly, the cells in a table are adjusted so that the added data can be viewed. Perform these steps to add text in a table:

1. **Open** a drawing in CorelDRAW X6. In our case, we open the drawing created in the previous section.

2. **Double-click** the cell in which you want to add text by using the Pick tool on Toolbox. As soon as you double-click the cell, the selected cell allows you to enter text in it and is shown by the cursor inside the specified cell.

3. **Click** the down arrow of the **Font size** combo box on the Property bar. Then **select** a value to specify the font size of the text you want to add to the table from the dropdown list.

4. **Type** the required text in the selected cell. The specified text inside the table drawn on the Drawing page appears on your screen.

Formatting Data in Table

The CorelDRAW application provides you tools to format the data of a table according to your requirements. Formatting gives you the freedom to make changes to the data so that it can be displayed in the exact way that you want them in the table. You can format the data creatively for not only attractive looks, but also make it help a user to understand the relevant information quickly and easily. Properly formatted table data is also easy to read. CorelDRAW provides you a range of features, such as select the font type, size, and color for your data, change the background color of table cells, and align the data in cells, which you can use to format the data of your table. In this section, you learn to change the font properties and learn to align data in a table. Let's now learn to change font properties in the next section.

Changing Font Properties

You can change the properties of text, such as styles and colors. By changing the properties of the fonts, you can make the table more attractive and user friendly to read. There are various tools in the form of font samples that you can apply on your table data. As the eye-catching strategy works well for users, this is the same when you work with text in graphical applications. In other words, the text in a specified font size, style, and color looks more approachable. The better the creativity you reflect in your work, the more appreciation you get. In this section, you learn how to change the font size and style of the text. Perform the following steps to change the font properties of the text in a table:

1. **Open** a drawing in CorelDRAW X6.

2. **Draw** a table on the Drawing page by using the **Table tool** on Toolbox. In our case, we create a table.

3. **Type** some text in the selected cells of your choice. In our case, we type in the various cells of the table.

4. **Double-click** in the cell containing the text whose font properties you want to format. The text gets selected.

5. Click the down arrow button of the **Font list** combo box on the Property bar. Then **select** the font type from the dropdown list. In our case, we select the font named **Blackadder ITC**. As a result, the font face of the text in the table changes to the selected font.

By the way, as browse the dropdown list and select a font, the font of the selected text in the table on the Drawing page automatically changes to provide a live preview of the selected font type.

6. **Click** a color of your choice for the selected text in the table, from the default color palette that appears to the left of the **Document window**. In our case, we select the **Red** color.

You will also see that a copy of the applied color appears in the default Document Palette, which preserves all the colors used in the working drawing.

Aligning Data in Tables

The CorelDRAW X6 application allows you to align your data by specifying certain attributes of placement, such as left, right, center, and justify. You can align the cell data of a table according to the space between the bounding boxes of the cells. The cells are surrounded by the bounding boxes, which enclose the data of the cells where data can be text or any object. CorelDRAW provides the following options through which you can align data. These options are available under the Text alignment dropdown list on the Property bar:

- **None:** Refers to the adjustment property of text that sanctions no alignment of data with the bounding box. You can also select this option by pressing the **Ctrl+N** keys in combination.
- **Left:** Refers to the adjustment property of text that aligns the data to the left side of the bounding box. It can also be done by pressing the **Ctrl+L** keys in combination.
- **Center:** Refers to the adjustment property of text that aligns the data to the center of the bounding box. It can also be done by pressing the **Ctrl+E** keys in combination.
- **Right:** Refers to the adjustment property of text that aligns the data to the right side of the bounding box. It can also be done by pressing the **Ctrl+R** keys in combination.
- **Full Justify:** Refers to the adjustment property of text that aligns the data, excluding the last line, to both the left and right sides of the bounding box. It can also be done by pressing the **Ctrl+J** keys in combination.
- **Force Justify:** Refers to the adjustment property of text that aligns all the data to both, the left and right sides, of the bounding box. It can also be done by pressing the **Ctrl+H** keys in combination. Now, perform the following simple steps to align the data of the table in CorelDRAW:

1. **Open** a drawing in CorelDRAW X6. In our case, we open the same drawing which was created in the previous section.

2. **Select** the cell from the table whose alignment you want to change.

3. Click the **Text alignment** button on the Property bar.

4. **Select** an alignment option from the dropdown list, to specify how you want to align the selected text in the bounding box of the cell. In our case, we select **Right** option.

As a result, the text of the selected cell in a table is now aligned to the right of the bounding box of the cell. In addition to moving data of a table according to your requirement, you can also insert and delete rows and columns from a table in CorelDRAW, as discussed in the next section.

Modifying Table Rows and Columns

In CorelDRAW, when you work with tables, sometimes you realize that the specified data inside the particular cells are not appropriately adjusted. For this reason, you want to insert or delete the rows and columns from the table according to your requirements. In case, there is only one row and three columns in your table and you feel that the extra data you have would be better displayed if there were more columns or rows in the table. In that case, you can easily insert the required rows and columns so that the information is represented in the best possible way.

In this section, you learn to insert rows and columns in table and also learn to delete rows and columns in table. Let's begin this section by learning the procedure to insert rows and columns in tables in the next section.

Inserting Rows and Columns

In CorelDRAW X6, you can either insert single row and column or multiple rows and columns in a table. The table rows can be inserted above or below the selected row, as per the requirement. The desired table row must be selected before inserting a row or multiple rows. Similarly, you can insert single column or multiple columns to the left or right of the selected column. Perform the following steps to insert rows in a table in CorelDRAW:

1. **Open** a drawing in CorelDRAW X6. Then **draw** a table on the Drawing page by using the **Table tool** on Toolbox.

2. **Select** the row in the table where you want to insert new rows. In our case, we select the **first row**.

Keep in mind that you can also select a row by clicking the mouse-pointer beside the row that you want to select. The shape of the mouse pointer changes to an arrow (➡). Now, click this arrow to select the desired row.

3. Go to **Table> Insert> Insert Rows** from the Menu bar to open its dialog box.

4. **Type** a value in the **Number of Rows** combo box in the Insert Rows dialog box, to specify the number of rows you want to insert in the table. In our case, we type: **3**.

5. **Select** a radio button beside the **Where** option to specify whether you want to insert the rows, below or above the selected row in the table. In our case, we select the **Below the selection** radio button to insert the new row below the selected row in the table.

6. Click the **OK** button in the Insert Rows dialog box. As a result, the table appears on your screen with three more rows inserted below the selected row.

Until now, you have learnt to insert rows in a table. The columns can also be inserted in the same way. Perform the following steps to insert columns in the same table:

1. **Select** the column of the table where you want to insert a new column. In our case, we select the **second column** of the table.

You can also select a column by clicking the mouse-pointer beside the column that you want to select. The shape of the mouse pointer changes to an arrow (➡). Now, click this arrow to select the desired column.

2. Choose **Table> Insert> Insert columns** from the Menu bar to open its dialog box.

3. **Type** a value in the **Number of columns** combo box in the Insert Columns dialog box, to specify the number of columns you want to insert in the table. In our case, we type: **4**.

4. **Select** a radio button beside the **Where** option to specify whether you want to insert the columns, below or above the selected column in the table. In our case, we select the **Left of the selection** radio button to insert the new column.

5. Click the **OK** button in the Insert Columns dialog box. As a result, the table appears with four more columns inserted to the right of the selected column.

Deleting Rows and Columns

Deleting is a property that allows you to permanently remove the element. In tables, you can delete the elements, such as rows and columns of the table. CorelDRAW X6 allows you to delete the rows and columns drawn on the Drawing page by using the Table menu available on the Menu bar. You can delete the specified rows, columns, and tables from the Drawing page. Sometimes, while creating tables, you may realize that you have inserted an extra row or column that you do not require. In that case, you can remove or delete the row or column from the table. Perform the following steps to delete a table row:

1. **Open** a drawing in CorelDRAW X6. In our case, we open the drawing created in the previous section.

2. **Select** the row or column you want to delete from the table. In our case, we select the **fourth row** of the table.

Keep in mind that if you are opening a drawing having a table, you can select rows or columns by using the Table tool. The selection of row is done by just a single click done after the arrow (➡) sign. Similarly, the selection of column is done by just a single click done after the arrow (⬇) appeared on the Drawing page.

3. Choose **Table> Delete> Row** from the Menu bar. As a result, the selected row is deleted from the table.

Formatting Tables

In CorelDRAW X6, the purpose behind formatting tables is to change their appearance and make them appear attractive and appealing to a user. You have already learnt the procedures to insert, delete, and align the properties of table in the previous section. Apart from these properties, CorelDRAW offers various formatting options that you can select and apply to your table. By using these options, you can change the border width and outline color of the table, fill colors in multiple cells of the table, and fit text along a path in a table cell. In addition, you can also merge and set margins for the text in the table cell.

In this section, you learn to change border outline of table, fill colors in cells, merge tables, split tables, and set margins for text in tables. Let's now learn to format a table by changing its border or outline in the next section.

Changing Border Outline of a Table

In CorelDRAW X6, the table is a combination of rows and columns that are linked to each other by using common boundaries. The boundaries that link each row and column of the table make up the boundary or outline of the entire table. You can modify the thickness of the borders of tables or cells, as well as their background color. Although, CorelDRAW is primarily known as a designing application, it comprises of several features that allow you to work with tables with great flexibility. Perform the following steps to format a table by changing its border and outline:

1. **Open** a drawing in CorelDRAW X6. In our case, we open a drawing having a table drawn on the Drawing page.

2. **Select** the table on the Drawing page by using the Pick tool.

3. Click the down arrow button beside the **Border selection** option on the Property bar, as shown in picture 12.0 with the red arrow. A dropdown list appears displaying the formatting options for the border of the selected table.

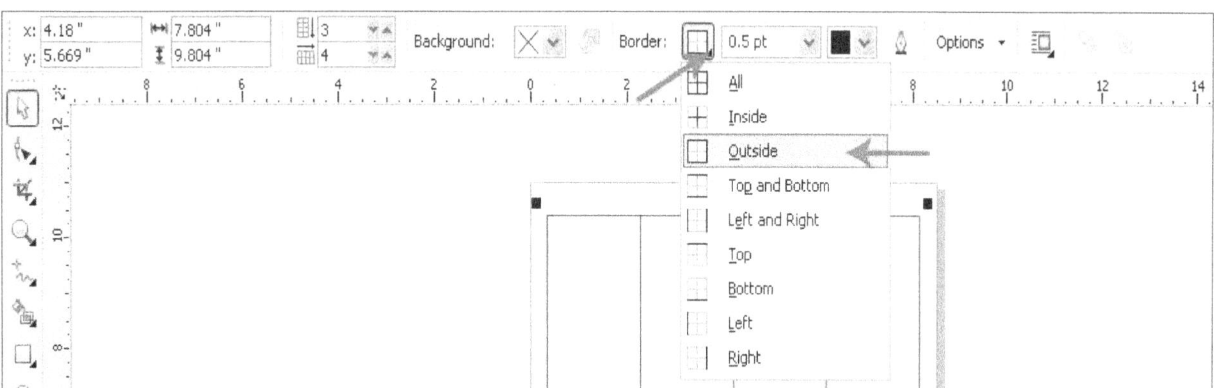

Picture 12.0

4. **Select** an option to specify where you want the border formatting to be applied in the table, from the dropdown list. In our case, we select the **Outside** option that allows you to manage the formatting to the outer outline or border of the table, as shown in picture 12.0 with the red arrow.

5. **Click** the down arrow of the **Outline width** combo box on the Property bar. It opens a dropdown list specifying the various dimensions of width.

6. **Select** a value for the outline width from the drop down list. In our case, we have selected the value, **24.0 pt**.

7. **Click** the down arrow of the **Outline color** button on the Property bar. Using this option, you will be able to specify the color for the outline of the selected table. It opens a color palette flyout on your screen.

8. **Select** a color that you want to apply to the outline from the color palette flyout. In our case, we have selected the **sky blue** color. As a result, the table appears with the specified width and color of outline, as shown in picture 12.1.

In addition, using the CorelDRAW X6 application, you can follow the same procedure to change the border or outline of a selected cell in a table. You will have various formatting options that you can select and apply to your table.

In this section of the lesson, you learnt to change the border outline of a table. After learning how to change the border or outline of a table, let's now discuss the procedure to fill colors in the cells of a table in the next section.

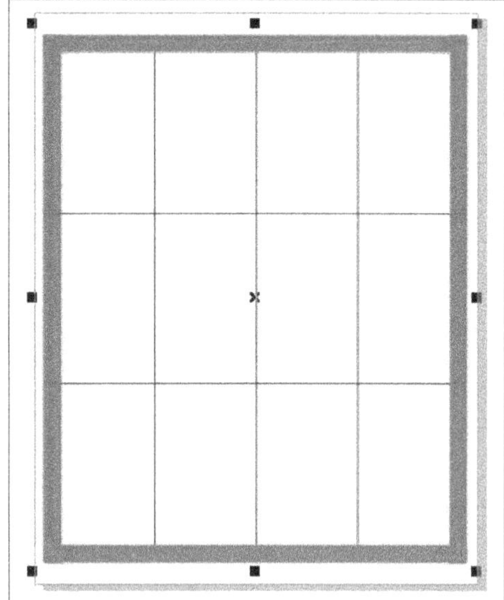

Picture 12.1

Filling Colors in Cells

The data in the form of tables are just the representation of figures and facts. You can introduce colors inside the cells of a table to make it more attractive and appealing. Tabular data is generally dry data, which appears monotonous and can bore the user easily. You can add colors in tables by using the default color palette available in CorelDRAW to apply the desired color in your table. In addition, the colors can be applied to the selected cell or cells of the table or to the entire table, as a background. Perform the following steps to fill colors in the cells of a table:

1. **Open** a drawing in CorelDRAW X6. In our case, we have opened the drawing created in the previous section.

2. **Double-click** the cell of the table in which you want to fill color.

3. Choose **Table> Select> Cell** from the Menu bar. The selected cell of the table appears with diagonal line.

4. **Click** the desired color you want to fill in the cell from the default **Color palette** located on the left side of the Document window.

As a result, the color is automatically applied to the selected cell of the table and also stored in the default Document Palette, that keeps a record of all the colors used in the current working document. Let's now learn to merge the cells of a table in the next section.

Merging Table Cells

Merging the specified cells of a table allows you to integrate several cells to form a single cell. While working with tables in CorelDRAW you may sometimes find that certain data in it would be better represented in an elongated and expanded manner. For this, you can merge the specific cells of a table that represent the data in a table without changing the original information in any way. CorelDRAW provides you a simple way to merge the cells of a table, as you will learn in this section. Perform the following steps to merge the cells of a table in CorelDRAW:

1. **Open** a drawing in CorelDRAW X6. In our case, we open the drawing created in the previous section.

2. **Select** the <u>cells</u> from the table, which you want to merge. In our case, we select the **first**, **second**, and **third** cells in the first row.

By the way, you can select the cells of a table by simply dragging the mouse-pointer in the cells you want to select.

3. Choose **Table**> **Merge Cells** from Menu bar. As a result, the selected cells merge and appear as a single cell.

Keep in mind that you can also merge the selected cells of a table by pressing the Ctrl+M keys in combination. The merged cells can also be unmerged. For this, you need to select Table> Unmerge Cells from the Menu bar.

Splitting Table Cells

In CorelDRAW X6, you can split the desired cells into a multiple number of respective rows and columns. Splitting cells help you to split a single cell into a specified number of cells, horizontally or vertically. To split a cell into numerous fractions is an easy procedure. All you need to do is select the location from where you want to split the cell in a table, and then use any of the two buttons from the Property bar to split the cell:

- **Split cells horizontally:** Allows you to split cells into a specified number of rows
- **Split cells vertically:** Allows you to split cells into a specified number of columns

After knowing about these two buttons, now you can perform the following simple steps on your computer to split a cell in a table:

1. **Open** a drawing in CorelDRAW X6. In our case, we open the drawing created in the previous section.

2. **Select** the cells from the table, which you want to split. In our case, we select the second column having five cells of the table.

3. Choose **Table**> **Split into Columns** from the Menu bar. The Split Cells dialog box appears.

4. Type a value in the **Number of columns** spin box, to specify the number of columns you want to split the selected columns into. In our case, we type: **4**.

5. Click the **OK** button in the Split Cells dialog box. As a result, the table cells split vertically into four cells.

Setting Margins for text in a Table Cell

You have already learnt the procedure to type text in the cells of a table. Sometimes, you are required to adjust the typed text inside the cells. CorelDRAW X6 allows you to adjust the text enclosed within the boundary of the cell. In addition, the application provides you four ways to set the margins of the data within the table. For this, you are required to access the Margins button on the Property bar, and then select the desired option from the list. The dropdown list that appears on clicking the Margin button contains combo boxes with the following options:

- **Top cell margin:** Allows you to specify the width of the margin of the top cell
- **Bottom cell margin**: Allows you to specify the width of margin of the bottom cell
- **Left cell margin:** Allows you to specify the width of margin of the left cell
- **Right cell margin:** Allows you to specify the width of margin of the right cell

After knowing about these options, now you can perform the following simple steps on your computer to set the margins for text in a table cell:

1. **Open** a drawing in CorelDRAW X6. In our case, we open a drawing having a table drawn on the Drawing page.

2. **Enter** the text in any cell of the table. In our case, we enter the text in the **third row** and the **third column** of the table.

3. **Select** the text by double-clicking over the text in the cell.

4. Click the **Vertical alignment** button on the Property bar.

5. **Select** an option from the dropdown list to specify the alignment of the text selected within the boundary of the selected cell. In our case, we select the **Bottom Vertical Alignment** option.

6. Click the down arrow of the **Margins** button on the Property bar.

7. Click the **Lock Margins** button to unlock the property to set same width for all margins.

8. Type a value in the **Top cell margin** combo box. In our case, we type **0.3"**.

9. Type a value in the **Bottom cell margin** combo box. In our case, we type **0.23"**.

10. Type a value in the **Left cell margin** combo box. In our case, we type **0.22"**.

11. Type a value in the **Right cell margin** combo box. In our case, we type **0.27"**.

12. Press the **Enter** button from the keyboard to apply the specified changes. As a result, now the text after specified margins within the boundary of the selected table cell appears on your screen.

Lesson 12
Mastering Layers in CorelDRAW X6
The layers in CorelDRAW play an integral role in handling the objects created on the Drawing page. In CorelDRAW X6, layers can be defined as invisible stages occupied with an object or collection of objects placed in stacks under the Object Manager docker. You can manage the stacking order of layers under the Object Manager docker that further contributes or affects the appearance of the objects visibility

and precedence in the drawing. Using layers, you can change the attributes of an individual object or a group of objects mutually. Layers allow you to easily edit and organize complex drawings, by dividing the drawing into multiple layers, with each layer containing a portion of the drawing. Apart from all this, the layers are also responsible for providing an effective way to handle and organize objects.

In CorelDRAW X6, you can create two types of layers, local layers and master layers. The local layer comprises of a particular page, whereas the master layer comprises of the content used in the entire drawing. Local layer, also called Layer 1, is the default layer, and all the components of a drawing are placed on this layer until a different layer is added. A selected layer always appears in a bold red font.

In this chapter, you learn to create a layer. Next, you learn to modify layer properties, in which we discuss the procedure to show or hide layer properties, set the edit properties of layers, and alter the position of layers in the stacking order. This chapter also discusses the procedure to move objects from one layer to another layer. At the end of this chapter, you learn to delete a layer, which is no more required for practicing the drawing. Let's learn to create layers in the next section.

Creating a Layer

Layers can be created in a drawing for managing the individual object properties. Layers allow you to collect the objects with similar properties under a specific name. You can create one or more layers to organize the content of your drawing and help you to work with large and complex drawings. You can create and manage layers by using the Object Manager docker from the Tools menu. The layer is visible in the Object Manager docker. Initially, all the objects are drawn in the default layer, named as Layer 1.

While creating a new layer, you need to decide what type of layer you want, that is, a master layer or a local layer. If you want the layer to repeat on every page of your drawing, create the master layer; otherwise, if it is a layer for a particular page, create a local layer. By default, if no layer is created in a drawing, all the objects drawn are placed on the default layer called Layer 1. Before working with a layer in a drawing, you need to first activate the layer by clicking the layer named in the Object Manager docker. Perform the following steps to create a layer in a CorelDRAW drawing:

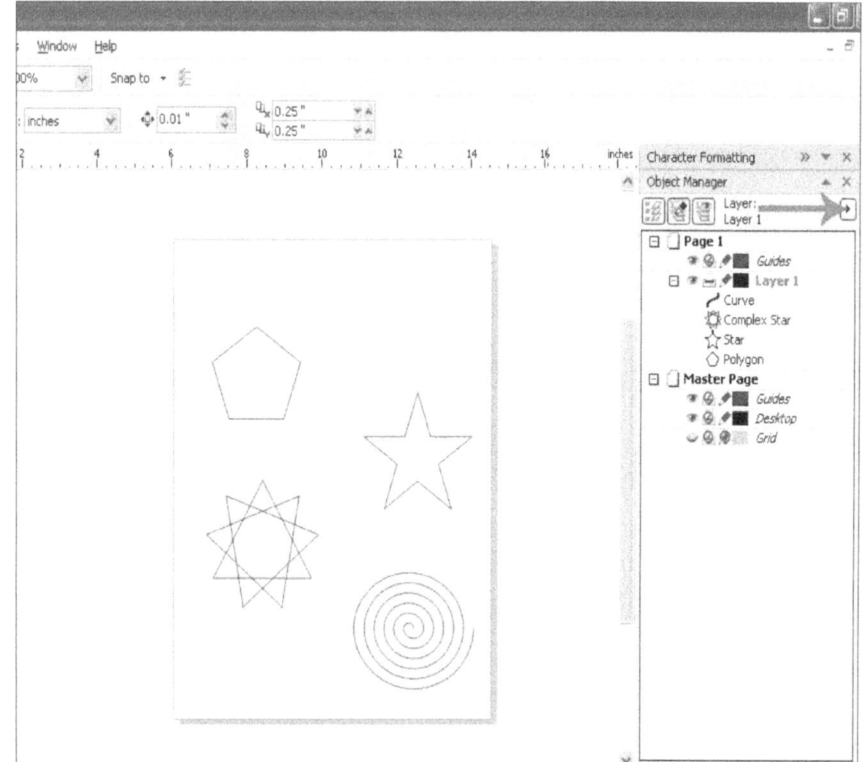

Picture 12.2

1. **Open** a drawing in CorelDRAW X6. In our case, we open a drawing having objects, such as **polygon**, **star**, **complex star**, and **spiral**, drawn on the Drawing page, as shown in picture 12.2.

2. Choose **Tools> Object Manager** from the Menu bar. The Object Manager docker appears to the right side of the Drawing page.

3. Click the **Object Manager Options** button in the Object Manager docker, as shown in picture 12.2 with the red arrow on the right side of the screen. It opens a dropdown list with various options.

4. Select the **New Layer** option from the dropdown list.

As you select the New Layer option, a new layer appears under the Object Manager docker. The new layer now becomes the active layer, and the objects drawn further on the Drawing page are embraced under this layer. You can notice that the name of the layer appears in red bold font because it is the currently active layer. In our case, now we draw a **rectangle** by using the Rectangle tool on the Drawing page, as shown in picture 12.3 on the Drawing page. This rectangle appears under the new layer, that is, **Layer 2**, in the Object Manger docker, as shown in picture 12.3 with the red arrow on the right side of the screen.

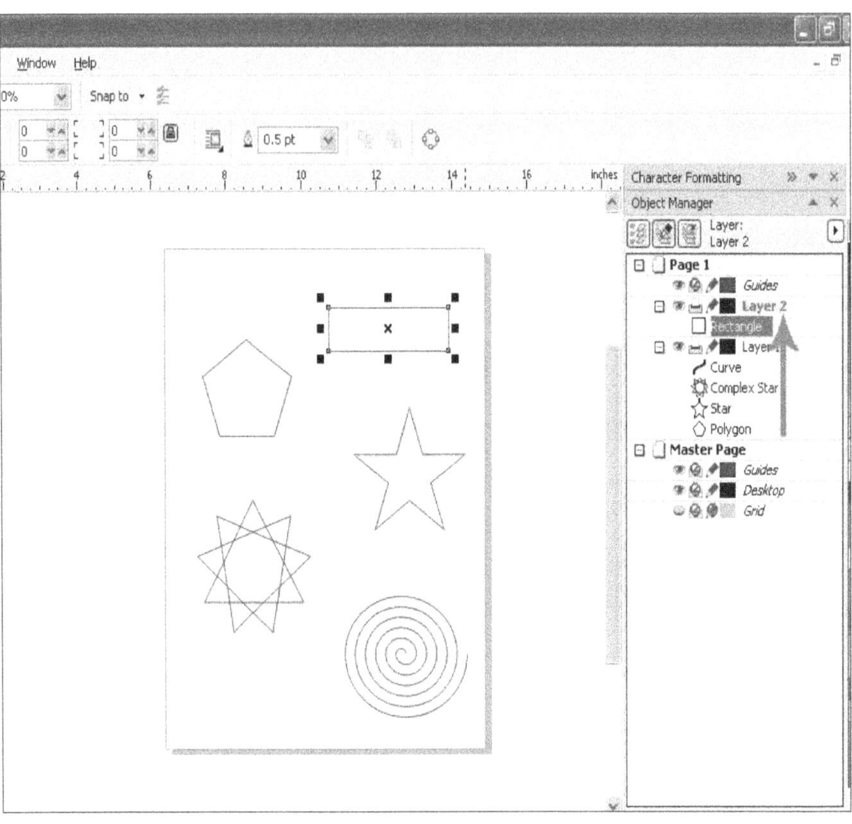

Picture 12.3

Keep in mind that in CorelDRAW X6, you can also create a master layer by selecting the New Master Layer option from the Object Manager Options flyout docker in the Object Manager docker.

Modifying Layer Properties

CorelDRAW X6 allows you to make changes in the properties of a layer in the form of visibility, name, and printability. You can also specify the layer as a master layer that manages and controls all the objects drawn on the Drawing page. Therefore, it is not necessary for you to work with only the default properties of a layer; you can also customize the properties according to your requirements. While working with objects, if you want to change the stacking order of an object, the change is applied to the layer on which the object is located. Similarly, you can also change the stacking order of layers, by moving them to the front or back of the stacking order as required. In this section, you learn to show or hide layer properties, set the editing properties of layers, and alter the position of layer in the stacking order. Let's first learn to show or hide layer properties in the next section.

Showing or Hiding Layer Properties

CorelDRAW X6 application allows you to show or hide the layer properties that affect the objects drawn under specific layers. You can make changes on specific layers without affecting the objects of other layers by using the Object Manager docker. The application allows showing or hiding the layer in CorelDRAW by using the Show or Hide icon in the Object Manager docker. When you hide a layer in a drawing, the objects present in that layer are not visible in the drawing. In this way, you can work with complex drawing by temporarily displaying only those objects that you need to work on while hiding the other objects in a drawing.

In this section, we use the Object Manager docker to show or hide Layer 2, which contains a rectangle. On hiding the layer, the rectangle will be no more visible on the Drawing page. In this way, you can change the properties of the other objects without affecting the objects on the other layers. Perform the following steps to show or hide a layer:

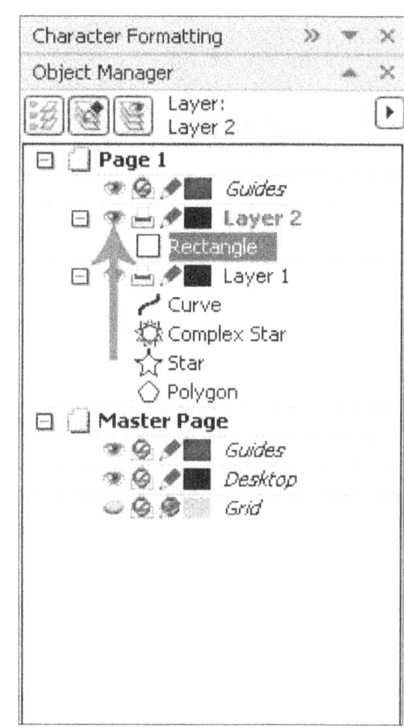

Picture 12.4

1. **Open** a drawing in CorelDRAW X6. In our case, we open the same drawing which was created in the previous section.

2. **Select** an object on the Drawing page by using the Pick tool from Toolbox. In our case, we select a **Rectangle** on Layer 2, as already shown in picture 12.3 on the Drawing page.

3. Choose **Tools> Object Manager** from the Menu bar. The Object Manager docker appears aligned in the right hand side of the Drawing window, (picture 12.3).

4. Click the **Show or Hide** icon beside the name of the selected layer that you want to hide, as shown in picture 12.4. In our case, we click the icon beside **Layer 2**, which contains a rectangle object.

As you hide the layer in the Object Manager docker, the objects under the layer (in our case, a rectangle) disappear from the Drawing page. Now, you can work on the objects present on other layer within the same Drawing page by editing the properties of the objects according to your requirements. You can make the object reappear by clicking the Show or Hide icon in the Object Manager docker.

Setting the Editing Properties of Layers

You can set the editing properties of layers in the same way you edit an object drawn on the Drawing page. In CorelDRAW, you can set the editing properties of a layer by certain ways, such as hide or unhide layers according to the objects you want to display and work on in the Drawing page. Hiding the objects from one layer allows you to edit the remaining objects drawn on the Drawing page. In addition, you can also lock or unlock layers. When you lock layers, you can display the objects present in the layer on the Drawing page. However, the properties of those objects cannot be modified in any way. If you want to make changes in the objects, you have to first unlock the layer. Perform the following steps to set the editing properties of a layer:

1. **Open** a drawing in CorelDRAW X6. In our case, we open the drawing created in the previous section.

2. Click the **Show or Hide** icon beside the Layer 2, to display the polygon contained in the layer on the Drawing page.

3. **Select** the layer from the **Object Manager** docker, which you want to edit. In our case, we have selected **Layer 1**.

4. Click the **Lock or Hide** icon beside the selected Layer 1 to lock the properties of the objects in the layer. The objects placed in Layer 1 are locked and are no longer available for editing on the Drawing page.

By the way, you would know that the Lock and Unlock button changes its icon as per the selection (when you click). The button appears in the unlocked state by default.

5. Click the **Object Manager Options** button in the Object Manager docker. A dropdown list appears.

6. **Clear** (uncheck) the **Edit Across Layers** option from the dropdown list.

Now, you can perform editing on all the layers and objects present on the Drawing page according to your requirements. Let's further learn to change the position of layer in the stacking order.

Altering the Position of Layer in the Stacking Order

In CorelDRAW X6, you can move one layer over the other layer within the same Drawing page. In this way, the objects drawn in one layer are stacked over the objects created in another layer. Moving a layer on a page or between different pages changes the stacking order of the layer, which in turn changes the appearance of the objects in the layer. In case, you draw a circle on Layer 1 and a rectangle on Layer 2, the circle appears hidden behind the rectangle by default. However, if you want to show the circle on the top of the rectangle, you need to alter the position of the layers, so that the circle appears on the top of the rectangle. Perform the following steps to alter the position of a layer in the stacking order:

1. **Open** a drawing in CorelDRAW X6. In our case, we open a drawing having a **rectangle** and an **ellipse** on Layer 1 and a **star** on Layer 2.

2. Select **Layer 1** from the Object Manager docker.

3. **Drag** Layer 1 on the top of Layer 2.

When you change the order of layers under the Object Manager docker to alter the stacking order of objects drawn on the Drawing page, the order of appearance of objects on the Drawing page changes accordingly, with the objects in Layer 1 (rectangle and ellipse) appearing on top of the object in Layer 2 (star). So, after learning to manipulate the stacking order of layers in CorelDRAW, let's now learn to move and copy objects between layers in the next section.

Moving Objects in Layers

Moving an object on the Drawing page can be done easily. For this, you are just required to move and place the object by using the Pick tool from Toolbox. On the other hand, you can also move an object or group of objects from one layer to other layer. CorelDRAW allows you to move the selected objects to different layers. You are required to select the specific layer under which the object that you want to move is placed. Next, you can simply drag and drop the selected object from one layer to the required layer. The process of moving the object from a layer to another layer is carried in the Object Manager docker. Perform the following steps to move objects between layers:

1. **Open** a drawing in CorelDRAW X6. In our case, we open the drawing created in the previous section.

2. **Select** an object on the Drawing page by using the Pick tool. In our case, we select the **ellipse** object.

Note that Layer 1 comprises two objects, a rectangle and an ellipse. Whereas, the Layer 2 comprises a single object, star. In our case, we have selected the ellipse on the Drawing page, which is in Layer 1. Now, let's move ahead.

3. Click the **Object Manager Options** button in the Object Manager docker.

4. **Select** an option from the dropdown list. In our case, we select the **Move to Layer** option.

5. **Select** the layer in the Object Manager docker from which you want to move the selected object (ellipse). In our case, we select **Layer 2**. As a result, the selected object (ellipse) is transferred from Layer 1 to Layer 2 under the Object Manager docker.

Deleting a Layer

While working with layers in CorelDRAW, you can delete the layer which is no more required for the drawing. In other words, if you do not need a layer in your drawing, you can delete the layer by using the Object Manager docker. In CorelDRAW, when you delete a layer, all the objects on that layer are also deleted. If you need to keep those objects, you are required to move them to different layer before deleting the layer. Perform the following steps to delete a layer:

1. **Open** a drawing in CorelDRAW X6. In our case, we open the drawing created in the previous section.

2. **Select** the layer from the Object Manager docker, which you want to delete. In our case, we select **Layer 1**.

3. Click the **Object Manager Options** button in the Object Manager docker.

4. Select the **Delete Layer** option from the dropdown list. As a result, the selected Layer 1 is deleted from the Object Manager docker and the objects in the layer are also deleted from the Drawing page.

Lesson 13
Working with Bitmaps and Export Options
CorelDRAW X6 is a vector drawing application in which the objects you learnt to create are vector illustrations. In general, the images are categorized into two types, that is, bitmap, and vector. Both types of images appear identical and the objective behind their difference is in the way they capture the color content. You can also note a basic difference in these types of images when they are magnified. Bitmap images comprises of dots or pixels. Pixels are nothing but small dots, which uniquely classifies the color codes of the image. The bitmap image captures colors of graphics in the form of a unique identity (pixels), however, a vector image can be stretched to any level as this type has no impact of dots or pixels for capturing colors.

In the previous chapters, we have worked with vector images on our Drawing page. In CorelDRAW, all the images are saved of .cdr format by default, and this format belongs to the vector image family. Bitmaps can also be defined as the images that can be used to store a location and account of pixels on a specific image. So, instead of describing images in terms of curves and lines, bitmap images are defined in pixels. You can produce the images of any size from a dot to a poster. The main difference between vectors and bitmaps are experienced when you attempt to edit them. This chapter discusses about working with the bitmap images. In cases, you may require the bitmap images that let you apply special effects to the objects within CorelDRAW.

In this chapter, you first learn to work with image type conversions in CorelDRAW, wherein we discuss the procedure to convert a vector image into a bitmap in the drawing as well as while exporting. You also learn to import a bitmap in the CorelDRAW X6 application. Next, you learn to transform a bitmap, in which you learn to resample and resize a bitmap. Further, this chapter discusses the procedure to work with page layout tools by using the default templates. Moreover, you learn to work with advance operations, in which you discuss the process to apply the 3D Pinch/Punch and Color Transform effects on a bitmap. Towards the middle of this chapter, you explore the Image Adjustment Color lab of CorelDRAW X6. This chapter also demonstrates the process to trace bitmaps imported on the Drawing page. At last, you learn to export a drawing in CorelDRAW X6, wherein you discuss to export drawing to PDF, for Web and for Office applications. Let's begin the chapter and first learn to work with image type conversions of the CorelDRAW X6 application in the next section.

Working with Image Type Conversions in CorelDRAW X6
CorelDRAW X6 provides the facility of converting vector images into bitmap images. You can prepare a drawing for printing by rasterization. In this process, the Raster Image Processor (RIP) of the application turns the text and images into pixels (or bitmaps), which you can display or screen and are ready to print. This facility is important because some features, such as 3D effects, can be applied to bitmap images only. The process of converting a vector image into a bitmap image is called rasterization.

In this section, you learn to convert vector images into bitmap images in a drawing while exporting a drawing. Let's now learn to convert a vector image into a bitmap image in the next section.

Converting Vector Images into Bitmap Images
In CorelDRAW X6, you can convert a vector image into a bitmap image. While converting a vector image into bitmap, you are required to select a color mode for the image. The color mode determines the

colors that constitute the bitmap. The size of your file may increase or decrease depending on the color mode you select, such as in case you create a simple bitmap file in MS Paint having a smaller file size with the RGB (Red, Green, and Blue) color mode as compared to a bitmap file created in Photoshop with the CMYK (Cyan, Magenta, Yellow, and Key) color mode. Perform the following steps to convert a vector image into a bitmap image:

1. **Open** a drawing in CorelDRAW X6. In our case, we open a drawing having a vector image, as shown in picture 12.5.

2. Choose **Bitmap> Convert to Bitmap** from the Menu bar to open its dialog box, as shown in picture 12.6.

3. **Enter** a value in the **Resolution** combo box to specify the resolution for the bitmap image you want to create. In our case, we enter **300**.

Picture 12.5

4. Click the down arrow of the **Color mode** list box in the Color section. Then **select** the desired color mode. In our case, we select **CMYK Color (32-bit).**

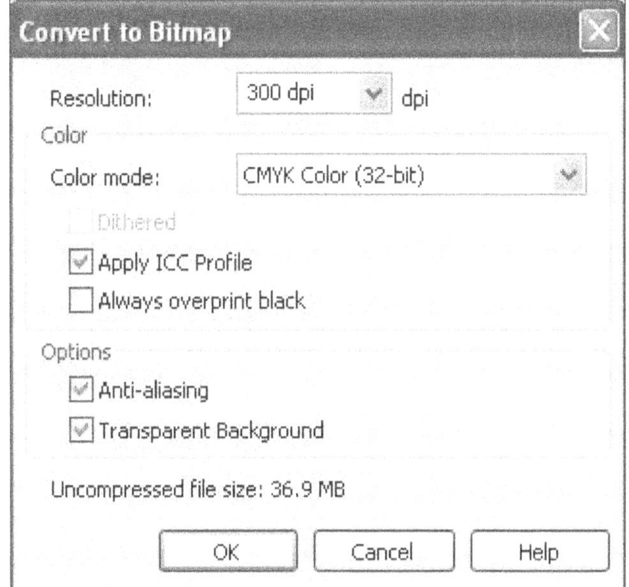

Picture 12.6

Picture 12.7

5. Select the **Anti-aliasing** check box in the Options section. Then select the **Transparent Background** check box also in the Options section.

6. Click the **OK** button in the Convert To Bitmap dialog box. As a result, the vector image is converted into a bitmap image, as shown in picture 12.7.

After converting a vector image into a bitmap image, you can also perform the conversion at the time of exporting the image, as discussed in the next section.

Converting Vector Images into Bitmap While Exporting

CorelDRAW X6 provides the feature to convert a vector image into a bitmap at the time of exporting the image. This process follows the conversion that is important for market leading professional, such as designers and publishers, as these professionals require a worthy command for handling the color managements to yield desired outcomes. In other words, by converting an image into a bitmap image while exporting helps you to work in an existing drawing without affecting the destination or the file type in which you have saved the current drawing. Perform the following steps to convert a vector image to a bitmap image while exporting:

1. **Open** a drawing in CorelDRAW X6. In our case, we have opened a drawing (image) on the Drawing page.

2. Choose **File> Export** from the Menu bar. It opens the Export dialog box.

3. **Navigate** to the location to specify where you want to save your bitmap image. In our case, the location is **Desktop**.

4. **Enter** the name of the image in the File name combo box. Then **click** the down arrow button of the **Save as type** combo box.

5. **Select** a file extension that you want to specify for the selected file from the dropdown list. In our case, we select **BMP-Windows Bitmap (*.bmp; *.dib; *.rle).**

6. Click the **Export** button in the Export dialog box. It opens the **Convert to Bitmap** dialog box.

7. **Enter** a value for the width of the exported image in the **Width** spin box of the Image Size section. In our case, we enter **11.95**.

8. Enter a value to specify the height of the exported image in the **Height** spin box of the Image Size section. In our case, we enter **16.0**.

9. **Enter** a value to specify the resolution for the image in the **Resolution** spin box of the Image Size section. In our case, we enter **300**.

10. Select the **Maintain aspect ratio** check box in the Image Size section to maintain the proportions of the image and prevent distortions.

Aspect Ratio refers to the relationship between the width and height of an image. If you do not want any changes in the size of the original image, you can select the **Maintain original size** check box.

11. Click the down arrow of the **Color Mode** combo box in the Color section of the Convert to Bitmap dialog box.

12. **Select** a color mode from the dropdown list. In our case, we select **RGB Color (24-bit)**.

13. Select the **Anti-aliasing** check box in the Options section to smooth the edges of the image after it is converted into a bitmap.

14. Click the **OK** button in the Convert to Bitmap dialog box. As a result, the image is exported from its original location and saved in the selected location.

After learning to export a vector image by converting it to a bitmap image, you can also import a bitmap image from other applications, such as Photoshop and Paint, and use it in your CorelDRAW drawing, as discussed in the next section.

Importing a Bitmap in CorelDRAW X6

In CorelDRAW X6, you can import the bitmaps on the Drawing page by using the import command. By using this command, you can accommodate the documents created earlier in the same application or in other applications, such as Adobe Photoshop or Corel PAINT. In other words, the importing process helps the professional users to import the bitmap files from different applications on a single workspace (in our case, CorelDRAW X6). You can also edit the imported bitmap files with the editing tools present in the Toolbox of CorelDRAW X6 application. In this section, you learn the procedure to import a bitmap in the CorelDRAW Drawing page with the help of the Import dialog box. Perform the following steps to import a bitmap:

1. **Open** a new drawing in CorelDRAW X6. Then choose **File**> **Import** from the Menu bar to open Import dialog box.

2. **Navigate** to the location in the Navigation section of the left side of the Import dialog box to specify from where you want to import the bitmap file (from your computer hard drive).

3. **Select** the bitmap image you want to import. Then click the **Import** button in the dialog box.

Now, as you drag the mouse pointer on the Drawing page, the shape of the mouse pointer changes and displays information, such as name and dimension, of the image you want to import as well as different ways by which you can move and resize the image on the Drawing page.

4. **Click** the location for the image on the Drawing page. As you click, the image appears on the Drawing page.

After importing a bitmap image into CorelDRAW drawing, let us now learn about the various ways to modify image in the next section.

Transforming a Bitmap

CorelDRAW X6 application allows you to use various tools and techniques to resample and resize the bitmap images. Sometimes, you may require enlarging an image without changing its resolution. However, enlarging spreads the available pixels of the image over a large area, resulting in the loss of image details. In such cases, you can resample the image by adding pixels, thereby preserving the details of the original image. In addition to this, you can also change the size of an image while maintaining the number of pixels and quality of the image by resizing the bitmap images.

In this section, you learn working with bitmaps, in which you discuss the procedure to resample and resize a bitmap. Let's first learn to resample a bitmap in the next section.

Resampling a Bitmap

Resampling is a process that improves the quality and results in the printing output. In other words, resampling refers to the process of changing the image by adding or removing pixels from it. As sampling affects the number of pixels in an image, the resolution of the image is affected in the process. The resampling also helps to reduce the file size when images are of extremely large size. The resampling process is commonly carried out by leading professional aspirants for resampling their high loaded designs in a desired size to publish as graphics. Perform the following steps to resample a bitmap image:

1. **Open** a drawing in CorelDRAW X6. In our case, we open the drawing having a bitmap image on the Drawing page, as shown in picture 12.8.

2. **Select** the image by using the Pick tool. Then choose **Bitmaps> Resample** from the Menu bar to open its dialog box.

3. Enter the value: **12.4** in the **Width** spin box in the Image size section to specify the width of the image. Then enter the value: **12.97** in the **Height** spin box to specify the height of the image.

4. Enter the value: **126** in the **Horizontal** spin box in the Resolution section to specify the resolution (pixel) of image horizontally. Then enter the value: **126** in the **Vertical** spin box to specify the resolution vertically.

Picture 12.8

5. Select the **Anti-alias** check box, and then the **Maintain aspect ratio** check box in the Resample dialog box.

6. Click the **OK** button in the Resample dialog box. The image, after resampling is shown in picture 12.9 below.

Working with Page Layout

The term page layout is referred to the organization with agreement to the image clips, text, and objects placed on the Drawing page. You can use the page layouts with different patterns and designs to customize the display for newspapers, magazines, books, publications, and websites. The layout structure encompasses all the objects placed on the Drawing page. The structure of layout on the Drawing page of the CorelDRAW application includes the additional elements, such as margins, text blocks, images, object padding, and any grids or templates used in the Drawing.

Picture 12.9

The page layout applications, such as CorelDRAW X6, allow designers to modify all of these elements for publishing the prints. In this section, you learn to design the page layouts by using the default template provided by CorelDRAW X6. Perform the following steps to work with layout styles in CorelDRAW X6 by using the default templates:

1. **Open** a new drawing in CorelDRAW X6. Then choose **New**> **New From Template** from the Menu bar. The dialog box appears displaying the default templates under the **All** category.

2. Click the **Catalogs** options to view the catalog templates under the Filter section in the New Form Template dialog box.

3. **Select** the required template from the list. In our case, we select **Craft Store NA-Catalog**.

4. Click the **Open** button in the dialog box to open the template. After the template opens on your Drawing page, then choose **File**> **Import** from the Menu bar.

5. **Navigate** the location in your computer hard drive to specify from where you want to import a file (an image).

6. **Select** a file that you want to import on the Drawing page. Then click the **Import** button in the dialog box.

7. Click the **OK** button in the Import Warning dialog box.

Now, as you drag the mouse pointer on the Drawing page, the shape of the mouse pointer changes and displays information, such as name and dimension of the image you want to import as well as different ways by which you can move and resize the image on the Drawing page.

8. **Click** the location for the image on the Drawing page. As you click, the image appears on the Drawing page.

9. **Resize** the imported image on the Drawing page by moving the corners of the image. The image automatically resizes according to the specification you provide at the time of moving the corners surrounded at the boundary of the imported file.

10. **Move** the imported file at the desired location to place inside the template. Then if you want, **insert** paragraph text on the Drawing page using the Text tool from Toolbox.

Working with Advance Operations on Bitmap Images

CorelDRAW X6 provides various special effects that can be applied on bitmap images. By applying the effects on bitmaps, you can change the appearance, color, and properties of bitmaps. Special effects change the appearance of the image to make it appealing or attractive, or simply arouse curiosity or interest by displaying the image in a different way. When you apply a special effect to the image, it changes the properties of the image, such as orientation and color. CorelDRAW application provides the following special effects to apply to a bitmap image, which are preset under the Bitmap menu in the Menu bar:

- **3D Effects:** Refers to the effects that you can apply directly on a bitmap image, such as 3D Rotate, Cylinder, Emboss, Page Curl, Perspective, Pinch/Punch, and Sphere. For example, you can apply the Sphere effect on an image to produce a spherical-shaped image.
- **Art Strokes:** Refers to the effects that created the effect of hand paint strokes on a bitmap image, such as Charcoal, Conte Crayon, Crayon, Cubist, Impressionist, Palette knife, Pastels, Pen & Ink, Pointillist, Scraperboard, Sketch Pad, Watercolor, Water Marker, and Wave Paper.
- **Blur:** Refers to the effect that creates a haziness or distinction around the outline of the bitmap image to make it appear dim or dull. The blur effects present in the application are Directional Smooth, Gaussian Blur, Jaggy Despeckle, Low Pass, Motion Blur, Radial Blur, Smooth, Soften, and Zoom.
- **Camera:** Allows you to create an effect similar to the one produced by a diffusion lens. There is only one effect under this special effect, namely diffuse.
- **Color Transform:** Allows creating photographic illusions by reducing and replacing the colors of the bitmap image. Examples of this effect are Bit Plane, Halftone, Psychedelic, and Solarize.
- **Contour:** Allows you to highlight and enhance the edges of the bitmap image. Examples of Contour effects are Edge Detect, Find Edges, and Trace Contour.
- **Creative:** Allows you to apply various textures and shapes to the bitmap image, such as Crafts, Crystalize, Fabric, Frame, Glass Block, Kid's Play, Mosaic, Particles, Scatter, Smoked Glass, Stained Glass, Vignette, Vortex, and Weather.
- **Distort:** Allows you to change the surface of the bitmap image by using various effects, such as Blocks, Displace, Offset, Pixelate, Ripple, Swirl, Tile, Wet Paint, Whirlpool and Wind.
- **Noise:** Allows you to modify the coarseness of the bitmap image. Examples of the Noise effects are Add Noise, Maximum, Median, Minimum, Remove Moiré, and Remove Noise.
- **Sharpen:** Allows you to enhance the edges of the bitmap image. The different Sharpen effects are Adaptive Unsharp, Directional Sharpen, High Pass, Sharpen, and Unsharp Mask.
- **Plug-ins:** Allows you to use third party filters to apply special effect to bitmaps. You can apply plug-ins through Digimarc by either embedded watermark or by read watermark.

After getting idea of some of the special effects available in CorelDRAW, let's now learn to use some of these effects on a CorelDRAW drawing in the next section.

Applying 3D Effects to a Bitmap

The CorelDRAW X6 application enables you to apply various effects under 3D effects, such as 3D Rotate, Cylinder, Emboss, Page Curl, Perspective, Pinch/Punch, and Sphere. By using 3D effects, you can create illusions to display the objects in three dimensions. In addition, 3D effects help you to create the illusion of depth in your CorelDRAW object or drawing. In this section, you learn to apply the Pinch/Punch 3D effect on a bitmap. Perform the following steps to apply 3D effects to a bitmap image:

1. **Open** a drawing in CorelDRAW X6. In our case, we open a drawing having a bitmap image on the Drawing page.

2. **Select** the bitmap on the Drawing page by using the Pick tool. Then choose **Bitmaps> 3D Effects> Pinch/Punch** from the Menu bar to open its dialog box.

3. **Enter** a value in the **Pinch/Punch** text box to specify the value of squeezing the bitmap image. In our case, we enter **100**.

4. Click the **OK** button in the Pinch/Punch dialog box to save the specified settings. As a result, the Pinch/Punch effect is applied to the bitmap image on your screen.

After learning to use the Pinch/Punch 3D effect on a bitmap image, let's now learn to apply the Color Transform effects to the bitmap image in the next section.

Applying Color Transform Effect to a Bitmap

In CorelDRAW, you can apply the various Color Transform effects, such as Bit Planes, Halftone, Psychedelic, and Solarize. These effects provide you the adjustment element for different categories. By applying color transformation on the bitmaps, you can create pictorial illusions with the help of color reduction and replacements. In this section, you learn to apply the Halftone color transformation on a bitmap on the Drawing page. Perform the following steps to apply the Color Transform effects to a bitmap image:

1. **Open** a drawing in CorelDRAW X6. In our case, we open a drawing having a bitmap image on the Drawing page.

2. **Select** the bitmap on the Drawing page by using the Pick tool. Then choose **Bitmaps**> **Color Transform**> **Halftone** from the Menu bar.

The Halftone dialog box sections enable you to adjust the Cyan, Magenta, and Yellow color range of the image. Moreover, you can also select the amount of matrix dot radius of image under the Halftone dialog box.

3. **Enter** the desired value **(61)** in the Cyan text box to specify the cyan color content of the image. Then enter the desired value **(20)** in the Magenta text box to specify the magenta color content of the image.

4. **Enter** the desired value **(30)** in the Yellow text box to specify the yellow color content of the image. Then enter the desired value **(5)** in the Max dot radius text box to specify the bitmap dots per inch of the image.

By the way, you can also adjust the value for the colors by dragging the slider provided beside the options in the Halftone dialog box.

5. Click the **OK** button in the Halftone dialog box to save the settings. As a result, the Halftone Color Transform effect is applied to the selected image on your screen.

Exploring the Image Adjustment Lab Command

While working with images with poor color balance and contrast, you are required to eliminate the flaws while working with them. For this, the CorelDRAW X6 application enables the Image Adjustment Lab command. This command allows you to use many different tools for making adjustments and also saves your valuable time. You can access the Image Adjustment Lab command from the Menu bar of the CorelDRAW application. By clicking this command, the Lab dialog box appears, in which essential manuals and automatic controls are provided that help to correct common color and tonal adjustments. You can use the controls of the dialog box for precise corrections in the images placed on the Drawing page. In this Lab dialog box, you preview the changes you make in your image as you make them in different ways, in a single window, view the original and corrected images in separate windows, or view the image split into original and corrected portions within one window. Perform the following steps to set the color and tone of a bitmap image by using the Image Adjustment Lab command:

1. **Open** a drawing in CorelDRAW X6. In our case, we open a drawing having a bitmap image on the Drawing page.

2. **Select** the bitmap on the Drawing page by using the Pick tool. Then choose **Bitmaps> Image Adjustment Lab** from the Menu bar.

3. **Enter** a value **(4000)** in the <u>Temperature</u> text box to specify the temperature of the colors used in the selected image.

In CorelDRAW X6, the temperature of a color can be referred to the way of specifying light in terms of degrees (Kelvin), where a lower value resembles to dim lighting settings that causes an orange color cast and a higher value resembles to intense lighting settings that cause a blue color cast.
The color cast is the presence of colors in an image that occurs as a result of lighting conditions when photos are clicked, where dim light corresponds to yellow color cast, and bright light corresponds to blue color cast.

4. **Enter** a value **(14)** in the <u>Tint</u> text box to correct color casts by adjusting the green or magenta color in the image. Then **enter** a value **(80)** in the <u>Saturation</u> text box to specify the vividness of the colors in the image.

5. **Enter** a value **(55)** in the <u>Brightness</u> text box to brighten or darken the selected image according to your requirements. Then **enter** a value **(40)** in the <u>Contrast</u> text box to increase or decrease the difference in the tone between the dark and light areas of the image.

6. **Enter** a value **(10)** in the <u>Highlights</u> text box to adjust the brightness in the lightest areas of the image. Then **enter** a value **(50)** in the <u>Shadow</u> text box to adjust brightness of the mid-range tones in the image.

7. **Enter** a value **(60)** in the <u>Midtones</u> text box to adjust the brightness of the mid-range tones in your image.

8. Click the **OK** button in the Image Adjustment Lab dialog box. The image, after applying all the changes made in the dialog box, appears on your screen.

Tracing Bitmaps

The term can be referred to the act of drawing a diagram or outline. When you trace a bitmap, it enables you to edit and scale the graphics in a vector format. In CorelDRAW X6, various methods for tracing bitmap images are available whose descriptions in brief are as follows:

- **Centerline Trace:** Allows you to trace maps, signatures, line drawings, and technical illustrations. This feature also makes the use of the unfilled, closed, and open curves. You can call this tracing method as Stroke Tracing.

- **Outline Trace:** Allows you to trace line art, logos, clip arts, and both low and high quality images. By using the Outline trace method, you make the use of curve objects with no outlines. It is also known as fill or contour tracing.
- **Quick Trace:** Allows you quickly trace a bitmap image without specifying detailed values to trace it. For this purpose, the Quick Trace command is helpful. By using this command, you can trace the bitmap without displaying any dialog box and specifying values.

After learning about the methods used to trace images in CorelDRAW, let's learn to use these methods in a bitmap image. In our case, we are showing how to use the Quick Trace command to trace an image. Perform the following steps to trace a bitmap image by using the Quick Trace command:

1. **Open** a drawing in CorelDRAW X6. In our case, we open a drawing having a bitmap image on the Drawing page.

2. **Select** the bitmap on the Drawing page by using the Pick tool. Then choose **Bitmaps> Quick Trace** from the Menu bar.

The application requires a few seconds to trace the bitmap and after some time, the traced bitmap appears on your Drawing page. The bitmap is traced swiftly by using this command. The image appears with low color samples which are automatically evaluated depending on the size and color depth of the original bitmap.

By the way, you can also trace a bitmap image by using the **(Quick Trace) Trace Bitmap** button on the Property bar. Let's now learn about the export command of CorelDRAW X6 in the next section.

Exporting from CorelDRAW X6

CorelDRAW X6 allows you to export the drawings in external file formats that support various applications, such as Adobe reader, Autodesk AutoCAD, Flash player, Adobe Illustrator, and many more. For instance, you can create multiple pages designed for the book in CorelDRAW drawing, and then export the drawing in PDF (Portable Document Format) that can be accessed through the Adobe reader. Technically, the drawings created in the application are converted to support other applications at the time of exporting. Using the Export command under the File menu, you can export the CorelDRAW drawing and layouts.

In CorelDRAW X6, you can export the drawing in numerous file formats, such as PDF, BMP, AI, CPT, JPG, PFB, BMP, CAL, CGM, CMX, CPT, CUR, DOC, DWG, DXF, EMF, EPS, FMV, FPX, GEM, GIF, ICO, IMG, JP2, HPG, MAC, PCX, PDF, PCT, PLT, PNG, PP5, PPF, PSD, RTF, SCT, SCG, SVGZ, SWF, TGA, TIF, TTF, TXT, WMF, WP4,WP5, WPD, WPG, WSD, WI, and XPM. In this section, you learn to export a CorelDRAW X6 drawing to PDF and for the Web. Let's now learn to export a drawing to PDF in the next section.

Exporting to PDF

The drawing created and designed in CorelDRAW can be exported in the PDF file format. The application allows you to select the file formats while exporting the file in the desired location of your computer system. In this way, the designs or layouts generated on the drawing can be read or viewed from a PDF reader, such as Adobe PDF reader. While exporting the drawing in the PDF format, you can specify the limitations for current document, selective documents, number of pages, and the compatibility for various applications that support the PDF format. In this section, you learn to export the bitmap image on the Drawing page to a PDF file format. Perform the following steps to export the CorelDRAW drawing to a PDF file format:

1. **Open** a drawing in CorelDRAW X6. In our case, we open the same drawing which was created in the previous section.

2. **Select** the image on the Drawing page by using the Pick tool. Then choose **File**> **Export** from the Menu bar. It opens the Export dialog box on your screen.

3. **Navigate** to the location in your hard drive to specify where you want to export the bitmap file.

4. **Enter** the desired name to the file in the File name combo box. Then click the down arrow button of the **Save as type** combo box.

5. **Select** a file extension that you want to specify for the selected file from the dropdown list. In our case, we select **PDF-Adobe Portable Document Format (*.pdf)**.

6. Click the **Export** button in the Export dialog box. It opens the PDF Settings dialog box.

7. Click the **OK** button in the PDF Settings dialog box to accept the default setting. As a result, the PDF of the current drawing is automatically saved to the specified location.

Exporting for the Web

The drawing comprises of objects, texts, bitmap, and effects that can be exported to various other application. The Web is one of the most popular medium for the drawing or layouts created in CorelDRAW. You can export an individual composition of drawing to be used in a website. For instance, you can design a logo for your company by using the bitmap images on the CorelDRAW Drawing page, and then export the designed logo to be used in the company's website on the Web. For this, you need to export the drawing in the GIF (Graphic Interchange Format) file format. The GIF format is widely used as vector graphic and for logo file in the Web. Web browsers can now access the drawing exported from CorelDRAW as a GIF file format for their use. Perform the following steps to export a CorelDRAW drawing for the Web:

1. **Open** a drawing in CorelDRAW X6. In our case, we open the drawing having a bitmap image on the Drawing page.

2. **Select** the image on the Drawing page by using the Pick tool. Then choose **File**> **Export For Web** from the Menu bar. It opens the Export For Web dialog box.

3. Click the **Save As** button in the Export For Web dialog box. Then **navigate** to the location in your hard drive to specify where you want to export the file.

4. **Enter** the desired name to the file in the File name combo box. Then click the **Save** button in the Export dialog box. As a result, the current drawing is saved for exporting to Web.

Exporting for Office

CorelDRAW application allows you to export native drawing for Office applications. You can export the drawings or layouts created in the application for further usage in MS Office products, such as Word, Excel, Access, PowerPoint, Publisher, and One Note. In this way, you can utilize external software to develop content for online or digital devices. You can export to office by selecting the Export For Office option under the File menu. Then, the Export For Office dialog box allows you to specify the properties for exporting the drawing in the desired Office application according to your requirements. In this section, you learn to export the bitmap image placed on the Drawing page into a PNG file format to be used in the Office (MS Word) product. Perform the following simple steps to export a CorelDRAW drawing for Office:

1. **Open** a drawing in CorelDRAW X6. In our case, we open the drawing having a bitmap image on the Drawing page.

2. **Select** the image on the Drawing page by using the Pick tool. Then choose **File**> **Export For Office** from the Menu bar. It opens the Export For Office dialog box.

3. Click the **OK** button in the Export For Office dialog box. It opens the Save As dialog box.

4. **Navigate** to the location in your hard drive to specify where you want to export the file.

5. **Enter** the desired name to the file in the File name combo box. Then click the **Save** button in the Export dialog box.

As a result, the current working drawing file gets exported for Office applications having Portable Network Graphics. In this way, you can use the drawing in MS Office applications.

Niranjan Jha Showman
Trainer, Author, Physician, Entrepreneur, Filmmaker, Activist
Cromosys Corporation
Education and Technology Research Center
www.facebook.com/cromosys
+91-9561450045
Nallasopara (W), Mumbai, India

NIRANJAN JHA SHOWMAN

Founder - Niranjan Jha Showman

Education and Technology Research Center

Patankar Park, Nallasopara (W), Mumbai. +91-9561450045

Education, Technology, Publication, Healthcare, Newsmedia, Realtor, Filmmaking

www.facebook.com/cromosys

Cromosys Publication
Teach
Yourself
German
NIRANJAN JHA SHOWMAN

Cromosys Publication
Teach
Yourself
French
NIRANJAN JHA SHOWMAN

Cromosys Publication

Teach
Yourself
Spanish

NIRANJAN JHA SHOWMAN

Cromosys Publication

English
Voice
Accent and
Pronunciation

NIRANJAN JHA SHOWMAN

Teach
Yourself
Autodesk
MAYA
Cromosys Publication
NIRANJAN JHA SHOWMAN

Cromosys Publication
Teach
Yourself
Autodesk
3ds Max
NIRANJAN JHA SHOWMAN

Cromosys Publication
CRIMINAL FACTORY
NIRANJAN JHA SHOWMAN

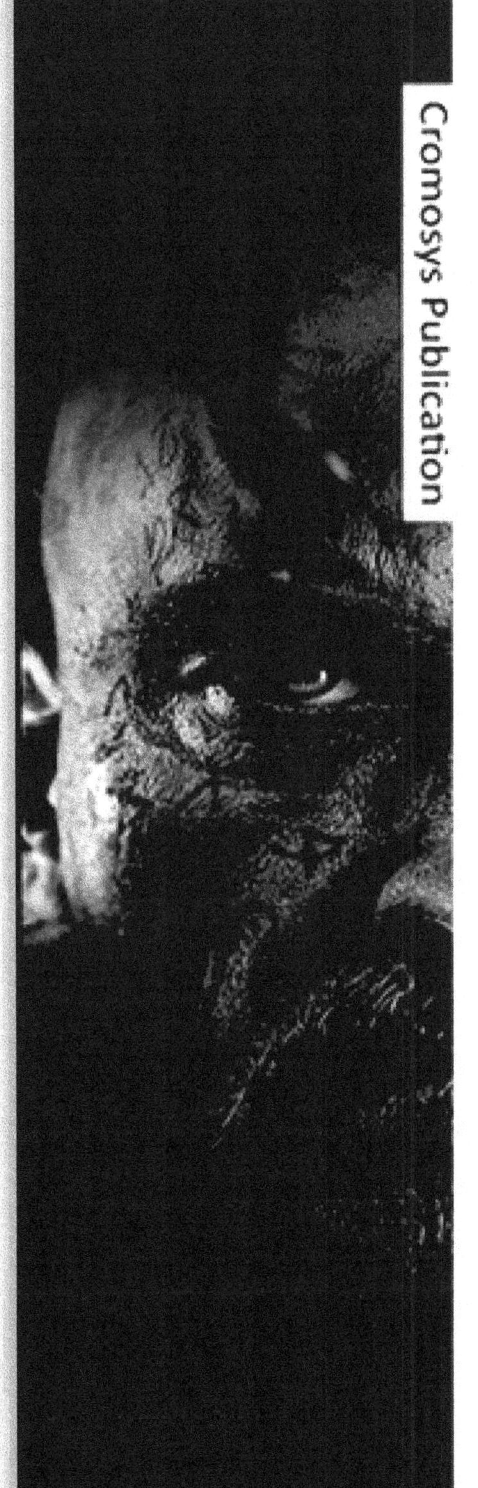

Cromosys Publication
FOCAL DISASTER
NIRANJAN JHA SHOWMAN

Cromosys Publication
Your talents will not help you succeed without your skill of using them.
NIRANJAN JHA SHOWMAN
BE
MILLIONAIRE
LIKE
ME

Extracts from the Register of Copyrights

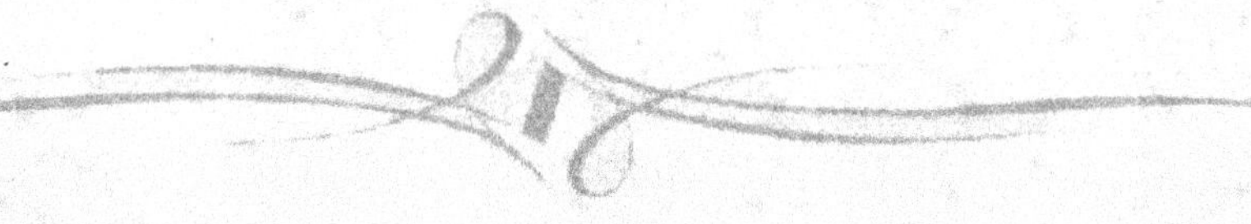

Dated : 22/07/2022

1.	Registration Number	:	**T-82782-2022**
2.	Name, address and nationality of the applicant	:	NIRANJAN JHA SHOWMAN, CROMOSYS PUBLICATION, 001, JAYSATYAM, PATANKAR ROAD, NALLASOPARA (W), MUMBAI, MAHARASHTRA - 401203. INDIAN
3.	Nature of the applicant's interest in the copyright of the work	:	AUTHOR
4.	Class and description of the work	:	LITERARY / BOOK
5.	Title of the work	:	**Teach Yourself CorelDRAW**
6.	Language of the work	:	ENGLISH
7.	Name, address and nationality of the author and if the author is deceased, date of his decease	:	NIRANJAN JHA SHOWMAN, CROMOSYS PUBLICATION, 001, JAYSATYAM, PATANKAR ROAD, NALLASOPARA (W), MUMBAI, MAHARASHTRA - 401203. INDIAN
8.	Whether the work is published or unpublished	:	UNPUBLISHED
9.	Year and country of first publication and name, address and nationality of the publisher	:	N.A.
10.	Years and countries of subsequent publications, if any, and names, addresses and nationalities of the publishers	:	N.A. SAME AS ABOVE
11.	Names, addresses and nationalities of the owners of various rights comprising the copyright in the work and the extent of rights held by each, together with particulars of assignments and licences, if any	:	
12.	Names, addresses and nationalities of other persons, if any, authorised to assign or licence of rights comprising the copyright	:	N.A.
13.	If the work is an 'Artistic work', the location of the original work, including name, address and nationality of the person in possession of the work. (In the case of an architectural work, the year of completion of the work should also be shown).	:	N.A.
14.	If the work is an 'Artistic work', whether it is registered under the Designs Act 2000 if yes give details.	:	N.A.
15.	If the work is an 'Artistic work', capable of being registered as a design under the Designs Act 2000.whether it has been applied to an article though an industrial process and ,if yes ,the number of times it is reproduced.	:	N.A.
16.	Remarks, if any	:	

Diary Number :   8523/2020-DF/T
Date of Application :   25/07/2020
Date of Receipt :   25/07/2020

DEPUTY REGISTRAR OF COPYRIGHTS